Destinations Past

Books by John Lukacs

The Great Powers and Eastern Europe

Tocqueville: The European Revolution and Correspondence with Gobineau *(editor)*

A History of the Cold War

Decline and Rise of Europe

A New History of the Cold War

Historical Consciousness

The Passing of the Modern Age

The Last European War, 1939–1941

1945: Year Zero

Philadelphia: Patricians and Philistines, 1900–1950

Outgrowing Democracy: A History of the United States in the Twentieth Century

Budapest 1900: A Historical Portrait of a City and Its Culture

Confessions of an Original Sinner

The Duel: 10 May–31 July; The Eighty-Day Struggle Between Churchill and Hitler

The End of the Twentieth Century and the End of the Modern Age

Destinations Past

Traveling through History with
John Lukacs

University of Missouri Press • Columbia

Copyright © 1994 by John Lukacs
University of Missouri Press, Columbia, Missouri 65201
Printed and bound in the United States of America
All rights reserved
5 4 3 2 1   98 97 96 95 94

Library of Congress Cataloging-in-Publication Data

Lukacs, John, 1924–
    Destinations past: traveling through history with John Lukacs.
      p. cm.
    Includes index.
    ISBN 0-8262-0956-4
    1. Lukacs, John, 1924–   —Journeys—Europe. 2. Europe—
Description and travel.   3. Europe—History—Miscellanea.
I. Title.
D923.L84   1994
940—dc20   93-45629
                                                          CIP

∞™ This paper meets the requirements of the American National Standard for
Permanence of Paper for Printed Library Materials, Z39.48, 1984.

Designer: Rhonda Miller
Typesetter: Connell-Zeko Type & Graphics
Printer and binder: Thomson-Shore, Inc.
Typefaces: Mistral and Times New Roman

For credits, see p. 220

To the Young Travelers: Paul, Karen, Helen

Contents

Preface

In 1966, when Harold Nicolson was eighty and ga-ga, his son Nigel published the three volumes of his father's *Diaries and Letters*. In one of his lucid moments the father told the son how odd it was to publish three books that he did not realize he had written. I shall be seventy when this book is published and (I hope) not ga-ga, but I think I know what Nicolson must have felt, since we may have had something in common. I am not thinking about the condition that his style was my literary model for many years, though perhaps no longer; and I am not thinking about the agreeable condition of seeing a book of one's being published without any (in my case, well, with a little) work on one's part. I am thinking about the impulse to write. In my *Confessions of an Original Sinner*, at the beginning of a chapter entitled "Writing," I cited Somerset Maugham, who once wrote that when a young author "discovers that he has a creative urge to write . . . [this] is a mystery as impenetrable as the origin of sex." I do not believe that this is so, I added. "Writing, after all, is yet another form of self-expression. The motive to write is the desire to vanquish a mental preoccupation by expressing it consciously and clearly." What Owen Barfield once said about a friend of his may be even more apposite. He is "a man of letters. He writes, not for a living, nor for reputation, but because he can't help it." Reading this I sensed a shock of recognition; I think that Harold Nicolson would have agreed.

We rarely see ourselves as others see us, which is a mixed blessing, but I had another shock of recognition a few years ago. I overheard what another historian said when someone inquired about me, during a coffee break at a symposium, after I had given a perhaps breezy, though not insubstantial, paper. He did not see that I was, accidentally, standing behind them. He said: "He is a historian; but he is really a writer." It may have been a shock of *non*-recognition; but there it was.

He should not have said "really." He should have said "also." Or, more precisely: "and." But that should not suggest a dual accomplishment. If a historian cannot write adequately, he is no historian at all. History consists of words, for many reasons, one of them being that facts cannot be separated from the words that express them. This is a shorthand statement of a realization about which I have written often, especially in my *Historical Consciousness*; but every one of my sixteen published books reflects this conviction, including this one.

Destinations Past. I am deeply, and I mean deeply, indebted to Beverly Jarrett of the University of Missouri Press, who found it useful and proper to publish this string (it is a string, rather than a random collection) of some of my writings about my travels, stretching out over forty years. They are written about certain places and about certain times. That accords with the realization that we travel in time as well as in space: 1994 (or 1894) in California is not 1994 (or 1894) in the Caucasus.* So this is not really a travel book, and this is not travel-writing. It is less (and perhaps, here and there, more) than that. Its contents comprise history and travel; travel because of history; travel to certain places because of their history, or because of a certain historical moment. Its elements are geography and history, simultaneously and together. There is nothing extraordinary about

---

*"What happens when we travel to new places, new scenes? Our mind flickers between the old-new and the new-old, rather than between *the* new and *the* old. Our pleasures spring not from wholly new cognitions but, rather, from our recognitions: for we recognize things that we had expected to see, things that we had seen somewhere (and, what is more important, *somehow*) before; things that we had imagined and anticipated more or less consciously. The wholly unexpected plays a relatively small part in these experiences. Now I believe that, were we able to travel not only through space but also through time, we would experience similar sensations: *if, instead of visiting Portugal or Greece, we could visit the 1750's or the 1880's,* the functions of our recognitions would be substantially the same. We would be fascinated and surprised by some things, repelled and disillusioned by others; we would encounter certain unexpected features of life that we would nonetheless immediately recognize; we would get used gradually to others; and the most interesting and vivifying experiences would probably involve the crystallizations, in our consciousness, of suddenly developing recognitions of things and ideas that, in some way or another, we may have already known (or that we would think we have known). But of course we do travel through time as well as through space . . . Amsterdam in 1966 is not only a Dutch city but it represents fragments and portions of the Bourgeois Age; the Spain of the 1840's fascinated Gautier and Borrow not only because it was 'exotic' but because it was 'backward,' Mozarabian and medieval." *Historical Consciousness,* p. 251.

that, just as the act of seeing involves imagination and perception together, and *simultaneously*—a condition inadequately recognized by determinists and positivists and, I fear, by psychologists too.

Description, not definition; geo*graphy*, not geo*logy*; historio*graphy*, not historio*logy*. Is this string of descriptions graphic enough? Is it well-written enough? I cannot tell. It is not a collection of the best of my writings, because of the necessary limits of its theme. I hope that its chapters hang together, but it has other limitations too. Most of the places are in Europe (and England), only two of them describe an American place and time (Philadelphia), even though a fair number of my books and other writings have dealt with the history of this, my adopted, country. It thus may seem a lopsided portrait of my interests. There may be a reason for this. It is not only that I am European-born (Europe is my mother; America is my wife); it is that there is such a thing as a discovery of Europe by ex-Europeans, and it was in America that I learned much about Europe, and it was not until I had lived for some time in America that I found myself to be a European, and it was America that made these travels possible for me. There is much about my American travels in my occasional diaries and in many letters. But this volume does not contain excerpts from my diaries and letters, even though I believe that snatches of my better writing may exist in diaries and letters, perhaps especially in the latter, including those written on the spur to my wife. There is another limitation. It is the frequent (but, I hope, not disagreeably repetitious) idea, or theme, that appears again and again: my emphatic insistence on the worthiness of the bourgeois values of the past. "Bourgeois," for a long time, was an adjective and an idea execrated not only by Marxists but by bohemians and intellectuals and artists, but this is fading now: the very word has risen lately in our estimations, and not only in mine.

Re-reading (rather than looking over) these writings during forty years: here and there I have been startled and worried because some of their youthful excrescences, and I have edited them, here and there, though not very much. I see how through the years my writing may have improved; the melodramatic impulse grew weaker—or, perhaps, more governable. Cervantes said that the road is better than the inn. That may—or may not—be true about traveling. It is certainly true about writing. Most (not all) of these pieces were published, in very diverse places, ranging from *Harper's Bazaar* to *Chronicles,* from *The New Republic* to *National Review*, from *Four Quarters* to *The New Yorker*, etc. I have to say something about the latter, because the pieces I wrote for *The New Yorker* I think are among the best of the lot. In 1984 William Shawn, the now legendary former editor of *The New Yorker*, became interested in my writing—indeed, so much that he was willing to publish some very odd pieces that I proposed to him, including that (here re-printed) walk across Switzerland with my teenage daughter. (And a profile of a Hungarian writer, entirely unknown to Americans—one of my best, though it does not fit into this volume. It was published in December 1986; a month later Shawn was dismissed from his editorship, whereafter my connection with *The New Yorker* ceased.)

In 1989 Richard Snow, the editor of *American Heritage*, asked some of his historian contributors, including myself, to participate in a series, "A Brush with History," to select an episode in their lives when they had brushed against great men or great events or both. My contribution was different from the others. It bore the title: "Enough for One Life." I wrote: "I lived through the Second World War in the middle of Europe. I saw the fiery retreat of the last German troops and the cautious advance of the first Russian soldiers on a dark, frozen morning. Twenty years later I went to Winston Churchill's funeral. I saw the London house where he died: I walked past his bier in Westminster Hall; I knew that I was a witness to the last great moment of the British Empire. Another twenty-four years later I walked in the streets of the small town where Adolf Hitler was born one hundred years ago. I think I've had enough brushes with history; I do not wish for more. But I am eternally thankful to God for having allowed my puny self to work with an inadequate little brush of my own manufacture; trying to present what certain people in certain places and at certain times did and said and thought and feared and hoped for." Re-reading this, I fear that it may be a tad too smarmy, while perhaps not sufficiently precise. "Enough for One Life"? I am seventy now, but I hope that God may still allow me a little more traveling, and perhaps even a brush with history, now and then . . . and a little more writing—because I can't help it.

"Pickering Close"
near Phoenixville, Pennsylvania

Destinations Past

Entering Venice

(1954)

When Venice was first shown to me, in 1936, Austrian and Hungarian chatter filled the cabanas and the Casino of the Lido, a Maharajah set himself up at the Excelsior, Americans and Englishmen were there, too, indifferent to Mussolini's wrath about sanctions because of his war on Ethiopia, the Venetian lagoons were clean and everything was cheap. I came three more times before the war. In 1937, when I stayed in a hotel with my aunt, I was attracted by a few place-names on the map of the lagoon: Malamocco, Pellestrina, Chioggia, which, to me, sounded more inspiring than Angkor Vat, Bali, Titicaca or Tahiti. (They still do.) On the maps they were yellow: sandy, sparely inhabited, roadless, marked with tiny circles, reserved for the smallest of habitations. Malamocco, San Pietro, Pellestrina, closing the lagoons south of Venice, except for two narrow passages around those spaghetti-like bodies. They had the fascination of desolate and unworldly spots, just around the corner from what is bustling and well-known. What was there in Malamocco, mosaics or mocca? Or Armenian graves? Were there nothing but sandy dunes, low grass, hiding-places for lovers paddling thereto? Now, seventeen years later, there arose a chance to satisfy this rosy curiosity, visiting as I was Europe with my American wife.

South of the two lagunar islands there is the delta of the Po, at the northern tip of which is Chioggia. Three hundred yards of more sand or silt between that small thumb of a peninsula, another quarter of a mile between the two lagoon islands, and the whole lagoon would be closed, and Venice imprisoned in a stagnant lake. We would approach Venice from Chioggia. Venice would be approached from the sea, in the morning. The faded pink of the Doges' Palace will glow. Bells will ring. We will enter Venice with the sun.

But I warned my wife.

Chioggia, on the map, looked like a trap. After Bologna the road runs across the Emilian and south Venetian plains, plains of dust and of passions, communistically inclined regions of Italy, of "Bitter Rice" and striking farmhands. The price of our aurorean entry to Venice may be heat, insects, flat tires, troubles.

We lunched at Bologna, after having driven across the mountain passes from Florence. I remembered Bologna from before the war. Besides the singular cathedral and the two leaning towers I remembered smart arcades, cloud-like snowy dumplings, Blackshirts, many of them. Now Bologna lay under the midday sun, without Blackshirts, but with many Communist inscriptions on its walls. Then we drove across the plains. There were old women with straw hats, moving slowly through the fields. It is all flat around Rovigo and Cavarzere, sleepy field towns, the name of the latter evoking to me, for no reason that I know of, the image of old Italian stationmasters with their funny, high, black Victor Emmanuel chakos, wizened faces, long chins, drooping white moustaches. Rovigo is already in southern Venetia. In the square a plaque commemorates the entry of Victor Emmanuel II in July 1866, the liberation from Austria, "dalla schiavitù straniera." That made me think. On that July day, eighty-eight years ago, the people of this town, save probably for a few grim Ultramontane families, came out from behind their shutters to greet their "liberation" with patriotic pride: yellow dust, purple speeches, and the green plumes of the Bersaglieri. Would they know that the defeat of Austria by Prussia and Italy in 1866 would lead to a Hitler, a Mussolini, a Stalin, and the same dust and the same poverty and disillusionment with the ideals of Italian greatness, of liberal democracy, of the monarchy? A small black cloud of a thought.

There were no black clouds over the road from Rovigo to Chioggia. There were canals with green water, tobacco, cotton-dust in the air, drawbridges, donkeys, roads with pollarded trees. The delta was verdant and fructiferous. The white towers of Cavarzere faded behind us. A pebbly and rutted road went on to Chioggia. We got there at six in the Italian mid-afternoon, and we left on the lagoon steamer at five-fifteen next dawn, in the fishermen's mid-morning.

Chioggia was a frontier place between small realms of land and sea, and between the larger realms of fantasy and imagination. It surpassed my expectations. It was a small Venice, touristless and shabby, and yet a real Venice. I had not expected white stone baroque bridges, with their black rain-stained stripes, arching over canals; large quadrangular paving stones; a bobbling mass of painted boats and barges with Byzantine hulls and prows, and their forests of thin masts over the green water; the peeling motherly churches, the warm, spicy darkness within them. The main street ran out to the sea. It was almost half as broad as St. Mark's Square in Venice, with provincial café terraces and their hundreds of tin tables. From both sides of that main street opened the alleys and coves where the fishermen's wives tatted their lacework, children ran around, nets dried, and everything smelled after the sea. There were radios blaring, a modern bus-line, a transmarine Lido that we saw later in the evening, a modern ochre-colored group of houses, marking the progress of postwar Christian Democracy.

The barges were moving down the canals; from out in the lagoon a steamer turned inward; the lights now came on in Pellestrina, to the north, and the strong lighthouse of Venice began to blink, twice a minute, far ahead of us on the left. The sun, as it went down, illuminated a scene worthy of the great Dutch landscape painters: a small island with the old ruin of a white house, with a blackened arch and two cows grazing on the scraggly grass under bulging clouds. It was a seventeenth-century scene, except now the triangular sails of the fishing-boats were all orange-colored. We had the obvious dinner of fried scampi and local wine at one of the fishermen's trattorias. There were the smells of a softening breeze, seaweed and frying oil.

My wife had a headache, and the steamer was to sail at the crack of dawn, so we went to bed early. I abandoned the sentimental inclination to wander along the winding streets, to sit with jolly fishermen, drinking red wine, listening to local songs in dialect, etc. This was 1954 not 1904; I was not a latecoming Bellocian; I was—perhaps regrettably—bereft of Belloc's perspective, or of his wish to shock the Protestantism and the philistinism of Liberal England, to proclaim the living virtues of a jolly Catholicism in France or Italy, glad to be away from a landscape of gas works and rigid factory chimneys, glad to drink honest red wine with the Catholic peasants. Here were the Italians of 1954, and *pibigas* and *frigori-feri* and *televisione* and the *filobus* and Italian magazines named *Quick,*

Intercom, and *Tentazione,* on the iron newstands of Chioggia. Before turning in, I leaned out of the large window of our room. The long ochre wharf stretched out below us. On it were painted, or scrawled, the inevitable murals of 1954 in Italy:

W PCI W PCI PCI DEMOCRAZIA MPCI VOTA COMUNISTA

W standing for "Viva!," M for "Morte!"—more than often in a fighting embrace with each other. The walls are also placarded with the posters of the neo-Fascists, the MSI, their symbol a ragged national flame. "I *veri* italiani votano MSI," meaning that *real* Italians, those not Communists, not Anglophiles, not clericals, not cosmopolitans, vote Neo-Fascist. I *veri* italiani must watch "the little spark" (i.e. the MSI) "from which will rise a great flame."

Oh, these W's and M's, abbreviations in an age of abbreviations of Long Live! and Death To! The best one I saw was in Florence (next to a M WINTERTON! GLI ITALIANI NON SONO DEI MAU MAU, addressed to the British military commander at Trieste); it read, simply and evidently aimed at all historic-minded Florentines,

M I GUELFI,

obviously put up by a Ghibelline.

PCI PCI PCI PCI VOTA MSI. Chioggia is still at night. Before falling asleep I heard the night vaporetto coming in from Venice, turning around the wharf with one long splash. The soft patter of walking feet (all in gum-shoes in modern Italy) died out soon.

During the night many fishermen put out to the lagoon. I heard the mild sputter-sputter of their engines. They went, old and young, in their black barges, with big miner's lamps in iron cages. They earned little, probably not enough to escape their rock-like tenements, whose walls were peeling through many dreadful layers of damp plaster, the ceilings mildewed, the solitary cord and the familiar nakedness of the electric bulb casting a strange unworldly light over their evenings in the autumns and winters, with fog, dampness, the fears of tuberculosis and of unemployment setting in. All of this in the shadow of the Lido, where clerks gamble on Saturday nights, the minimum bet is 3,000 Lire, a good week's pay for some fishermen. But the rumbles of class struggle are elsewhere. Apartment houses are rising in Chioggia. Many of the young fishermen are perched on their motor-scooters, in their sack suits, on Saturdays, that is.

When the dawn came with the breezes and the hooting of a motor-barge, the small canopy of the Venetian sky was brightening fast. The strings of lights at Pellestrina were still blinking. Many fishermen had stood out to sea. There were long minutes of an ominous and beautiful silence, and the chub and pull of the rowboats, six or seven of them, winding their way out on the verdigris waters. The steamer still slept, empty and black, under our window. Meanwhile the façade of the crumbling church across the small canal, and the small arched bridge leading to it, had become a pearly grey, an unworldly hue, Aurora's pallor on this rising day.

The last barges were now moving out. Their men rowed standing, with the peculiar backwater stroke of the Venetians, only slightly faster than their second cousins, the gondoliers. But in these still waters they moved fast, they were far out in a minute or so.

Around the stone wharf the first of the night fishermen were returning, their big white lamps were still burning, but they threw no more big holes of light into the inky night sea; halos, rather, which, already pallid under the whitening steps of a church, gained a last strength as they swept over the last black shadows under the bridge. The day boats were moving out, the night boats were coming in; the circle was closing on the calm surface of the captivated sea here.

There was this palpable presence of wet rot; but not of decadence, for that is dry and turns into dust, and then is blown away to nothing. Out of wet rot comes ferment, and the human yeast, and passions that mature into something rational, not exotic passions symbolized by sails in the sunset in Oceania. Particles of the romantic temper of life were still here, in this climate of a hard Mediterranean realism: a ferment of life, like subterranean marshlands with vast hidden deposits of gaseous energy. These people were hard enough to survive the rise and the fall and the disappearance of vast and distant Empires.

On a brick wall of Chioggia:
W LA MADONNA   W LA MADRE   W MARIA
painted with strong masculine letters.

Before we boarded the ship, I looked back to the broad, curving main street of Chioggia. The dominant color was already a mix of white and grey. From this background of fine light shadows, on which the uneven walls and arcades of the shambling houses emerged like a pencil-drawing, came the black figures of a few men, their steps clattering in that wondrous silence of the dawn hour.

Within five minutes the lagoon steamer left Chioggia far behind. The morning sky was now all light and open.

We wound, in two hours, along the thin coastline of those two stringlike lagoon islands, in and out of Pellestrina, S. Pietro, Alberoni, Malamocco. They were all, as I now, after Chioggia, imagined them to be: one or two round temple-like churches, the pastel houses, the leafy truck gardens, the uneven stone walls. The human ferment trickled on and off the ship at the ramshackle wooden piers and stations, most of them sweatered workers, swinging their arms in the cold. The captain, in his shiny and worn blue uniform, offered us coffee in the tiny wheelhouse. Again we wound away from the shore in a lagunar arc.

He said that it was difficult to navigate this small ship in the winter fog, and that the run was kept up by the company, though there were few passengers.

"What are these workers doing in the winter?"

"Many are out of work around here. There is not much work, everything is small, just enough to provide Venice. They used to work in the Arsenal. There is little work there now. You know where the Fleet is." A gesture downwards. "Don't they go to look for work elsewhere?" "Not many. They are not the kind. They stay here."

We were now passing, still very silently, three small islands very near Venice, just behind S. Giorgio Maggiore: a hospital for the incurable; an orphans' home; a mental institution. These islands are not visible from Venice, hidden from tourists and from the jolly traffic of the Lido, while the Chioggia steamer passes by them. They stand in the lagoon, with their high walls and small stone piers, partly covered with wisteria: bastions of charity, not yet abandoned as are two other bastions, half-sunk and desolate, full of stones and lizards, the earlier bastions that once used to guard Venice seaward from the Turk. The captain and his helmsman came out from the wheelhouse to shake hands with us. We stood on the bridge, in the soft but chilly sea-breeze, with the bitter Italian national cigarettes in our mouths. We had turned in from the Channel of St. George, and all that Venice is so well-known for, the Campanile, St. Mark's, the faded pink façade of the Doges' were straight ahead of us, as in a painting. (So much of the past twelve hours reminded me of paintings, but, then, the cliché is true, so much of Italy resembles canvases, and so many of her people move on a stage.) We stepped off the landing, onto the stones of Venice. Already in that very early hour the square was beginning to be infested with tourists; the faces and thighs of film and soccer stars shone from magazine stands that were opening. Errol Flynn and a Midwestern bishop were safe and snug in the Danieli. All over Venice pigeons rose with the sun, and thirty thousand German cameras in German hands began to click.

Conversation in Vienna

(1958)

I arrived in Vienna on a bright June evening. The air was liquid and sweet.

The last time I saw Vienna was 1946, when I escaped from a Hungary that was gradually falling under Soviet domination. Vienna was dark, hungry, gloomy. I stayed but two days and went on west, toward America. After me came thousands and thousands of Hungarian Displaced Persons, during 1947, 1948, 1949, when the frontier was still open, here and there, for a few minutes a day, between two patrols, or for a considerable sum. The Hungarian bourgeoisie oozed through, oozed on to the West. Among them was my mother, already very ill with the tuberculosis she had contracted in a damp, cold cellar during the siege of Budapest. She died in Vienna, in 1950.

Those were the days of the "Third Man." Half-occupied by the Russians, an island surrounded by the Soviet zone in Austria, Vienna was the classic scene for Graham Greene or Eric Ambler: spies and spivs, professional black-marketeers and prostitutes with large liquid eyes, zither players and Siberian infantry. On the body of a beaten Europe Vienna was a soft, sordid scab.

Today the Siberian infantry is gone; and the fact that the Stalin-Platz is once again Schwarzenberg-Platz is a symbol, a great and important symbol. The Russian occupation left not one spiritual mark, not a scar. For ten years the soldiers of the largest land empire of the world held on to one-third of a small nation of seven million people; now it is as if they had never been here at all. The Austrian Communist Party is a dull, rather than a bad, joke. Vienna is European, super-European; Western, very Western. This should be a lesson for those who still keep prattling about the terrific *spiritual* impact of the Communist "idea"; or to John Foster Dulles, who at the last moment was reluctant to quit Austria in exchange for the Russians' quitting their zone, for one never knows: the brilliant, the devilish machinations of the Communists, the Russians. . . . But they *are* gone, after all. The shops on the Kärnterstrasse are smarter than their New York counterparts; and doe-eyed Viennese girls look alluring and sensuous in the chemise. (That Dean Acheson has made a recent statement against the chemise confirms my notion that Secretaries of State should confine themselves to things like legal briefs and classic diplomacy and not pontificate about movements either of the spirit or of the flesh.)

There remains a large but, however. The Russians are only fifty miles away, to the east. We drove to the Hungarian frontier, and walked up within ten feet of the seven-foot-high double barbed-wire fence. The girls took a few pictures, and we looked at the soldier climbing up the watchtower on the other side. There is such a watchtower, a good fifty feet high, every half mile. Soon an uneasy patrol came down the Hungarian fields, carefully rounding the plowed-up strips and the land mines.

This I saw but a day after I learned of the brutal execution of Nagy and Maléter. Back in Vienna gleamed the bright glass and the yellow tiles of the rebuilt Westbahnhof, and the old houses stoop peeling and stolid in the evening, and the baroque majesty of the Burg shone buttery and white, bathed in brilliant spotlights that illuminate the Latin inscriptions for the glory of Hapsburg Emperors . . . but the Russians were only an hour away. And my homeland was cut off by barbed wire, perhaps forever. The superiority of the European spirit? Perhaps. But there stood not a single European soldier between the frontier and Vienna. Instead, the evening lamps were lit and everywhere Austrians and tourists ate their large platters and drank the fresh green wine of Austria. We did, too. We went to the first inn and drank a lot of wine and tried to forget things and were all quite silly.

And then, next morning, I met a Russian Agent.

He was an old family acquaintance. Descendant of a well-to-do Hungarian bourgeois family; rather handsome even now, in his fifties; dark glasses, silvery hair, just a tiny bit unshaven; the gambling type, the *faiseur* type, the type of the cashiered officer, just one notch above embezzler or gigolo. In another time or different circumstances he might have turned up, in the Twenties, for example, among The Hungarians Of Hollywood. But his days were the Forties, not the Twenties.

Having survived the war, he occasionally did errands for my family in Budapest, for he was fond of us, in his way. At that time he was a sort of curbstone banker. Soon afterwards he became a Russian Agent. Not a Communist Agent—a Russian Agent. And not a Political Agent—a Purchasing Agent. Like Wolfsheim in *The Great Gatsby,* this man had "gonnegtions." He smuggled, bought and sold all kinds of materials for the Russians in Vienna, in true Third Man style; at times he was rich. I remembered some of these things from my mother's last letters. Now we were sitting and drinking coffee together.

He was—momentarily—down and out. He had had a partner in some peculiar business venture and the man had quit with most of the money. Subsequently he succeeded in shaking me down for a forty-dollar "loan."

"Forty dollars!" he said, with a dramatized sigh. "You know what forty dollars meant to me eight years ago? When your poor mother was still alive? Nothing, my boy, nothing! An evening's entertainment. This last thing has been an unexpected catastrophe. Still, ever since the Russians left, my business has not been the same."

"But why do you stay in Vienna, then?"

(I had been surprised to find him in Vienna; I had thought he would be running an Export-Import firm somewhere in Rio de Janeiro.)

"There's still business to do with the Russians. And who knows? I, personally, think that the Russians will be back."

"Back?"

"Back. Back all over. Not only in Vienna. In Austria. All over Europe. The future is theirs. For a while I thought that the Americans had beaten them to it. But no. You have no idea of what's going on in the Soviet Union. What these people have produced within one generation is incredible; they're coming up fast."

There was no use arguing with him about politics. We ordered another coffee, with whipped cream.

He then told me that he took frequent trips to Hungary; that Budapest was now miserably poor; but that this was the fault of the revolution; the revolutionaries were fools, absolute fools. They didn't have a chance, not the slightest. There was no question but that the Russians would never let the revolution succeed.

"But wasn't the whole population against them?"

"Yes, of course, but they were misled. Everyone was misled. They were gamblers. Crazy gamblers. Everybody."

"How can you say that? With such certainty, I mean?"

"I was there, you know! I was there during the first five days of the revolution. I had arrived in Budapest a week before the outbreak, on business.

"You say that everything was in vain, that the revolution could not but fail?"

"Of course. You don't know. You don't understand. The Russians work slowly. The strength is enormous, something that you in America cannot imagine. . . ."

"Tell me about the Revolution. About your own experiences. What was it like? What did you do?"

"Well, I could hardly walk much in the streets; there was constant firing, you know."

I wanted to hear something personal, something immediate, from this intelligent and dissolute man, a fragment of the picture of our native city where he had stood, in the flesh, during those supremely exciting days of the revolt; an anti-Communist revolt seen by a Russian agent; a Hungarian national rising seen by an ex-Hungarian, by a native who now believes only in a Soviet future, whose last sparks of patriotic feeling must have died out long ago. . . .

He lit a cigarette.

"On the twenty-fourth of October," he said, "I was walking down from my hotel. . . . But it was incredible! You won't believe it."

"What was it? Go on."

"You see, I wanted to go across that little square but there was a big demonstration before the monument that's standing there. You could still hear the shooting but there were thousands of people on that square, women, children and old people. You couldn't get through. You couldn't get through at all. They sang the National Anthem; many of them were on their knees. . . ."

"And what did you do?"

"I knelt down, too; and I cried."

Philadelphia
Franklin and Penn in the Fifties
(1958)

Philadelphia is a very large provincial town with patrician touches.

In a democratic age and in a democratic nation such patrician touches are the first things that meet the eye of the outsider. They stand out against the broad flatness of the human landscape; they *seem* to give form to content. Thus their real proportions are frequently exaggerated: to these patrician impressions such formative influences are attributed which they no longer possess.

I made this error ten years ago, when I first came to Philadelphia. Immediately I was reminded of London. I have learned since that I was in reputable company; this was the impression of a string of eminent visitors, from the Duke of Liancourt in the eighteenth century to André Maurois. Here I decided to settle. It took me ten years to find out that my impression was not altogether correct. Here, nevertheless, I stay.

I remember that autumn, ten years ago. I remember the leaves, the Georgian doorways, the Adam mantels through the glistening windows of the Delancey Place town houses, the fine rain, the English bookshop. Behind me were the war years of Central Europe, the terrible siege of my native city of Budapest, the Communist ascendancy in my native country, and a hot and horrid first American summer in New York. My soul craved the English patrician air with an immense thirst. I was twenty-four years old.

The green leaves and the Georgian mantels and the Palladian windows are still here, in Philadelphia. The old cracked-leather armchair touch still exists; it is something which, despite its new cosmopolitan residents and its neo-classical architecture, the shiny plasticity of Washington does not and will not have. There are the handsome Anglo-Saxon faces of upper-class Philadelphia men and women; "handsome" is the *mot juste,* not "attractive" or "beautiful," since they are Anglo-Saxon faces. There is that hardly visible but essential touch of self-assurance in some of the surviving patrician pretensions: the genuine quality of ama-teur horsemanship, the determined separation of men from women after dinner,* the love for stone and for brick walls, the hidden houses with their rich gardens. There are the Philadelphia oddities: the First City Troop, "city square" instead of the all-American "block"; "pavement" instead of the New York "sidewalk"; odd old clubs. There is that pecu-liarly puritanical upper-class custom of hard play: instead of luxuriating on Rivieras, these Philadelphians go on walking-tours through the Alps.

Most of these qualities are the marks of an autumnal civilization, of the bourgeois age, of an age now closing everywhere in the Western world. It is perhaps symptomatic that, like most patrician cities, Phila-delphia is best in the autumn. Then the fine, smoky air of the American fall pervades the city, and while at the seashore October means a forebod-ing chill, Philadelphia swiftly becomes cozy and warm. The dining-room of the Barclay is full;** the Opera is on its way; after the last siege of the customary Philadelphian hot-September spell, the downtown streets tin-kle with vigor. The shadows softly spread over the cracks in the pave-ment, and there is even a bright little impression of cheer. I like my week-end guests to come down in the Philadelphia autumn, when the suburbs are splendid with the stunning colors of the sap-rich trees of the Ameri-can Eastern Seaboard. It is then, and perhaps then alone, that I can feel without reservations that America is, after all, the transatlantic product of an old and ripe civilization: for, despite the now so fashionable assertions about the "unity of Western civilization," I do have my doubts.

II

Certain clichés about Philadelphia are literally inevitable. "An old-fashioned city"; "with Boston, the most English city in all America"; "the pervading influence of old family habits"; "the fine glow of old furniture"—they contain a good deal of truth. They are, nevertheless,

*1994. No longer.
**Ditto.

just a little more than half-truths. There is a good deal in the historic character of Philadelphia which is German rather than English, philistine rather than patrician, radical rather than conservative. Scratch the Philadelphia "old English stock": you will frequently find the German ancestry. Scratch the Philadelphia "patrician": not infrequently you'll find the philistine. Scratch the "conservative citizen" in Philadelphia: you will often find the radical underneath.

Hidden under the Anglo-Saxon front there is a German facet to Philadelphia. It is historic, essential, original, and enduring. It goes deeper than the circumstance that, like every American metropolis, Philadelphia has a large German sector in North Philadelphia, for there is an even larger Italian sector in South Philadelphia and yet it is not possible to speak of an Italian stamp on the Philadelphia character, while the German stamp is there.* Within two years after Penn came to Shackamaxon, German immigrants settled in "Germantown" and Cresheim. Divert your eyes from the English country-gentry attributes, from Chinese Chippendale, from the tales about old Madeira stocks, from the early hunt clubs and look into many an old Philadelphia family-name: you'll find the German origin.** Behind the façade of English names, a little historical scratching will reveal the heavy German plaster: Pfeiffer for Pepper, Pfannebäcker for Pennypacker. There is a German touch about Philadelphia food: cream cheese, scrapple, biscuits, and buns. Until about 1914 German brass-bands were a local attraction on Sunday afternoons. Even the Philadelphia policemen look somewhat un-Irish: they wear a rather unbecoming octagonal white cap for the most part of the year. From their shoulders down they are American city cops, from their necks up they might as well be the beach patrol at Swinemünde. Philadelphia is also a brewery town: and the latest promotion is a *Steinie-Pak.*

---

*1994. Wrong again. The opposite is now true.

**A significant exception were the early Philadelphia Jews, who seem to have been not German but Spanish and Portuguese in origin. Some of the oldest Philadelphia families, now Protestant, probably come from this Sephardic Jewish stock: Madeira, Seixas, Lavino, Markoe. The high social position of some of the Dutch and German Jews who came later is indicated by Rebecca Gratz, who inspired Scott's Rebecca in *Ivanhoe.* Philadelphia may have been the main bulwark of the old conservative and Sephardic tradition against the modernistic and secular tendencies of the later German-Russian Jewish immigrants. It should be also noted that, unlike anti-Catholicism, anti-Semitism as a visible and popular movement has never appeared in Philadelphia.

The social patronage of culture has, again, a Germanic tinge. In at least two famous local autobiographies, the authors proudly point at their systematic determination to keep up with culture by the rather incredible method of keeping a weekly list of the number of pages read from different books. In Franklin's so scientific-serious societies, in the sentimentalities of John Greenleaf Whittier, in the scholarship during the relatively short efflorescence of the University of Pennsylvania (around 1910), in the fervor of certain patrician literati for Science, Anthropology, Excavations (one meets society matrons who, at parties, suddenly announce that they have just returned from a Yucatan or Iranian "dig") there gleams a Germanic respect for Knowledge, immediately beneath the English veneer. It is a culture which patronizes Russian musicians but which is insensitive to irony and is baffled by criticism; a stodgy culture with a radical tinge which will rather pay lip-service to Zola than bother with Flaubert. Unknown, too, are the best of Philadelphia's own. Agnes Repplier was one of the finest essayists of American literary history; she wrote the finest book about Philadelphia. This book, as most of her writings, is wholly forgotten today. Nor were her refined, conservative, patrician talents recognized by the allegedly so refined, conservative, patrician Philadelphians of her own day. Which, of course, is typical of Philadelphia. The same thing happened to another native Philadelphian, to that exceptional American painter, Thomas Eakins, about the same time: but Philadelphia has always favored the second- if not the third-rate, due to a sort of provincial suspicion well hidden behind a successfully maintained pose of patrician reserve.

It is very easy to be deceived by this pose, as if it were the natural reserve of confident and cultural patricians. Here even the best observers slip a little; even Seán O'Faoláin who, in an otherwise excellent article written for *Holiday* magazine, said that Philadelphian patriciandom corresponds "to that great core of French society, the *grand bourgeois*— wealthy men of long lineage, whose conversation is also a blend of the good works of the conscience and the good things of life." I am rather inclined to agree with Hilaire Belloc, who felt that the only thing he could do to enliven a Philadelphia dinner-party was to take off his shoes and dance a jig. I do not say that good talk cannot be found in Philadelphia; I only say that it is not very typical of Philadelphia. The same thing is true about other qualities attributed to local patrician refinement. It is well-known that, for a city of her size, Philadelphia is practically devoid of first-class restaurants. This is usually explained by Philadelphians by saying that Philadelphia is a "homey town" (which is true) and that it is among the private walls of old clubs and old homes that exceptionally good food may be found (which is not true). Among the younger generation of Philadelphia society families there are many men who would not be caught dead saying "suspenders" for "braces" but who have a very poor knowledge of even the essentials of wine. In a full-page color photograph in that same *Holiday,* one of the oldest members of what is called the oldest social club of the English-speaking world—of the dreadfully exclusive Fish House or State In Schuylkill, devoted to fine cooking (the caption reads: "the ultra-select association gathers at its riverside Castle outside the city to feast on old traditions, good food . . .")—stands proudly posed against the blackboard where members write up the menu, which is as follows:

Boola-Boola Soup
Lamb Chops
Mint Jelly
Corn-off-the-Cob
Carrots
Lettuce and Tomatoes
Cheese and Crackers
Coffee

It is good and healthy and wholesome, but not what one would call a *grand bourgeois* menu.

Nor is it a Tory one. The cliché about Philadelphia being a "tory" city is quite off the mark, despite that happy breath of ease which visiting Englishmen get who always feel so much at home (since they are always welcomed) in Philadelphia. "Philadelphia is one of the few Tory cities left in the world," said a visiting English bishop not so long ago, "Birmingham being the other." He was curiously right about Philadelphian affinities with Birmingham, with that sort of puritan-radical philistinism, with the Toryism of the Chamberlains which, of course, is not really Toryism at all. The so-called patrician and conservative spirit of Philadelphia, if translated into English terms, comes closest to Gladstone. Gladstone would have been right at home here, while the Philadelphian reaction to a Disraeli or even to a pre-1940 Churchill would have been profound and uneasy embarrassment. It is this embarrassment which lies behind the provincialism of Philadelphia "culture," despite the long traditions, the many excellent clubs and private libraries, the many widely read and highly cultured lawyers. It is this embarrassment which has resulted in a peculiar sort of local gracelessness: and, indeed, the history of Philadelphia may be summed up in saying that it represents the rise and decline of much gentility without much grace.

There is a decent, a cozy character in this American Gladstonism. It is there in Philadelphia architecture, even during the worst late-Victorian period: in the unimaginative but never ugly brick rowhouses with their famous marble steps, representing the dogged determination to keep Philadelphia a "city of homes," which she has always been. Of course, by now the ranch house, in the form of a laminated cigarbox, appears all around Philadelphia, sordidly bespattering the lovely landscape of the Philadelphia suburbs. Yet in this so-called "conservative" city little is done to halt this scabrous development: for it represents, after all, "Progress." And the civic-spirited Philadelphian, whether rich or poor, Episcopalian, Quaker, Catholic, or Jewish, will do everything to avoid the impression of impeding "Progress."

But this deep-down Philadelphian uncertainty, this beating of the radical systole under the conservative face of the Philadelphia heart, is not new. The image of a Philadelphia full of stateliness and conservatism, breathing that reserved and patrician spirit into the so sensible Constitution of the United States, is a very nice image: but it is, also, considerably false. The populace of this outwardly so placid city has broken out in some of the worst riots in American history, while the cowed "élite" kept judiciously silent. There was a Committee of Public Safety operating in Philadelphia fifteen years before the more infamous Parisian one: though the British occupation of the city during the winter of 1777–78 was, for reasons politic, remarkably gentle, there followed "an ignoble reign of terror" which, in the words of an American historian, "had not even the saving grace of mistaken enthusiasm." The mob demanded Tory heads, and the city fathers decided that the selection of a few victims was necessary "to appease the people." What may have been the worst religious riots in American history took place in Philadelphia in 1844, when Catholic churches were burned (significantly, only Irish Catholic churches; the German Catholics were spared by a population which, I hasten to add, numbered mostly anti-slavery voters). And during the height of the McCarthy wave in 1954 (when Philadelphia was universally hailed by liberals across the country for just having turned Democratic after almost seventy years of Republican city rule), an editorial writer in the Philadelphia *Bulletin,* weighed down by the overwhelmingly McCarthyite stream of letters coming in, helplessly asked: "What has happened to the people in Philadelphia?"

The standard attributions to Philadelphia ought, therefore, to be qualified. The "Englishness" is no longer unqualifiable (someone told me how, in the best among the three Cricket Clubs still sported by Philadelphia, it was not possible to get a cup of tea on a summer afternoon). The attribute of "patrician civic-mindedness" has been weakened long ago: for decades now, the Philadelphian élite have moved far out of the city (with the wholehearted approval of the machine politicians). Nor is the "conservative" attribute very valid today, when the main morning newspaper of this traditional city, of the erstwhile Athens of America, is the Philadelphia *Inquirer,* owned by an unscrupulous press magnate, and probably the worst morning paper of any great city in the Western Hemisphere.* (The point is not that the *Inquirer* is scandalous: indeed, perhaps the first sensational scandalmongering paper in America, Duane's and Bache's radical *Aurora,* was started in Philadelphia in 1800. The point is that in 1800 Philadelphia patricians and Pecksniffs sniffed at the *Aurora* with disgust, while their descendants take the *Inquirer* complacently for granted, as *the* classic Philadelphia morning paper.)

III

A curious feature in the modern history of Philadelphia is that she has been frequently just about twenty years behind the rest of the United States. It was during the Civil War that the great cities of the Eastern

---

*No longer—though perhaps not *much* better.

Seaboard went Republican; Philadelphia went Republican twenty years later, in 1884. The country went dry under Wilson; Pennsylvania was the only large state that voted for Hoover and for the drys in 1932. And it was twenty years later that Philadelphia's own New Deal arrived, turning out an entrenched and corrupt Republican administration. This local New Deal was headed by Richardson Dilworth, a vest-pocket Franklin Roosevelt. Like the national New Deal, the Philadelphia reform crusade swept in a coalition of civic-minded descendants of old local families, liberal lawyers, happy and corruptible ward-leaders, determined city planners, and a whole bevy of hard-faced sharp young men. And throughout the United States liberals, with their political ambitions parched in these seven lean years of the Republican-Eisenhower comeback, have depended on this trickle of a Philadelphia New Deal to slake the thirst of their anxious souls.

There is no doubt that the Democratic victory in Philadelphia marked a civic turning-point, and that many of its reforms were useful, overdue, important. But there is another side to its story. It is that, being twenty years behind the times (American times, that is), the Philadelphia New Deal has engaged in some of the same illusions and errors which now mark the Rooseveltian spirit in retrospect. I shall not go into politics; I shall only suggest what this local New Deal has done to the face of Philadelphia. After 1952, Philadelphia turned to hustle and bustle. There are whole batteries of city planners, entire flying brigades of public-relations-men, official city ambassadors flying back and forth between Paris, Amsterdam, Monte Carlo, and Philadelphia (the very name of the city now being progressively obscured by the "official" slogan: DELAWARE VALLEY: U.S.A.). Big buses have replaced the trolleys (and the traffic situation is considerably worse); Interracial Non-Discrimination Commissions have been formed (and racial skirmishes have become much worse); Youth Study Centers and Community Centers have been built (and the juvenile delinquency situation has become very much worse). In some of the old side-streets the old and lovable gas lamps have been replaced by hideous aluminum dragons with fluorescent teeth, transforming the nocturnal landscape of this otherwise so placid city into a moonscape, into the anteroom of some gigantic atomic dentist. Old Broad Street Station and the so-called Chinese Wall were demolished; expressways bore deep into the clayey soil of Philadelphia; but it is by no means certain that the change is propitious. Despite its pompous exaltation, the new Penn Center in the middle of the city is really an esplanade of stiff-sack skyscrapers, about which many people have now second thoughts. They are office buildings which are not only unimaginative but outright ugly: large concrete bird-cages in the Bauhaus style of the 1930s; but, of course, the modern-angle functional architecture of the early 1930s has a way of growing out-of-date faster than the worst Gladstonian building.

Meanwhile there has been a tremendous surge of re-decoration, very much out of keeping with the older Philadelphia tradition of letting good (and, at times, also bad) enough alone. The lovely green Louis XV dining-room of the Barclay has been repainted in Mediterranean blue, with the mirrors removed, and Spanish iron grillwork mounted in their stead, in what may be called the Mrs. Luce style of 1956. There is a new hotel in the middle of Penn Center, the Sheraton, which opened with a tremendous hullabaloo: Sherman Adams represented the President, Danny Kaye led the Philadelphia Orchestra (true!), with Philadelphia society gaily partic-ipating in this spectacle with the Gabor Sisters. It is a hotel where every detail is furnished in the most execrable taste.* Architecturally at least, the New Philadelphia Spirit may have already produced many a mad, if not sad, failure.

For the changing face reflects the changing spirit of this city. In-deed, the early impression according to which the Philadelphia New Deal meant a return of the old patrician interest in city affairs has largely evaporated now, when even the average resident of the Main Line is probably an advertising executive born in Cleveland. Advertising execu-tives have already muscled their way into the Philadelphia civic front. It is now the ex-bricklayer John B. Kelly and the ex-Russian immigrant Albert Greenfield who might vie for the honor of being "Mr. Philadelphia." In this there is nothing wrong, except that in the past few years one heard many a joke cracked at the expense of Messrs. Kelly and Greenfield by

*Examples: There is a Connie Mack Room, with the rug in the form of a baseball diamond; a fake-Parisian outdoor café which bears the name of The Indian Queen and which, besides, is indoors; a Ye Olde Cheshire Cheese and a London Tavern where waiters wear red stocking-caps and emerald-green silk trousers, etc., etc. (Gone now.)

some of the same old-Philadelphia-society people who were delighted to get invitations to that Monte Carlo wedding and who will not fail to attend Mr. Greenfield's very large New Year's receptions. It is somewhat like the attitude of those *ancien régime* families who, whatever their virtues, tried hard in 1800 to wangle invitations to Bonaparte's levées. And it is because of these things that by now it is quite an exaggeration to speak of the formative influence of Philadelphian patriciandom today.*

It is always at the height of the new tides of the democratic flood that nostalgic evocations of the old patrician habits appear. It was at the height of the national New Deal, in 1936, that John P. Marquand's *The Late George Apley* came out; and recently there has been a veritable literary preoccupation with themes about the Philadelphia "aristocracy": a brace of plays, a couple of pompous architectural articles, a string of novels of which perhaps the most typical is *The Philadelphian*. Written by an advertising executive, full of stereotypes of the proud-old-family theme, on its cover the silhouette of a man in a Brooks Brothers suit, it is also frequently in error about those details which are so essential in this kind of sociological literature. Now, when this image of Philadelphia (and no longer Boston or Southampton or whatnot) forming the last bulwark of American social aristocracy has emerged, it may be instructive to compare these literary representations with the portraits by a local writer coming from a patrician Philadelphia family, with the novels of Livingston Biddle Jr. who, after all, should know what he is writing about. In his books, and especially in his first, *Main Line,* the majority of the society people are warped, useless, snobbish, selfish (he seems to have a particular dislike for Main Line mothers), while he extols the virtues of a golden-hearted and manly proletarian, of a city-desk newspaperman. Moreover, while the other writers desperately labor to establish the image of an American past full of noble refinement, there is in Livingston

---

*This is also true of the Philadelphia accent. Regional accents in the United States are rapidly disappearing and only traces of an English accent remain among upper-class Philadelphians (what I, for example, call the High Episcopalian "a"). There is, on the other hand, a formerly lower-class and, by now, middle-class Philadelphia accent which is among the ugliest forms of English diction. Its main mark is a flat, twangy, semi-nasal "a": i.e., "aysk," "mayd," and "clayss" for *ask, mad, class.* The most offensive and vulgar English diction I know is that of two Philadelphia radio disc-jockeys.

Biddle's books a constant hankering after Europe. This is, of course, going to the opposite extreme; yet, no matter how overly sentimental the spirit in his books, they reflect something of the spirit of William Penn. And here I arrive at what may be the source of so many of these Philadelphia contradictions.

IV

It seems that through the dim, grey, democratic years we can still distinguish the outlines of two figures that stand out against the receding past. It may be around them that all of these so contradictory Philadelphian impressions gather. For Philadelphia has a dual character, a split mind. Its character has been shaped partly by William Penn, partly by Benjamin Franklin. One was the contemplative humanitarian; the other the utilitarian eager-beaver. One, despite his brooding Quakerism, essentially an Englishman with an almost medieval soul; the other, despite his cosmopolitan repute at the French court, essentially the *bourgeois gentilhomme*. Penn was that peculiarly Anglo-Saxon case of the Rich Young Man Turned Humanist; Franklin was the more Germanic ideal, the Poor Apprentice who became a Famous Scientist. It is easy to imagine Franklin speaking to the Lions or addressing the Miss America contestants in Atlantic City; it is difficult to imagine Penn doing anything of the sort. The shy, the gentle, the introvert, the myrtle-and-brick Philadelphia, where houses are named Strawberry Mansion and Solitude, is that of William Penn. The city of the first utilitarian prison (a failure), of the concrete highways, of the anthropological institutes, of Art and Civic and Community Centers is that of Benjamin Franklin. Franklin represents perhaps the Philadelphia intellect, while Penn has given what is best to the Philadelphia heart. It is a pity that, by the twentieth century, the great majority of Americans associate Philadelphia with Franklin rather than with Penn: in their minds the *Saturday Evening Post* is vaguely but indissolubly connected with such images as Independence Hall and Valley Forge.*

---

*They have a point. Before me lies a picture of the Independence Hall restoration project, a "Prospective view of future development recommended by the Philadelphia National Shrines Park Commission." It is an instructive picture. In it, Independence Hall is a well-scrubbed, lovable toy, a colonial doll's house in the shade of the

Penn was the founder; Franklin, after all, a newcomer; but it is by no means true that newcomers to Philadelphia have such a hard row to hoe. One of the worst disasters that befell Philadelphia came in the person of a man, Edward P. Bok, about sixty years ago. This Victorian Franklin, a young immigrant with heavy feet and with a lot of cheek, came to Philadelphia as an apprentice. With the help of a successful marriage he souped up the whole *Saturday Evening Post* complex, founded the *Ladies Home Journal,* made thereby Philadelphia a magazine city, established lecture forums, orchestras, Americanization awards, and whatnot. He was the civic-minded eager-beaver at its worst. He also represented the Franklin spirit at its worst. But even at its best, the Philadelphia tradition has something of the Franklin spirit. The radicalism of the enlightened scoutmaster breaks through the patrician surface. It is in the Foreword of the autobiography of the otherwise so admirable George Wharton Pepper, written in 1944, that I read: "Perhaps it is only *wishful thinking,* but my belief is that as America goes so will go the world." The italics are mine: they wish to emphasize that these were not the words of a radical Wilsonian but of an isolationist, of perhaps the most eminent and most conservative Philadelphia lawyer.

Yet, perhaps because of its often vapid nature, the Franklin influence does not always endure. Whereas Penn's original constitution for Pennsylvania is an extraordinarily sensible document, the constitution which Franklin drew up during the Revolution had to be discarded within a few years. At first sight, compared to the sensitive Penn, Dr. Franklin seems to represent the great American virtue of robust common sense. At closer examination, however, this impression rapidly disappears. Somehow, somewhere, the tolerant spirit of Penn, less in the form of an image than in the sense of an instinct, meanwhile continues to prevail. His peculiar mixture of pallid purposefulness, of deep-seated melancholy hidden behind the benevolent vigor of action, is the mysterious inheritance of Philadelphia to this day.

It endured through the years when brown-stone castles and Masonic

---

monstrous, twelve-story façade of the Curtis Magazine Building, housing the *Saturday Evening Post* and the *Ladies Home Journal.* And across the square are the new, air-conditioned offices of *Holiday.*
No longer.

Cathedrals were erected in the middle of the city, and when a tremendous iron-and-marble civic cathedral was built to honor poor Penn in the form of a monstrous City Hall. Yet even at that time, in "corrupt and contented" Philadelphia, it bred manly virtues stronger than those of the present, liberal-politic, city-planner generation. It is true that around 1900 the touch was Germanic, and they drank schooners of beer to the Boers, but they also read Kipling and their image of England was not represented by the Schweppesman. From books, walking in town, talking to old lawyer friends of my Philadelphian father-in-law, I can still sense that cigar-smoke, the steamed clams, the cracking jokes, that red-cheeked, gartered, democratic touch of easy-handed corruption but also of easy-minded tolerance, the smell of the sea in the little restaurants (so unlike the modern drugstore smell of restaurants), the high whistle of the Reading locomotives (unlike the false beep of today's Pennsylvania diesels). It was a Philadelphia world all very different from Penn, and yet still closer to his large tolerant spirit than to the little crackerjack rules of Benjamin Franklin. This was fifty years ago; and since then the voice of Benjamin Franklin had become the Voice of America; but somehow, here and there, the unspoken voice of William Penn still echoes in Philadelphia.

Grand Mountain Hotel
New Rich and Old Hottles*

(1959)

The thin rain was falling as we drove across the cold little Swiss village square, with the geraniums around the central fountain, up toward the Grand Mountain Hotel.

A mile above the village, anchored on the mountain, rides the Grand Mountain Hotel in the evening, with a hundred yellow lights lit: a rich and safe ship for the rich and safe, above avalanches and wars, indestructible. A *Titanic* without smokestacks. It rides the indigo waves of the Alpine night.

It has entered European history: the Grand Mountain Hotels of Locarno, Lugano, with their Disarmament and Reparation and International Conferences; the resting and meeting-places of Stresemanns, Adenauers, Briands. It has, of course, entered literary history: scores of novels have been written about Grand Mountain Hotels and sanatoria, among them, *The Magic Mountain.* The Grand Mountain Hotel is a symbol. It represents a period, an age.

I have been here before, before the Second World War, perhaps twice, with my parents. I was very young then. We stayed no longer than a week, perhaps a fortnight. But the memories spring up, in disciplined order, as I pass through glass-and-mahogany doors, as I glimpse the long oblong veneering of the dark banister of the stairs, as I recognize the thin-lipped Swiss smile above the golden keys embroidered on the black lapels of the concierge. I deposit my passport. I shake hands with the Manager. On Turkey carpets I walk toward the little mahogany elevator. I enter the Grand Mountain Hotel.

*"Hottles" still exist, but the word for them is gone.

My parents are dead; Russian armies sit astride half of Europe; atom bombs are regularly exploded somewhere; some of my schoolmates ride official jeeps in Florida, working on the first rocket-shot at the moon. The Grand Mountain Hotel is the same.

All the things in it are the same. The long red runners on the floors of endless corridors. The brass key-hooks between the double doors of the rooms. The breakfast terrace in the morning, where a white-coated drove of Ticinese waiters stand on guard while through the insectless air flow the radiant waves of the mountain sun, softening the crystal butter, warming the cold strawberry jam, tempering the best morning coffee in the world in the proper proportion. The hushed tingle of the luncheon terrace— different from the determined tingle of the silver in the luxury restaurants of France—where from under small silver domes these Italian waiters, now in black, pull out veal steaks, roasted capons, thin red-veined cold ham. Inaudibly they snarl at each other in Italian; inobtrusively they consult with the guests in French, emulating the deference of personal servants. In the afternoon it is all light blue and light gold, white tennis sweaters and reddening faces returning from mountain walks, the some-what plaintive air of the hotel quartet playing under garden umbrellas on the terrace. The whine of the violin mixes with the sound of regular splashes coming from fountain and swimming pool. In the evening, sit-ting after dinner in the hall, I contemplate the ugliness of the furniture, the oak panelling all the way to the top, the Edwardian milk-glass bulbs and thin brass arms spreading their particular kind of light, dull rather than soft, into the dusky-plushy corners of that enormous, irregular hall. The black, shiny waitresses, with their white butterflies, bringing tiny drinks in pony glasses to a few tables. A little cigar-smoke is rising. A few people play bridge. By midnight, the hall is empty, since this is a hotel of comfort rather than of luxury. Unlike other sorts of luxury hotels, it fulfills but two-thirds of the French poet's wish: it stands for *luxe* and *calme* without *volupté*. I am whirred upstairs to my great soft crypt of a white Swiss bed.

These hotels have a smell of their own. No matter when one enters, over the dustless odor of the porous carpets wafts a faint smell of fine consommé. It wafts above furniture polish and kirsch, and a tinge of it is even detectible beyond the aromatism of the after-dinner coffee. Then, one flight above, commences the peculiar, Mountain Hotel odor of freshly scrubbed, damp wood: a fine smell of steam, even on the coldest and clearest of mornings. And there is an electric smell all around the terraces, balconies and gardens; it is there mixed within the clay-and-canvas odor of the tennis court, and the wet wood smell of the swimming pool. It is the ozone of the prickly, crackling Swiss mountain air, somewhat softened as it is streaming through this high valley, coming down to manageable proportions for the physical benefit of the guests of the Grand Mountain Hotel . . .

For a hundred years now people have been coming here for this air. There are also sulphuric waters, radioactive baths, massage rooms, vapors and excellent medical services; but the main asset is the divine mountain air. Toward the end of June the pilgrimage of the rich begins. Down the Rhine Valley, wending their way through the thick traffic of rainy Zurich in shiny automobiles; bumping in the jetstream toward Geneva Airport in transoceanic airplanes they come, toward the Grand Mountain Hotels of Switzerland, to restore their health, and to restore their spirits. The first task is manageable; the second is more difficult. The air does different things to different people, and the rich are different now.

They are not different in the sense F. Scott Fitzgerald was supposed to have meant it. They are different from the old rich, from the real rich. Not that they are parvenus. They are timid, they have less of the zest of life. They have little of the confidence of *nouveaux riches;* they are, rather, newly comfortable. They are not at ease. They are nervous. "The clientèle is changing, Monsieur." But of course.

The world wars changed not the Grand Mountain Hotel but the grand mountain clientèle. At first only the top of the clientèle. Even the First World War changed but little: the Russian noblemen were the only ones who disappeared. In the Twenties and the Thirties, the Anglo-Saxons were on the top: in the Grand Mountain Hotel Englishmen and Americans were prominent. The sun shone for longer periods. The stones shone yellow and red. English newspaper magnates, in houndstooth knickers, strode out late every morning to play golf; the children of New England fortunes won the hotel tennis championships, lanky American youngsters with rosy-red faces, successfully imitating the driving shots of Don Budge. As the Bright Young Things of the Twenties grew into their own thirties, they sat late in the bar drinking exotic cocktails, played bridge for very high stakes, and on golden afternoons raced down to St. Moritz to flirt and dance into the night. There were French and Dutch bankers, and *grand bourgeois* families from Central Europe; and ambitious young lawyers from Budapest on thin budgets, but already knowledgeable of the marks of *grand bourgeois* living.

There are very few Englishmen now: the war and taxes changed many things. There are fewer Americans, and among them the transient type predominates, the executive on his way back from Düsseldorf or Dhahran, stocking up on a little comfort that his timetable cannot stand but for a few days.

The new rich are Germans, and South Americans. The rich Germans, with their myopic eyes, with their large wives. They are good guests, dependable guests; they do not gamble and drink little. In the evenings, they sit self-consciously in their very dark suits, in their very polished black shoes, their necks craning above those silver four-in-hand ties which, in Central Europe, mean the acme of sartorial elegance. They smoke one Hamburg cigar a day, and on Saturday nights, when the hotel orchestra strikes up the airs of a Viennese *Abend,* they dance a little with their wives. They take the cures very seriously. Every morning they ride down together, on the hotel bus, to the *Trinkhalle,* to get their daily little cup of sulphuric water in that echoing big vault of a pump-room. In three weeks, they are pounded and massaged down; having become almost grey in the smoky air and new glass-enclosed offices of Frankfurt and Essen, their Hessian and Westphalian cheeks grown pallid-rosy again.

The South Americans are different. There are two kinds of them.

There are the native South Americans, old brown men with beautiful silver hair (why is it that South American men are seldom bald?); thin young men with white teeth. The descendants of the greatest plantation-owners of the universe: their minds and tongues fully Latinized but with a trace of Indian blood still singeing their olive cheeks. Their French is impeccable; they know their wines; they are perfect tippers. With the children all is cashmere and suede and hand-knitted pullovers in which their avian bones seem to disappear; the older men wear those peculiarly stooped black suits specially custom-made for them in Madrid or London. Only in the older women, as they throw shawls over their round shoulders under the dull haze of the globular lights, is there a touch of something not European, clannish, hen-like, Indian.

The neutral rich of the cold war; but they are near the end of a long line of thin castes. Perhaps more interesting are the new South Americans.

For they are not South Americans at all. They are Austrians, Rumanians, Hungarians, Poles, Czechs, a few Italians, a few Germans: the refugees and escapees, literally the displaced persons of the Second World War. Ex-Europeans who made out well in South America. How much worldly knowledge the Manager and the chief clerk of the Grand Mountain Hotel must have in these days, to match passports with nationalities! The names are still Central European names; but the passports are Venezuelan, Argentinian, Brazilian, Cuban. Ex-lawyers, ex-bankers, ex-merchants, ex-engineers: now they are South American industrialists or Export-Import wizards. They are different from the immigrants of the past: those had burned their bridges as they set off from the Old World. They are different from the refugees of old: those seldom grew rich within one generation. They are different from their friends and relatives who came to the United States: unlike them, the new South Americans do not really like their new fatherlands, no matter how much money they may make there. They are drawn back to Europe, to their bourgeois memories. They tell themselves that they have come to restore their health; they complain of the South American climate. But there are mountain resorts all over South America, cheaper and easier to reach. No: they come back to the Grand Mountain Hotel, to this old European hot-water bottle, to warm their souls growing cold in the hot shadows of South America.

So, in the 1950s, in the Grand Mountain Hotel there appears the same Prague corporation lawyer who twenty years before came to climb the mountain paths with his young wife and friends, in Tyrolean outfits. Then he may have been a little too loud in spots, a bit too demanding with the waiters; now he is wrinkled and stooped as he takes the short afternoon walking-route over the hilly path covered with pine-needles to the village terrace café, two miles away.

This oxygenation of a European summer draws people from all over the world to Switzerland. This has been going on for a hundred years now. Two hundred years ago it was the aristocratic Grand Tour and Italy; then came the long patrician interregnum of the vogue for watering-places, whose fame spread slowly eastward across the continent, from Bath and Spa through Evian and Baden-Baden to Gastein and Karlsbad. It was not until about 1850 that enterprising Swiss peasant families began to discover that, in the Bourgeois Age, hotelry and tourism may become a great national industry. Remember that not so long ago in Europe *hôpitals* were dreadful dying-places for the poor, and *hôtels* were but overnight shelters. The rich lived, traveled, lodged and died privately. About a hundred years ago this was beginning to change. It is still changing now; but the content changes more than the form.

In this century a number of European bottles were broken; and even from the unbroken ones a lot of old winey blood poured out. The *Titanic,* symbol of the faulty complacency of the Bourgeois World, a black-and-red iron cathedral, manufactured in Protestant Belfast, sank in icy waters in 1912; it was a premonition of the savage disaster which was to overwhelm that world two years later. But the Grand Mountain Hotel still stands.

For this is the old European story. Now wine in old bottles. New rich and old hottles.

On my last morning I go out on the wooden balcony of my room. The air is frozen and sunny at the same time. Outside everything is sharp, clear, cold. Inside the red comforter hangs bulbously over the bedstead: everything is thick and warm. Twin peaks sparkle; I can see far and wide, through the dark green valley shot through with sunshine, toward the blue opening at its end, promising Italy. I recall the Swiss tourist-office slogan: "The balcony of Europe." The view is superb; but I shiver in my pyjamas. I make for the room. Hot water is pouring into the tub. There I recall this philosophic sentence: "The spirit of Europe still warms the world." Right now it is my flesh which is warmed by the hot waters of the Grand Mountain Hotel. "Balcony of Europe?" No, rather the Hot-Water Bottle of the World.

Andorra
The Catalan Switzerland
(1964)

"La dernière cellule du monde féodal en Occident."
(From the Michelin: Pyrénées.)

There are two ways to get to Andorra. There is the High Road from France, and the Low Road from Spain. This is in accord with the romantic condition: the High Road is better, though it is often impassable. The Low Road is open more often than the high one but it is a lumpy bad highway rising gradually from the dry tablelands of Navarre: the approach is long and dull. The High Road is better. It is a road with an unusual attraction: it presents the Pyrenees in something like a natural cinemascope.

About thirty miles south of Toulouse there appears a dark blue line of hills straight ahead. In about a minute one sees a lighter blue range beyond them; and then another, grey-blue, continuous strip. In another minute something new appears: the unearthly glistening of the snow (at first as if the sky above the highest blue range were patched with white by an impressionist painter). Two, three more minutes on the road to the south and there it is: a whole, unbroken mountain panorama, a wall of mountains rising up in front of us, and the Route Nationale 20 is rushing straight south against this wall.

Even on a cloudy day the highest part of the wall is visible as one drives into Pamiers. This is a portion of that part of France which ever since 1814, when Wellington's army had camped through it, basking in the sunshine of easy romantic victories, has attracted many Englishmen. (Some of them have written very well about these towns, as, for example, an Edwardian Anglican rector, the Reverend S. Baring-Gould, about Foix:

"a very dull place, its sole feature being the castle, like a plain man with a prominent nose.") I was charmed by a curiosity in Pamiers: a row of nineteenth-century houses separated from the main road by something like a narrow canal which must have been one of the castle moats. The housedwellers cross through little cast-iron footbridges, and over this row of houses hang the branches of enormous plane trees. After that, Foix and Ax-les-Thermes, with its odor of rain and sulphur and its ancient Roman baths.

But somewhere between Pamiers and Foix that curious sensation: the first mountain village. For some reason one senses, even as the car scoots forward in the narrow streets, a feeling of sudden closeness: the color of the stone is different; there is that imaginary impression of low red fires inside the grey houses and dark wood. This is the Ariège, with its tradition of a strong, intelligent and tolerant peasantry; it is a country of dark rocks, thin pine forests, and the Pyreneean wild boar, the *sanglier.* The River Ariège runs north, coming down from the Andorran border, gurgling icy and white, romantic and shivery, as all mountain rivers should. After Ax-les-Thermes the road really begins to climb; it is cold; even under the hot mountain sun it is best to close the sunroof. Unlike the Alps, there are few mountain chalets, only the hydroelectric stations and here and there a stone chapel in ruins, high on the mountainsides. The first French customs station is at L'Hospitalet (a rather inhospitable-looking place). There follows now a very long and difficult mountain road, the highest one in the Pyrenees and one of the highest in Europe, closed from November sometimes into late April. At the Col d'Envalira, with eternal snow, the highest point (about 7,400 feet above sea-level): large sheets of snowy mountainside all around, frozen and still.

Then we descend into the narrow, green, different and unexpected valleys (there are two of them) of Andorra. And, in less than an hour, as we drive into the twinkling valley towns of Les Escaldes and Andorra-la-Valls (twin cities, these) there rise around us the inviting marks and signs of sensations of traveling in the twentieth century: the pleasures of arriving in a mountain town, the modern agreeableness of a mountain civilization. From the dark and the cold we are moving toward the interior prospects of glowing comfort: that sudden rush of heat and as one passes into the lobby of a bright hotel from the frozen mountain air of the parking-space, the steam-smell of the bathroom, the electric arclights of the town blinking through the large windows against the blackness of the conifers; beyond that, the prospects of large meals, strong spirits, a fire-place. Wending our way towards that through the streets: many people, and eternally lit shop-windows showing the riches of Europe and the wealth of America, people and cars, cars and people, including large black Ford station wagons and Cadillacs, driven slowly through the often very narrow streets by a race of small, brown, stocky people, with the permanent thin stubble on their mountaineer faces: a Spanish Switzerland.

This is broad, and not very precise, this term of a Spanish Switzer-land. It will do for a superficial impression but not for a definition. For the purposes of the latter, Andorra is a Catalan Principality.

We might as well go on with this business of Principalities and Powers. We might as well go on and say what Andorra is not. It is not a republic; it is not a democracy; strictly speaking, it is not even a state. Not a Republic: because Andorra is a Co-Principality, ruled by two sover-eigns, one of whom is a Spanish Bishop (the holder of the See of Urgel), the other the French Chief of State. Not a democracy: because according to her constitution her two Princes are absolute monarchs, either of whom still possesses the right to dispose at will—*à son bon plaisir*—of the life or death of any Andorran. According to certain categories of interna-tional law, not even a state: because Andorrans are not citizens of An-dorra: they are subjects of the two Princes: there is such a thing as Andorran citizenship but there is no sovereign state of Andorra.

According to modern international law, that is. The ancient laws of Andorra: that is another thing. It is all the difference between what is legal and what is real. It is in this respect that, save for her size, Andorra does not really fit into the category of the Quaint Minuscule States of Europe. Unlike Andorra, Monaco or Lichtenstein or Luxembourg or San Marino is a sovereign state; on the other hand one really can't speak of a Monagasque or a Litchtenstein national character. Supermodern Monaco and "European" Luxembourg are not "last cells of the feudal world in the West."

All of the Pyrenees are saturated with the memories of Charlemagne and Roland: the Andorrans, too, claim that Charlemagne stood and fought (he never seems to have slept) here and there. These are legends. For our purposes, the history of a distinct Andorra begins with 1278 and 1288, when two treaties, the so-called Pareatges, define and establish the dual rule of the Bishop of Urgell and of the Count of Foix over Andorra. Little more than three hundred years later it was a Count of Foix, the marvelous Henri IV, who became the King of France. After that, such diverse personages as Louis XIV, Bonaparte, the radical and anti-clerical Presidents of the French Republics, Marshal Philippe Pétain and General Charles de Gaulle—they have been, all of them, one time or another, one of the Princes of Andorra.

One ought not dwell upon the curiosities of Andorra's history of long ago. As late as a century ago the map of Europe was still dotted with many remnants of the Middle Ages, with green little islands of duchies, with colorful principalities. Until recent times there was little that was unique in the Andorran condition. The interesting part of Andorran history belongs to the twentieth century: it is contemporary. Unlike the Swiss or the Monegasques who were growing prosperous during the nineteenth century, the Andorrans lived a harsh and backward existence, sheltered but by the rigid securities of their patriarchal customs. In contrast to the rest of Europe, the population dropped; Andorrans were leaving their country. (The population in 1880 was 5,313; in 1936, 4,321.) At times during the Carlist Wars ripping Spanish Navarre, the bands of the Carlist chieftains with their extraordinary names (Zumálacarregui) roamed through the Andorran valleys at will. At times the Andorrans quarreled with their Bishop; on other occasions, the Bishop quarreled with the French—he once had all of the telegraph poles pulled down that the French had been putting up. The High Road connection with France did not yet exist; there were no railroads within a hundred miles, and no postal service. In the *Casa del Vall,* the Andorran government house, there is still a large kitchen, on the first floor, for as late as 1934 the august members of the council of state had to come on muleback, and some of them had no way of getting home the night of the meeting. During the First World War the Andorrans, perched between France and Spain, made some money by smuggling: but nothing like the riches of the comfortable bourgeois cove of Switzerland. The real connection with the outer world, and with the twentieth century, did not reach the Andorrans until the

Nineteen-Thirties. During the First World War the Bishop of Urgell had the Low Road built with his own funds: it is said that His Eminence, Cardinal Beulloch, the very shape of whose name suggests a very ponderous personage, could no longer stand the fifteen miles on muleback from Urgell to San Juliá. In the Twenties the Andorran Hydroelectric Company was built, with French capital; in return for the concession the Andorrans demanded that the Company undertake the construction of the High Road. It was completed in 1933.

Then came the Spanish Civil War; then the Second World War, with the German invasion of France. During the first war came hundreds of poor refugees; then, during two sunny, dramatic weeks in June 1940, came thousands of rich ones, their Panhards and Delahayes one after the other, churning up the dust on the Pas d'Envalira. In France now reigned the darkness of defeat and misery and inflation. The golden era of smuggling had begun.

But this English word "smuggling," with its wry, diminutive, Scottish-Celtic sense of something hidden, requires qualification. In the case of Andorra, "contrabands," with its Latin roots, is better, Contraband, for the Andorrans, has not been only a tradition; it has been the very root of their existence, and far from being illegal—because of the curious duality of Andorra's international situation. It was, and it still is, illegal for a Frenchman or for a Spaniard to take certain things out of Andorra across the frontier; but an Andorran may carry into Andorra whatever he wants from France or from Spain, and he can sell it to anyone, *in Andorra,* that is. And the Andorrans know their frontier region backwards and forwards, which is not a mere cliché, because the frontier does run backwards and forwards: there are few customs' stations: the herds wander peacefully from France to Andorra and from Andorra to Spain and back to France, their composition changing on the way. During the nineteenth century the principal objects for contraband were tobacco and livestock. Also, the principal direction of the traffic went south, from France through the Andorran valleys to Spain. That was the case during the Spanish Civil War, too; but in June 1940 all of this suddenly changed. There was the smuggling of refugees, of Allied agents, of escaping British pilots southwards, to the neutral safeties of Spain and Portugal. This traffic came to an end in 1944, with the liberation of France. But the other kind of traffic, that movement of goods and of goodies to France, did not end with the war. In Andorra there now piled up the goods of the neutral world and of the Americas. The result was a constant minor hemorrhage of the pallid postwar economy of France, from whose financial veins a strong little trickle (more than one billion francs in 1947, for example) was dripping into the Andorran receptacles.

This spectacle was sufficiently exciting to make the prose of a learned French professor break into a nervous trot as he was describing the geography of Andorra in a scientific publication of the *Institut de Géographie de Clermont-Ferrand:*

> Now the three or four wooden stores on the Andorran side of the frontier cracking at the seams with all that wasn't available in France, sardines, soap, hams, cigars, cigarettes, coffee, bananas, nylons, woolens . . . How to describe this atmosphere! Piled up in the most astonishing disorder, boxes of cigars next to shoes, liquor next to nylons. Klondyke and the Gold Rush! (*Un air de Klondyke du temps de la ruée vers l'or! Ou d'un poste du Far-West au siècle passé!*)

It was at that time that Andorra became something like Switzerland: but the similarities may be deceiving.

The Golden Age of Smuggling died down to more normal proportions more than a decade ago, with the gradual stabilization of the French (and of the Spanish) economies. Andorra did not become, and seemingly does not intend to become, an international financial center.

The character and the institutions of the Andorrans changed little. They may ride in Buicks, but their government and their way of life is still largely patriarchal. The former consists of a council of twenty-four men who are elected by the heads of families living in parishes. Their administration is composed by local officials with curious names and no less curious functions: the *Nunci* (the chief magistrate), *Les Banders* (who must be the very opposite of bandits, since they are the official communal shepherds), *Manadors* and *Vehedors; le Mostafa,* who is nominated by the parish and who is supposed to be in charge of verifying weights, scales and measures ("he tastes the wine which is sold in the inns; he must assure the quality of the bread, of the wine, and of the olive oil"). *Les Curés* are not what one would think: not the parish priests but the official notaries of Andorra, in charge of wills and testaments; *les Notaires* are the two registrars of Andorra, the only two officials who are named by the two Princes. There is a lovely calligraphical tradition respecting their official signatures, of which there must be two: their regular signature, called the *rubrica,* together with a kind of signed seal which is the *signo.* Some of these *signos* resemble the fine wrought iron which is so characteristic of the decorations of these mountain people.

Unlike the Roman law of most Latin countries, Andorran law is common law, its basic documents being the so-called *Politar* and the *Manual Digest* of 1748 which is a manual digest all right but no, not in English: the term is Catalan. There is no civil marriage; there is no divorce; there are no poor, no hospitals, because it is taken for granted that the parish organization, the *Comú,* must take care of the poor and of the indigent. There is no Andorran army, and no compulsory service; there are twelve Andorran policemen to whom recently a thirteenth one was added, the solitary traffic policeman of Andorra-la-Vella. Andorrans pay no taxes and no licenses for their cars, for their hunting, for their fishing. Their telephone service costs fifty cents a month. But there are no foreign firms in Andorra, nothing like Switzerland or Lichtenstein; and, except for the many summer visitors, no foreign residents. No matter how rich you are, you cannot become an Andorran national except in one event—if you married an Andorran girl with her parents' consent, and then only after your first child reached the age of fourteen.

So the Andorrans, these Catalans of the Pyrenees, live on, in their now electrically heated houses (they drove a hard bargain with the hydro-electric company: their rates are the lowest in the world, and their yearly consumption consequently the second highest, after Switzerland), in their new white concrete apartment buildings stocked with the comforts of a bourgeois civilization, with their wrought iron balconies and the heavy rustic imitation furniture inside. Between them, in the twinkling streets, the shops are full of radios, watches, perfumes, spirits; they are open every day, including Sunday; so are the banks. You may wander into a sports store and express your desire for a case of sherry: they may get it for you. For $1 a bottle (the best Spanish sherry, that is); scotch for $1.50; and the usual (or, rather, unusual) array of things from Swiss watches to Havana cigars. But when the evening of the day and the evening of the year falls, one senses the existence of a closed and patriarchal world, seeping even into the well-lit stores, when the streets are full not so much of tourists but of dark bony men, talking Catalan. The same feeling on Sunday, in the church of Les Escaldes, newly rebuilt in grey stone, and thus curiously similar to certain Irish parish churches in the United States, with that Celtic-Romanesque imitation architecture: the same serious congregation, without that shuffling in the back and without the baroque altars which are characteristic of their Spanish cousins further southward. The inscriptions, too, are in Catalan, like the cardboard tacked over the box at the statue of a rather primitive Madonna:

MISSES DEFUNTS

—in Catalan it means Masses for the dead, in English it sounds like a dirge for departed spinsters.

Except for the potential buying spree, which inevitably includes perfumes and expensive liquors, there is nothing deluxe in Andorra. There are a number of hotels, clean and comfortable ones, but only one of them which is good enough to deserve the red print in the Michelin. The *Parc* is a beautiful modern mountain hotel, with every room having a balcony and a view, and an excellent kitchen. It has an unusually lovely swimming pool which, for once, fully merits the natural-shape adjective, since it is hewed out from the flat rocks of the hillside, its steps and bottom slightly undulating, pebbly-smooth. For an apéritif or a cognac, before or after lunch, one may sit outside on a really emerald-green lawn; beneath are the narrow streets of the town, and above one's head rise the two tremendous sides of a green and rocky mountain; all around flows the cold, clear air, warmed by the mountain sun.

The Gran Valira and some of the smaller streams are supposed to be rich in trout. Hunting is not expensive but wild game is much less abundant than in the past: weeks may pass until someone bags a specimen of the now elusive but beautiful Pyreneean chamois, the *isard*. The last bear was shot in 1942, a fact which appears in both Andorran guidebooks: it is curious to see this association in the chronology of this mountaineer people with what was otherwise the year of Stalingrad, Treblinka, Guadalcanal. Terrains for ski abound; but it is only recently that the Andorrans have begun to exploit them; moreover, not only is the High Road impassable in winter but on the French side of the pass ski-tows have been installed, so that the enthusiasts need not drive further up, into Andorra. There are two or three old buildings, and an interesting rough Romanesque church in the village of Canillo, but that is about all in the way of institutionalized quaintness. What are not merely quaint but vivid are the curiosities of modern Andorran life.

They couldn't be less French, in attitudes and customs; they are jealously, proudly Andorran; still their passports are issued by the préfet of the Pyrenées-Orientales, and their diplomatic interests are represented by the Foreign Ministry in Paris. They couldn't be more Catholic, serious, rigid and patriarchal as they are: yet they have been always, and are still now, sensitive and recalcitrant about their prerogatives of independence which they think are often menaced by their Prince, the Bishop of Urgell. Their relations with France are no less suspicious and mercurial: up to this day, for example, they have refused to establish a telephone service with France so that, except for a few special coin boxes, it is not possible to call France a few miles away (and it is impossible to telephone to Andorra from France), while all of Spain is dialable, including the Canary Islands. On the other hand, they let the French take care of all of the postal service, except for the postmen, who number two. The Andorrans are supermodern in the sense that fuel injection and transistors and kilowatts are the subjects of their everyday conversation: but they have stuck to some of their weights and measures which are still medieval, with curious names (the *canne,* about 3 feet 8 inches, composed by several *pans,* about nine inches—which, however, is not the same as the *canne de Barcelona,* nine feet six inches; the *caballon,* whose official description is seventeen sheafs of wheat, and which with great difficulty was agreed upon to mean one thousand eight hundred and ninety-one square meters; and there are *arrobas, mitgeras, porrons, paucans, sisterons* and *punyeras*).

There is, finally, Radio Andorra. Shortly before the Second World War a canny French capitalist, part-owner of what was then Radio Toulouse, wanted to place some of his capital outside the reaches of taxability. With the help of an Andorran friend, he obtained with some difficulty the permission of the Andorran government council in order to set up a radio station in the hills. Radio Andorra was an immediate success, for two reasons. First, it carried certain commercials, something that was not done by any of the other Western European government-owned radio networks. The second reason was the personality of the principal announcer, of a young woman, whose melodious voice: *Aqui Radio Andorra!* became a modern Roland's horn. She received hundreds of letters every day, from admirers all over Western Europe, including countless marriage offers. Then came the war; Radio Andorra, expropriated by the Andorran government, remained studiously neutral; it went on broadcasting its pacific programs, music, music, music, a few commercials but not a single newsbroadcast during the war and after. To Radio Andorra listened now millions of Western Europeans in the years of darkness, including those millions whose simple radio sets could not pick up London. It was a thin but strong little shaft of Latin sunshine, that music. The sweet alto announcer married an Andorran. After the war Radio Andorra, prosperous as all get out, became Radio des Vallées: a new and more powerful station was built, the highest one in Europe, whose musical sounds can be heard far into the plains of Central and Northern Europe and to the Levant.

For Andorra, as for Radio Andorra, the historical circumstance created the economic condition: uniqueness, neutrality, prosperity: whether all of this made the people "progressive," that is another question. Radio, automobiles, electricity, yes: but no railroad has come close to Andorra, the Pyrenees are a wall blocking out television, and there is no place for an airfield. Perhaps the helicopter, hopping and buzzing above the Envalira, will change the latter, and Andorra will become an International Ski Paradise: but I am inclined to doubt it. The Andorrans are a shrewd race, and they know the advantages of being underdeveloped. One goes into a wineshop on one of the neon-lit streets of Les Escaldes and there they are, gathering around the vinegary barrels talking Catalan, with their belts and heavy leather purses, suspicious and confident. One senses that the world of the long mountain nights, and the frozen trips of contraband, the oil-lamp time of the last century, is still very close, a part of their lives, as some of them go out into the evening street, climb with their short legs into their black cars and drive away.

Three Days in London
Churchill's Funeral

(1965)

January Twenty-Ninth
Friday

It is a very quiet London, a humdrum day. No sense of crowds, no excitement, no feeling of something big and ceremonial. Even at the airport there are not many people; it is a winter arrival day; the kings and the prime ministers are driven away quickly, silently, there is little of that raincoated and gumsoled rushing around them of slovenly photographers with their hanging ogling equipment. The English are, of course, very good at this quick and efficient whisking of important people out of sight. Still it is very different from the June atmosphere of coronations, and even of royal funerals.

That grey airport bus, through the western suburbs of the great city. It is a long and humdrum approach through what were not so long ago solidly respectable rows of houses but which bear some of the outward marks of social decay. There is not much traffic in this snow and driving sleet. Past the huge dumb-impassive square aluminum buildings set up by construction companies, indistinguishable from American ones. And then, rather suddenly, near the end of the new concrete highroad, rows of brown brick buildings, a Victorian English sea of houses after the grey wintry continental cloudiness of the motorway. The lights burn yellow through the mist now, at eleven in the morning. And everywhere what, for a writer, must be one of the most evocative things of all: the inscriptions of London. The street signs and the shop fascia, the Bus Stops and the public lettering, most of it in that already traditional and very English modern sans-serif which Eric Gill had created in 1928, I think, for the

London transport system and which was, indeed, one of the few fine achievements of the English creative spirit between the wars. Of all countries that I know England has the finest public lettering.

At first this is curious that this should be so, for an un-rhetorical and un-intellectual people. At second thought it is perhaps not so surprising at all. This people, with all of its Old Testament traditions, is not really a pharisaic people: with their respect for The Law there is mixed a deep strain of their love for The Word. That is just why Perfidious Albion is, really, a mistaken phrase; that is why this is the Shakespearean nation; that is why they understood Churchill when he had to be understood, in that dramatic moment of their long existence.

But there are very few signs of the funeral now, less than twenty-four hours before it will begin.

The flags are at half-mast, of course. But there are not so many of them.

Noon. We walk out from the hotel, not quite sure where we shall presently head to.

It is still sleeting and grey. Hyde Park stretches out, green, wet and empty. The traffic on the great street has dropped down to a Sunday-afternoon level; many empty cabs and only the red busses lumbering past without rumbling, much like English middle-class spinsters who had grown to maturity in the King Edward age, with a Queen Alexandra bearing, and now often their conductors are young black women and men.

We walk somewhat hesitantly eastward, into the wind. Then one notices the many different national flags, at half-mast, flying from the buildings. This row, fifty years ago the town houses and the flats of a rich upper-middle-class, during the short peachy-creamy period of Peter Pan Kensington, houses many consulates now; the banners of many unknown new African countries, and Tito's red star flapping in the wind. (He, too, owes much to Churchill.)

There is something else, too. Something that towers, kindly, over the white Kensington houses with their now tattered fluorescent and bureaucratic insides. This thing stands above the intrusive, the uncomfortable thoughts of what the James Barries and the inevitable reaction to them—

Bloomsbury, further down—had done to the spirit of England. The building which now houses the Dutch Consulate. It is a large red apartment
building, built in the Queen Anne style, I presume, around 1910; its white
curved roof-gables have a Dutch impression, though this is surely coinci-
dental. Set back from the pavement behind a low wall and a small gravelly
courtyard this house stands like a large solid ship, anchored forever. Its
brick walls have a tinge of vermilion; like all colors, this impression is
inseparable from the association which goes with it, and this is that of
quiet, reddish small square rooms inside, with dark comfortable furniture
and brass fenders. Above the doorway, with its crest with the Royal
Netherlands seal, flies the bourgeois red-white-blue horizontal flag of
Holland, half-mast, in mourning.

It stands but a few hundred feet from Hyde Park Gate, from another,
even more English, red-brick house where Winston Churchill died. And
now, for the first time, I am gripped by the kind of emotion which is
compounded by historical memory and personal association. This London house, and the Holland Legation, and Churchill—they are, all three,
a monument of decency, commingled now in my mind and before my
eyes. Large, tolerant, solid and decent—this is what they stood for. Houses
like this have buttressed the now so ramshackle edifice of a thousand
years of European civilization, during its last great Protestant and Northwestern and bourgeois phase. Holland and England. Marlborough and
Churchill; Holland the first England; England the second Holland; brown
warm rooms and Edwardian Queen Anne; nations of families, presided
over by royal families, by decent and unpretentious ones. The Dutch
mourn Churchill, they understand how he tried to save a certain kind of
civilization.

From the house of the Holland Legation we now drive to Westminster Hall.

The cab rolls by an endless queue. We come upon it suddenly, on
Millbank, as it stretches out of the New Palace Yard and from Westminster Hall; its thousands of people stand straight and somber, huddling
from the wind, scuffling slowly, close against the iron railings, way down
Millbank; and then the queue is turned inward, through the small flat
garden between the street and the eastern end of Westminster and the

river embankment; and then it turns back again, a little sparser but long, very long. It goes all the way to the Lambeth Bridge. This will take hours. My eight-year-old son is wearing cotton socks. Still, we'll see. With a cold empty feeling in my stomach I pay off the cab on the Lambeth Bridge and there we are, in the queue.

It is a good queue because it is moving. The wind is awfully cold, blowing from the grey sheet of the Thames, but there is not that sense of hopeless democratic impatience as when one has to stand and wait and stand and wait for what seem to be endless minutes without explanation. I am surprised how far we have progressed in fifteen minutes, how long already the queue is behind us. And it is a good queue because it is an English queue, disciplined and good-natured, without jostling. After fifteen minutes I know that we'll go through with it. Behind us a group of schoolgirls, with impossibly long scarves, are joking and occasionally snickering, but somehow this does not seem out of place here: a grim, self-conscious solemnity would be. We are standing and walking and standing and walking, surrounded by a variety of people, most of them working-class, charwomen perhaps. They must know that we are not English. Paul wants to tell them that we have flown over from Toulouse for the funeral but I dissuade him. We are not English. I came because of my conviction of respect and my sentiment of gratitude: to suggest their appreciation of us would compromise the conviction and the sentiment.

The papers wrote later that in the crowd lived the spirit of '40, that there was a great democratic upsurge of Englishmen, with men in bowler hats and elegant women standing in line with the cockneys and the steve-dores. Perhaps. I don't know about that. It might have been that way, in the cold evenings and at night, in the pubs and the teashops behind West-minster where the frozen fragments of the crowd went to restore them-selves with a warm cup of something. The way I see this queue is that of pale knots of different people, a long quilted afghan made out of patches of multifarious humanity: schoolgirls, working-people, businessmen, and the cheap-furred, straight-backed women of the conservative middle-class, a few foreigners here and there, including a few dark faces, smiling Pakistanis or Malayans or whatever they are. For a moment I feel a slight irritation: what do *they* have to do here? mere curiosity-seekers, that is, wanting to be present at the ceremonies of the Great Imperial Guru? But I dismiss the thought in a moment: because it is ungenerous and unreasonable: in *this* cold wind, through *this* frozen garden, for such hours, it is wrong, absolutely wrong, to question motives.

The working people. We have now made the first turn in the queue and people are talking. The charwomen. (But are they charwomen?) In their greenish old tweed coats, the brown wool scarves, the little glasses resting on the bumps of their pale faces, their bad teeth, their thin mouths. "I was here in 'Forty." "There was St. Paul's with all the City blazing around it, you know." But these are standard memories which have been repeated over and over again, presumably in the papers all through this week. How much of the memories are real? How much a mixture of associations? It doesn't matter. What matters is that they came, in this cold, which is no ceremony and no coronation, a hundred thousand of the working people of England, with their good nature and their knobby faces, out of a still living feeling rather than of memory—to the bier of a man who led them not to a great victory but who saved them from the worst of possible defeats, from the collapse of English self-respect.

Now their houses are warm and their television is going and they live better than ever before . . . Better: well, in a way. And they sense, too, the transitory malleability of this comfort, the old working people of old England, the tired members of the island race even in this airplane age: still members not fragments: selfish but self-respecting: unimaginative but fair. *Fair.* One day when the last portions of the green fairness of England will be gone or meticulously fenced in by planners and antiquarians that old green fairness will still exist, I think: it is the green copper bottom of the hearts of the working people of England.

But the middle-class is here, too. And my heart goes out for them.

I mean the middle-class, and not the more elegant members of the upper-middle-class. I mean men in their thin towncoats, women with their bony cheeks and blue eyes who have already lived longer than they shall live, erect and tired; I do not mean the children of Saki, the men and women of the once world of Evelyn Waugh and of the boring world of Anthony Powell. I need not describe them. I mean the people who were once the backbone of England.

It is a strange thing: but they, the upholders of the Conservative Party and of the once Imperial Spirit and of the Country Right Or Wrong were not those to whom Churchill meant the most. Like all of the really grands seigneurs, Churchill was closer to the aristocracy and also to the lower classes of the people. To the lower classes not because he had much of the vulgar demagogue in him (earthy he could be but rarely vulgar) but because the lower classes sometimes instinctively understood him even on his terms, on his own level. (In a news film I once saw a flick of a Churchill gesture that I cannot forget. He is coming through the ruins of an East London street after one of the bombardments. There are people, including a woman, with blowing hair, like the spirit of a proletarian Boadicea, running up to him from the ruins, gathering around him as he marches through the rubble in his tall hat and coat and cane, smoking with his incomparable chewing smile. As one of them runs up, he pats her on the back with his left arm, with an All Right! All Right! gesture. It is an amiable, patronizing and nonchalant everyday gesture. For a moment one senses that feeling of utter trust and confidence which only certain grandfathers can give.)

It was at that time—October 1940?—that the grey ice on the faces of the middle-class melted enough to reveal a racial facet of their true selves. He infused some kind of a sense into their long decline, from Kensington to Kensington. They were not the lot of hard-faced men who had made out well from the first war: but they were, let's face it, the people of Baldwin and of Chamberlain, stiff and unimaginative, with a tight kind of patriotism that was no longer enough. It was not merely a clique of narrow Germanophile politicians who distrusted Churchill in the Thirties, it was the once large middle-class of England who instinctively distrusted him: they were the people who had a natural trust in the Chamberlains: Churchill's pugnacity, his rhetoric, his brilliance, his Francophilia and his Americanisms, these were things they shunned, uneasily, stiffly, shyly. Then, in 1940, all of this flashed away. Even then they did not quite understand him: but in this country of common sense this was irrelevant then, and it is irrelevant still. For, after the war, it was this thinning and threadbare and sorely tried middle-class that continued to believe in some of the older patriotic virtues no matter how out of date these seemed to have become. Slowly, instinctively, through their bones—their bones warmed by this feeling through the chilly austerity years of British decline—their minds received Churchill, with his prose and through the memories of the war.

Oh, this shy race of men and women, how very different they are from other middle-classes of other nations, from the bourgeois of the continent! They are shy because they are kind. Kindness is not yet generosity, just as fairness isn't all honesty. But it is still from among their children that there may come forward one day an angry and generous Englishman, at another great dark hour of civilization, an avenging angel remembering Churchill.

Now, in his death, the pomp means less to them than to the others; it is not the might and the parade, the flags and the bands that impress them, but they, perhaps for the first time, have an inner comprehension of the magnanimity of this man now dead. Now, in his death, he belongs to them perhaps even more than to anyone else in England.

1940 is close now: the volunteer vans. We have turned away from the Thames; we are in the line moving slowly toward Millbank. There are three old blue vans of a volunteer service parked on the grass, and old small women address us with paper cups, offering blackish tea and Bovril. Two of the vans bear these inscriptions in small white paint: "London 1940–44. Coventry 1940. Bristol 1941." 1940 is close now; and the soft little rumble of the long queue seems to have dropped.

It is perhaps an appropriate thing that the American delegation to this Churchill funeral, because of some kind of Washington complexity and confusion, is unimpressive and second-rate. It is appropriate because 1940 has no great meaning for Americans. 1940 is a high year, an historic date, a sharp and poignant association for Britain and for Europe, not for America. There was, of course, Churchill's romantic Americanism, the very, very necessary help that Roosevelt chose to give him at that time, the sympathy, the interest, the willingness that millions of Americans had for Britain's struggle late that summer. But 1940 was still the peak of the European War, before America, Russia, Japan entered the scene; it was the gripping great crisis of the civilization of Europe rather than that of the "West" (a word hurriedly resuscitated and put into currency only after 1945) or, at that, of the United Nations. The lines were clear in 1940.

Hitler, Mussolini, Stalin, the Japanese, the opportunists as well as the Jew-haters, the Anglophobes of the lower-middle classes, greasy Spanish functionaries as well as the dark peasant masses of Russia, they, all, had their mean little enjoyments in witnessing the humiliations of Britannia. The other side was incarnated by Churchill, simply and clearly. It was good to know that summer—and not only for the British—that the struggle was ineluctable; that even in this century where everything is blurred by the viscuous wash of public relations, there were still two camps as close to Good Versus Evil as ever in the terrestrial struggles of nations.

All of this touched the United States but indirectly. This is even true of the great English speeches of Churchill that year. Despite the evocative power of the same—or, rather, of almost the same—language, his great June and July resolution meant something much more to certain Europeans than to Americans then. I say "certain Europeans" because at that time many of them were only small minorities, those who knew they lived in the dark, who had lived to see Hitler triumphant, who had experienced the quick sinking of a new kind of iron night on their once civilized evenings. They were the ones who needed the most that spirit of defiance and of inspiration and of British self-confidence which Churchill alone gave.

Westminster Hall. First there is the sense of relief from the cold, the sleet and wind dropping behind one in an instant; it is mingled with that other sense of relief that the long cold progress is over. Here, for the first time, the gestures of the policemen are quicker. The crowd surges forward for a moment, many abreast, on the steps—and there we are, formed into two lines, in a hall. We are already moving to the left. It is very simple. In that enormous hall, under its English Gothic beams, a very tall catafalque, like a great memorial stone cut in dull black, and his coffin under a large generous British flag. The rest is what one would expect: the four Royal Marines standing like statues, and the tall candles burning.

So there we go, rather quickly now; and as we come closer I sense that the catafalque is perhaps purposely higher than usual, the flag larger than usual, which is why it is so fitting. There lies an old corpulent man whose flesh had begun to dissolve some time ago. He loved life very much; and he made life possible for many of us because he had a very old, and very strong, belief in the possibilities of human decency and of human greatness. History is not a record of life but life itself: because we are neither human animals nor perpetual slaves. In the long and slow and sad music of humanity he once sounded an English and noble note which some of us were blessed to receive and to remember.

Now up the stairs and before us we see the open door where the crowds file through and immediately dissolve, taken up by the stream of everyday London. But:

instinctively, at the top of the stairs, everyone of us turns around, for a moment. I wrote "us" because, for the first and only time, I felt that I can write this honestly: not an Englishman, my grief was different from theirs, but at this moment—this very individual moment, since there is, curiously, not a speck of crowd psychic reaction in this turning around—we are all one. Again the tall catafalque and the candles blowing and the four ceremonial guards and the flag covering the coffin, all palely shining through the thin light which comes in through the large window, with its small and reconstituted unimpressive stained-glass panels. It is not perhaps the scene which is unforgettable: it is the occasion. Farewell Churchill. Farewell, father of a foreign family. Farewell British Empire. I loved you once. I love you still.

January Thirtieth
Saturday

The thirtieth of January. Dawn thoughts. On this day Franklin Roosevelt was born in 1882, and Adolf Hitler came to power in Germany thirty-two years ago.

Roosevelt and Hitler died within the same month, in April 1945. Churchill survived them by twenty years. His relationship with Roosevelt was a complex one: a mixture of genuine affection (on Churchill's part, that was), a strong recognition of obligations, a sense of loyalty together with what was a very Churchillian unwillingness to fight for certain things. It is difficult to say what were the deeper sources of his unusual deference to Roosevelt during the last two years of the war: his absolute conviction of the necessity of American benevolence for Britain, together with a certain weariness, played a role in that. Roosevelt, in turn, was the smaller person of the two—not because of his breezy American seignorialism shining at times on his face (that Churchill liked) but because of a certain uneasiness toward Churchill (and toward Britain, Europe, history)—a compound of sentiments of inferiority and of superiority, the by-products of a Rooseveltian intellectual attitude which professed to see the twentieth century as The Century of America and Of The Common Man: in these terms Churchill was a brave roast beef Tory, an almost Dickensian figure. This was the same kind of American myopia which made Oliver Wendell Holmes consider Harold Laski to have been the greatest brain in England. Still, in 1940 at least, Roosevelt's heart was in the right place. Hence Churchill's enduring gratitude too.

Much has been written about Hitler's love-hate relationship to England. In reality, this theme is overdone. This evil genius, capable of great instinctive flashes of comprehension when dealing with some of the motive forces of various national characteristics, never understood the English, and least of all did he understand Churchill. He did not understand that behind This Far And No Further there was something more than a stubborn dumb pragmatism; he could not understand the romantic springs of English sentiment; he mistook Churchill's bravery for mere panache; Churchill's peculiar compound of resolution and nonchalance was one of the few things which remained far beyond the reach of Hitler's wild and powerful mind.

Churchill and Hitler were, at any rate, the two protagonists of the dramatic phase of the last war, even though Roosevelt and Stalin played the decisive roles in its epic phase, in the end.

A young man was supposed to have said yesterday: "Let's hope that Hitler can see this now."

But the crowds are not big. Four, five deep at the most. And how silent they are. We had risen early, in a black dawn; dressed and walked down to the Gloucester Road. The streets had a quiet Sunday feeling. A few polite posters telling motorists that some of the Thames bridges will be closed for the funeral. But the Underground is running—the Underground, with its sultana-cake plush seats, with its peculiar coal-and-cocoa smell. At Westminster Station we rose to the surface, into the jaws of the large long crowd—and great, great quiet, well an hour before the great procession was to move out of the New Palace Yard.

I read later, and heard it discussed on the plane back to Paris by a famous American reporter, that what had impressed him was the pride of the crowd, that this was a day of great inner pride, that the people of England had pulled themselves up this week and showed a proud face to the world in their mourning. This is not what I saw. Perhaps certain foreigners, television reporters, Americans felt this, because of some of their preconceived ideas: but foreigners, and especially Americans (this is strange) are prone to mistake the English aloofness for some kind of haughtiness instead of seeing what it is: the essential shyness of this people. I saw less pride than a kind of disciplined resignation, and a respectful sadness: a sadness full of the remembrance of the past for those who had memories of 1940; and, for the young, full of a strange, vague, almost medieval respect for a distant and legendary figure, someone removed even from their parents' generation, someone with real authority, someone they could respect . . . That was strange: the papers remarked it, too: the large number of young people in the crowds, long-haired, sad-faced young barbarians, in search for something, with their strange, watery eyes.

For the others self-respect rather than pride, and a self-respect tinted with the sense of passing time. There was in this a thin thread of resigned realization that for *this* England, in her present situation, the Churchillian generation was too old: that he was the right man at the right time but not for the grey, the difficult, the technical present. I do not think that there are very many Englishmen, including Conservatives, who regard the election of July 1945 which turned Churchill out of power as some kind of a national disaster. They have an instinctive feeling that he was right for the war rather than for the postwar time. (And this is true in a way: with all of his great gifts, with his great understanding of world history, with his great insights into movements, connections, correspondences, tendencies, Churchill was not a good diplomatist—especially not when it came to dealing with Americans . . .)

A Churchillian generation: there was, really, no such thing. Eden, Beaverbrook, Macmillan, Duff Cooper . . . Of all of them the latter was closest to Churchill in spirit: but he never had more than a minor position. The shock that grips all of England at this moment is the sight of Macmillan, Eden, Attlee, among the honorary pallbearers. How infinitely old they look! Attlee is bent over twice. He has to sit down in the cold wind, in a big black overcoat, protected carefully by a tall guards' officer. Then, for a moment, Eden—infinitely old, infinitely weary, too—bends over Attlee with a kind of great solicitude. It shows how far away we are now from the Churchillian Days, from the time of the Low cartoon of May 1940, "We're all behind you, Winston!"—Attlee, Bevin, Morrison, Eden, all of them rolling up their sleeves and marching in a broad file behind Churchill. Low drew them (how well I remember that cartoon) in a somewhat unimaginative outfit, like English shop-stewards in their Sunday best they looked. But they were, at that moment, the good, the reliable, the last best hope, the shop-stewards of European civilization.

The RAF pilots escorting the coffin. "Never in the field of human conflict was so much owed by so many to so few." That was, to some extent, a Churchillian exaggeration. (His 1940 rhetoric was not always exaggerated, the "We shall fight in the streets" passage, for example: there are witnesses to whom he had said in May that if the Germans were to land and push into London he would go with a rifle to the sentry-box at the end of Downing Street and keep firing at them 'til the end.) Would the Battle of Britain have been won without American support? I do not mean the material support which was not decisive at that time; I mean the knowledge, by Churchill and by the people of England and by the world, that America was moving away from neutrality, toward their side. And the legendary figures announced in '40 *were* exaggerated. "You can always take one of them with you": the RAF pilots *did* take more than one of them but not five or six. The score was a little less than two to one. Still it was an appropriate thing to have the officers of the 1940 fighter squadrons form the first escort. They are grandfathers now, most of them; slightly corpulent training officers in pacific command posts; it is not difficult to imagine their suburban homes, their habits, their families. They have nothing of Valhalla heroes' marks on their faces. They, in 1940, they only did their duty, they would say. Now, too.

The Polish officer. He is in the crowd, with his Slavic, creased face, in an angular black suit, wearing the ribbons of his medals. So this man came to pay his respects, too. For a long time the exiled Poles were bitter about Churchill. They had reason to be. From the very beginning he had found it necessary to compromise with Stalin. He wanted to let the Russians have the eastern portion of Poland up to the Curzon (or, rather, Lloyd George) Line, in exchange for a Russian agreement for a Russophile but free Polish government. In this he failed: in the end Stalin got both the frontier and the government he wanted, a big Soviet Ukraine and a subservient Communist regime in Warsaw. At Yalta, too, Churchill fought for the cause of Poland and lost (he won for France instead). Having lost, he put up a good front and went far in defending Yalta in the House of Commons. How bitter it must have been for the brave Polish exiles, with their large wounded army, these months in the ruined 1945 landscape of London! They had fought and bled in three continents, for six years, and they were abandoned in the end: large Russian armies installed forever in the terrible landscape of their ravaged country, and with the acquiescence of Churchill. (The Yugoslav exiles fared worse: Churchill had put his chips on the bandit Tito well before the end of the war.)

A German Christian-Democrat newspaper in Bonn, paying homage to Churchill, wrote among other things that he was nevertheless responsible for the division of Europe, having let Stalin come too far into the heart of the continent. And yet that is all wrong. Churchill tried to save what he could. At least his basic idea was right, as it was indeed in 1915, in the Dardanelles business, even though he could not carry it out—in 1915 because of the British government, in 1943–45 because of the distrust of the American government. Churchill knew that a price had to be paid in Eastern Europe for the Russian contribution to Germany's defeat; also, he knew the Russians better than did Roosevelt, knowing that this price ought to be fixed in advance, since with the Russians no postponing of unpleasant things and no vague declarations of universal goodwill would do. He was more concerned with the tragic destinies of Poland than Roosevelt, who was, at worst, concerned with his Polish-American voters, and Hull, who pleaded moral indignation in refusing to enter into Territorial Deals. And when in October 1944 Churchill, exasperated with American procrastination, sat down with Stalin and divided with him on a sheet of paper the rest of Eastern Europe, only a simple-witted person or some kind of a special pleader may see in that the evidence of Traditional and Perfidious Machiavellian Diplomacy: for at that time, as indeed on other occasions, what Churchill did was to try to save what was possible. And he did. He made sure that the Russians won't interfere in Greece, which he then saved from a Communist revolution. His support of Tito, too, paid off in a way: it contributed to Tito's sense of his independence: surely this made the latter less dependent on Stalin: it helped to make his future break from Moscow possible. Even Poland remained a nation, after all, far from being independent but, still, a nation and a state at a time when Stalin could have done anything he wanted in that part of Europe: he did not incorporate Poland into Russia, after all.

In that way, too, Churchill was a great European. But how bitter and lonely must have been those exile years to men and women such as this angular, wooden Pole, alone for more than two decades now in this grey and unemotional London! And yet he is here, on this icy street, silent and stolid. What must be the thoughts and the memories that burn slowly in that creased, war-worn skull! Churchill and he *were* fighting comrades in a great European War, after all. And when I read in the paper, next day, that Poland (Communist Poland, that is) was the only East European nation that was represented by a cabinet minister, and that he sat in St. Paul's among the official guests, and so did the old spare leaders of the Polish national army, Anders and Bór-Komorowski, I thought that this was only fitting and just, and that in issuing the invitations to the latter the British had, instinctively, done the right (and not merely the proper) thing again.

The monarchs of Northwestern Europe. Olav of Norway (rubicund); Frederick of Denmark (genial); Baudouin of Belgium (still like a student); Jean of Luxembourg (looking surprisingly like Otto of Hapsburg); Queen Juliana (surprisingly heavy). It is right that they should be here. Churchill saved their countries twenty-five years ago.

And, so, this is a sad family occasion. They have an instinctive tie of memory with Elizabeth, who, like some of them, was very young at that time. They know what they owe to this great commoner now dead. That there is this great array of royalty paying their respects at the bier of a statesman is not the important thing. The important thing, again, is the memory of 1940: those dazzling, feverish evenings of the brilliant and deadly May and June of that year. Four times in six weeks King George and his Queen had driven in the evening to Victoria Station, to greet the fleeing monarchs and presidents of Europe with dignity, sympathy and solicitude. The sky was enormously blue in London, the German air attacks had not yet begun, unlike those black clouds that had risen from the fires of Bergen, Rotterdam, Antwerp. In the white rooms of London hotels these royal persons of Europe were surrounded by gentleness and courtesy, by the fading flowers of a civilization. They had come to be thus received in its then last island house.

They are respectable men and women, these constitutional monarchs of the small democratic nations of Northwestern Europe. For a moment, as they stand, some of them uneasily, on the steps of St. Paul's, they are a family unto themselves. They represent those lands of the world where there are still many living movements to an older kind of humaneness. On the surface map of the world they represent the central cluster of decency, these bourgeois monarchs of Northwestern Europe. Churchill knew that: for he was a monarchist not merely out of sentiment but because of his deep historical reason. In a fatherless world they are sources of a certain strength and of a certain inspiration. May they live and reign for long! May their presidency over the Sunday afternoons of Western Europe be prolonged!

Above them towers now de Gaulle. "The Constable of France": thus Churchill saw him in June 1940. The constable of a new Europe, now? There is something to this. His presence is regal: naturally, without the slightest pomp. There he stands in his ill-fitting French army greatcoat, blinking occasionally, putting on his glasses, leaning down to Prince Jean of Luxembourg, saying something with a bearing that reflects a familiarity and solicitude. Many, many people in this great royal assembly look at him often. Later the London papers describe him in terms of unstinted admiration and respect. Very little of that uneasy suppressed dislike with which some Americans regard de Gaulle. But, of course, their quarrels and the phrase of the heavy burden of the Cross of Lorraine notwithstanding, Churchill understood and respected de Gaulle; so far as their conceptions of history (and of human nature, too) went, Churchill and de Gaulle, two national leaders of the Right, had more in common than Churchill and Roosevelt. This is what most intellectuals failed to understand: that in 1940 the truest opponents of Hitlerism were men of the Right not of the Left: Churchill and de Gaulle, each representing a certain superb kind of patriotism not internationalism.

A ragged group of Frenchmen. They, as well as groups from Denmark and from elsewhere, flew over here representing their Resistance. Their silken tricolors wave smartly as the coffin moves by. These colors, together with the few red-and-white-crossed Danish flags, enlighten for a moment the somber tints of the procession, beneath the cold blackened imperial buildings of Whitehall. They are a ragged group of men and women, marching disordered as in any French civic parade, many of them paunchy, with their rimless glasses: small *fonctionnaires* and *propriétaires* (one old Frenchman with an angelic white beard shuffles on, pink-faced, waving an enormous flag).

The French owe much to Churchill. Unfortunately not many of them recognize this. (De Gaulle does: despite the struggles and the quarrels and the high-hatted arguments in his *Memoirs* he did write down a crucial sentence that without Churchill he and Free France would have been nothing, nothing. "Shipwrecked from desolation," he wrote, "on the shores of England, what could I have done without his help?") It is a curious thing that while elsewhere on the continent the national traitors and the Fascist politicians were the Germanophiles, in France the party of surrender, the nationalist party, consisted of Anglophobes. Anglophobia, not Germanophilia, was the key to the behavior and to the attitudes of Pétain, Laval, Darlan. They had had reasons for distrusting Chamberlain: unfortunately they distrusted Churchill even more. That tremendous, ill-considered but genuine Churchillian offer for an Anglo-French Union, uttered on the sixteenth of June in 1940, was one of the gravest pronouncements in modern history and in the history of Great Britain. How different would the United Europe look today had the French accepted it at that time! Throughout his life Churchill was a genuine Francophile. This shines through not only in his great generous gestures of 1940 (that inimitable broadcast to the French in October: *Dieu protège la France!*) but in the way he fought for France and for de Gaulle five years later, at Yalta, and six years before '40 as he spoke in the House of Commons: "Thank God for the French Army!" he said. (He also noted the utter annoyance and disbelief on the faces of the Members.) This was more than a political choice for Churchill. He belonged to a generation of aristocratic and patrician Englishmen who, coming to maturity in the Edwardian Age, were, among all British generations, the most conversant with the political history of the continent and the most deeply attuned to the delights and civilities of French culture. Churchill was never prone to take a philistine view of Europe, not even when the continent was ruined, when the governments of the ancient states of Western Europe had been reduced to the role of tattered suppliants, when it seemed that America and Britain and Russia would rule the world. His distaste for the Birmingham municipal radicalism of the Chamberlains was part and parcel of his distaste for the Germanic inclinations and sympathies of that kind of British middle-class. (His artistic inclinations reflected these tendencies, too: his disinterest in music, his painting in the manner of the French impressionists.) Unlike those of some of his Edwardian contemporaries, Churchill's Francophilia was more than an acquired taste for certain pleasant and civilized delights. He enormously admired Joan of Arc and Napoleon, two of the greatest opponents of England. He understood something of what D. H. Lawrence once noted, that the Rhine was a peculiar frontier of the European spirit. He believed in the alliance, in the necessary alliance, of St. George and St. Denis; and he represented that short-lived Anglo-French conflation of spirit which, with its elegance and nonchalance, marked some of the highest levels of European civilization early in this century.

The Churchill family. Despite his aristocratic inclinations (among them his thoroughbred characteristic of impatience: the most aristocratic and least helpful of his characteristics) Churchill had a deep understanding of the patient virtues of patrician family life, of that fragment of bourgeois civilization. One must know something of the English aristocracy to recognize how unusual that was. Thus the beauty and the dignity with which his family walks behind his coffin is a living apotheosis to his personal ideals. Not a trace of that self-conscious pride which would make them a center of attention. Suicide, divorce, degradation, they have all fallen away. There are no signs of the ravages of life, only the tragic quiet of discipline on Sarah Churchill's pale jewelled face. (She is fifty years old now!) Her father would have been solicitous of her on this day.

On this day of Sabbath the British people mourn a great David-like figure who is buried with the pomp and reward of a great Old Testament Patriarch. It being Sabbath, the President of Israel couldn't ride in a car, he had to walk to St. Paul's.

That, too, is fitting for the occasion. The heads of the state of Israel walking, small and solemn, to Churchill's funeral. Enormous are the debts that the people of Israel owed, and still owe, to Churchill. I am not thinking of his support for the Jewish State, which goes back a long time. It is, all, a one-way debt. Unlike Roosevelt, he owed little to Jewish political support. Churchill had few vested interests in supporting Israel; he was a new King Cyrus without an Esther. He saw the evil incarnated in Hitler instantly, immediately. Then he rose like a hero, highest in those months in 1940 when the future of human decency was at stake, and when Jewry and Christianity were on the same side, which was the side incarnated by him, which was his side. It is therefore that no Jewish intellectual should ever call Churchill "a splendid anachronism"; it is therefore that every conscientious Catholic should pay respects to this Englishman who, in a supreme moment, saw Evil even clearer than had the Pope.

The procession has reached the Thames.

We are told that this is the end of the state funeral, and that from now on the private progress of mourning belongs to the Churchill family. In reality there is no frontier between the two portions of the procession. But the progress is thinning out. The crowds are lighter; on the bridges, closed to traffic, there are not more than three deep, and some of them will scurry across the width of the bridge to follow the watery wake of the launches.

And it is because of the royal procession melting away in the City that, somehow, the funeral becomes sadder and more poignant. There is the wail of the bagpipes, keening across the cold river: but their impression is only aleatory now. There is something very sad in the aspect of this river, and in the small neat launch that will carry Churchill's coffin upstream. It is said that he himself, in instructions he had left for his funeral, wanted his coffin to be carried up the Thames, as was Nelson's. But how different is the Thames now from Nelson's, or even Wellington's time! Two hundred years ago Canaletto himself painted it and wondered at it, when it was a great green river, ample and rich like the empire, with gardens and rich terraces on its borders. Now it is a grey and narrowing flow, with but faint memories of the ocean sea whose scummy tides race inland on dark evenings; the once rich shipping of the Port of London is sparse and far downstream. No longer could a warship, even a destroyer, come upstream for Churchill. The *Havengore* is a launch used for hydrographic tasks by the Port of London Authority.

Swiftly she sails up the cold narrowing river, bordered by warehouses, barges and cranes. And as she is small, the coffin, covered and now protected by that large and lovely flag, is visible to all.

The train. In a black automobile, simply, the coffin is now driven to the train. The crowds are very sparse now: but, still, that enormous silence, all over London.

Up to now everything connected with the arrangement of the funeral was stately and appropriate; now it has become appropriate in a familiar sense. The midday silence of the great iron railway hall, for example. Waterloo Station. That peculiarly English, steady stutterless hissing of the steam locomotive. Far on the other side of the station other trains are standing and people moving, the regular Saturday traffic of the British Railways. The train is appropriate: it brings to life the Edwardian memories, the comfortable English patrician tastes of Churchill's age: those butter-and-chocolate British Pullman cars, including the van in which the Irish Guards will place the coffin, painted cream and maroon, including the momentary sight of the tables laid in white napery with their little yellow fringed lamps in a dining-car for the family, including the portly engine. In the procession there is now the sense of the few small hitches of a family occasion: the Pullman waiter, standing respectfully but somewhat uneasily in his white spencer jacket, the nervousness of the stationmaster who looks at his watch too often, because, for the first time, this perfectly managed timetable is a minute or two late.

Then—and how appropriate this is!—the locomotive blows twice. The sound of the whistle is melancholy and raucous at the same time. The steady hissing of the steam valves remains the same; there is no dramatic huffing and puffing as the train gathers speed and glides out of the iron station into the pale sunlight of the Western Saturday afternoon.

In a minute its rumble dies away; the end of the last coach vanishes; now, for the first time, we are face to face with the emptiness of the afternoon.

That afternoon and evening I walked in the streets and across the squares of this great city.

Everything resumed now its course, the theatres and the cinemas and the shops were open, the football matches were played and there was racing in the wet parks, the crowds filled the streets but the sense of silence remained. I felt nothing of that inner, quiet glow of relief that so often follows funerals and other ceremonial occasions. I am sure that there were few gatherings in great houses this day; that, instead, at the same time, the inner silence was something oppressive.

There was now, in London, some of that yellow fog that, in the cold, reminds one of what one knows of the nineteenth century; of imperial London with its large Roman paving-blocks, and the black processions of thousands of cabs, and the great throngs of people in the cold shadows of the stony classical buildings built by an imperial race. This dark-bright evening of London was closer to, say, 1875 than to 1935. Now the city was full, fuller than a century ago, and yet there was a sense of emptiness or, rather, an emptiness of sense: something had gone out of the spirit of these imperial buildings: Trafalgar Square was brilliantly lit but it was not Nelson's Column and the lions which were strange: it was Admiralty Arch, that well-proportioned Edwardian building with its proud Latin inscription chiselled large and deep over the seething roadways, it seemed ancient and emptied out now.

It was because of Churchill that Macaulay's awful prediction still had not come true, that tourists from New Zealand standing on London Bridge may contemplate a large living metropolis and not merely a few broken buildings. London had risen from her partial ruins, and her imperial monuments, lit by floodlights and by the eerie sideglows of her cinemas, still stand. But it was a purposeless crowd who swirled among them on this silent evening.

Meanwhile I had a sandwich in a place called a Wimpy. The waitress in a wimpy maroon uniform was very English, with her bun-like face and her shyness and adolescent incompetence. I thought of the fat-faced Advertising Managers and the horde of public-relations-men who decide on names such as Wimpy, who spread the cheeseburger all over Britain, and the end-result of their American publicity bang being a weak British wimpy.

There came in a man, a fortyish man with glasses and a mouse-colored moustache, and a turned-down mouth between a woolen scarf and his grey tired face. He may have been a teacher in a poor school in the Midlands. He looked at the plastic menu for a while. Then he said to the waitress: "A Wimpy, please." As he said that there passed a shadow of embarrassment, a flicker of resigned disturbance across his face. I thought that I could detect something of the same on the otherwise nearly vacuous, pale face of the little waitress too. *That* embarrassment they shared in common. Surrounded by Wimpies and the cheap metallic filth of plastic dishes and the sex magazines, in the midst of this vast process of thin liquefaction that flicker of embarrassment was a faint sign of the atavistic resistance of the race: a faint sign but a sign nonetheless: a weak glow but still a glow of the once fire, of some kind of a fire below the ashes.

January Thirty-First
Sunday

The Sunday papers. In the quiet of the morning, the Sunday papers. (All of the weariness in the civilization of the great English-speaking cities in the twentieth century lies latent in these two words and in their associations: Sunday papers.)

The long accounts of yesterday's funeral and the excellent photographs are there but, somewhat surprisingly, the articles are not very good. There are slips even in the evocative details—one of the young leader writers saying, for example, that as the launch moved off Tower Bridge Pier, "a band crashed out with the tune that was a last Churchillian brag: 'Rule Britannia'": how wrong it is, the crash instead of the muffled keening across the long dampness, and the Last Churchillian Brag, as if it had not been something infinitely different and melancholy. There are also such things as the article by the Fellow and Director of English Studies (in reality a New York intellectual eager-beaver) at Churchill

College (in reality a Lord Snow institution), ending with a real Madison Avenue phrase: "Given the tools, Churchill College can do its part of the exciting job."

All through the week the writers of articles did capture many of the fragments and some of the atmosphere of the occasion: but now the reminiscences have a curious kind of nervous tiredness about them. The more intelligent among the commentators, thus, write that this funeral was indeed a proud and ceremonial occasion but the last occasion for something that is irrevocably past, the last time when London was the capital of the world: for after this last solemn homage to the glories of a British imperial past the worn weekdays of a compressed modest England begin anew. This may be true: but it does not quite explain that slight awkwardness of the eulogies by some of the more perceptive younger writers. I think I know the sources of that awkwardness of sentiment: it is the knowledge, especially of those who had grown up in the postwar years, that the Churchill victory of the Second World War was, after all, not much of a victory indeed.

That, too, may be true. But this intellectual recognition, lurking uneasily beneath the immediate impressions of the occasion, does not really conflict, for once, with the sentiments of the people: the sense of gratitude by this unemotional people of England which is now untainted either by nostalgia or by self-pity: because it has little to do with the glory of victory. It is the sense that *Churchill had saved them from defeat* rather than the knowledge that he had led Britain to victory. This is, I think, what accounts for the absence of any amount of nostalgic jingoism among the people—who, even more than the journalists and the statesmen and, of course, than the intellectuals, may feel in their bones how close England was to disaster in 1940.

Now this seems to be rather obvious: but few people, I think, comprehended its historical portents.

To most people, in England as well as abroad, the Thirties are, in retrospect, something like a rather incredible episode, an era of philistine stupidity. The older generation who lived through it are not prone to analyze it in any detail, partly because of the fortunate British mental habit of letting bygones be bygones, partly because of the less fortunate British unwillingness to face certain unpleasant truths. To the younger generation it is yet another example of the myopia of the then governing classes. The consequence of these beliefs is, then, that Churchill came forth, at a time of great distress, to attune the spirit of England to its standard condition.

But was this really so? As one contemplates the devolution of Britain during the last half-century one gets the impression that it was the lassitude which was the standard condition, in the Twenties and the Thirties and the Fifties and the Sixties. The Bonar Laws as well as the Lansburys, the donkey generals of 1917 and the asses of the 1935 Peace Ballot, the Chamberlains as well as the Ramsay Macdonalds, the spirit of Harold Laski as well as the Great Ideas of Lord Snow: what did they, what do they, have in common with Churchill? In one of the few fortunate phrases in the post-mortems Dame Rebecca West wrote that she remembers Churchill in the Twenties shining with vitality as if it had been sluiced over him with a pail. This at a time when the spirit of England had begun to smell like weak cocoa.

This does not mean that Churchill was completely isolated, absolutely alone: he was out of spirit with *The Times,* he was out of spirit with "the times" (whatever that is), but there was something else: he knew that he could bring an entire people with him, in 1940. This was one of the great differences between Churchill and de Gaulle at that time. But even this does not mean that 1940 represented England in her standard conditions. And the people know this better than the intellectuals. Hence their deep emotional regret. They know how there loomed in 1940 the possibility of something that is still unspeakable and perhaps unthinkable: that England, despite her island situation, despite the riches of her then Empire, despite the aid from the United States, could have indeed collapsed before the strong and purposeful Germany, because England already then was at the tail end of a long period of lassitude and of abdication, because in the spirit of England, then as now, the vitality of aspirations shimmered very low.

To the present generation it seems unthinkable that Hitler could have ever won the war at all. To the intellectuals Hitlerism represents a strange and perhaps fascinating, barbaric and reactionary episode of a temporary madness going against the broad stream of the twentieth century, against the long and broad history of mechanical progress. England, together with the United States and the Soviet Union and the Progressive Forces of the world, was bound to defeat Fascism: foolish and stupid statesmen and vested interests had led her close to great painful disasters, whereupon Churchill, who only did in great style what had to be done anyhow, restored the balance of reason and of democratic virtue with Shakespearean words and gestures; that was his role; that was all. But that wasn't it at all. People still do not know how close Hitler and his cohorts came to winning the war in '40. Certain men and women who are attuned better to the listening to the movements and the sentiments of large masses of people in Europe know this better than do the intellectuals, including certain professional historians; and the common people of England who had lived through the war sense it better, too.

They could have been conquered. Their island history would have come to an end. Their self-respect would have gone for good. Churchill saved them from this fate: and he had appealed to them as he did so. It is a mark of the decency and of the common sense of the people of England that they were not, and are not now, puffed up with pride in remembering those days, and that the stillness reigning over Churchill's funeral reflects their now profound sentiment of still gratitude to him for having done so.

Several of the men now writing about Churchill's life say that he was at his best, at his most courageous, when he was alone in the Thirties, the lonely political Cassandra, the warning trumpet, the voice in the wilderness. This is an arguable proposition. Churchill, though of a small minority, was not entirely alone in the Thirties; he had certain newspaper columns at his disposal; and there is, at any rate, a difference between speaking out when one has no official position at all and between leading a half-armed nation, urged by instinct, on a proud course of defiance in face of the strong possibility of disaster. And: is it really true that Hitler could have been stopped easily in 'Thirty-Eight or in 'Thirty-Six, at the time of Munich or at the time of the Rhineland? I am not so sure about that. Of course Churchill was right. But who would have followed him in Thirty-Six? Not Baldwin. Not Chamberlain. Not the Liberals. Not the Laborites. Not the Trade Unions. Not the Fabianists. Not the Socialists. Not the Pacifists. Not the Popular Front. Not the Commonwealth. Not the Americans. Not Roosevelt. And why?

Why? Why did they—an enormous, a heterogeneous *they* —distrust him so much? with an emotional as well as an intellectual distrust whose echoes lived strong in England until the gunfire drowned them out in the high summer of 'Forty, and which was to flare up again, across the ocean, later in the war. *They,* all, distrusted him because he was uncategorizable. He was the kind of person whom mediocrities instinctively fear. "He was not steady" said conservative respectability. "He is a reactionary" said progressive intellectuality. But at the bottom the sources of their distrust were much the same. Neville Chamberlain and Eleanor Roosevelt, Harold Laski and Edward Stettinius distrusted Churchill out of the same human motives. He did not have the kind of intellect that has a natural appeal to Overseers of Harvard University and to deans of womens' colleges in New England. At the time when Churchill began to sputter against the Hitler German danger he was dismissed not only by the stolid dumbness of the Baldwins and the Chamberlains; it was at that time that Harold Laski wrote that Hitler was not much more than a tool in the hands of German capitalism, it was the time when Alger Hiss was the chief advisor of the Nye Committee, investigating the misdeeds of British militarism left over from the First World War; ten years later the same Hiss was to sit on Roosevelt's right at the Yalta table, with his long ambitious Quaker face, that intellectual mug, calculating, self-conscious, and smug.

Professor Rowse, the famous British historian, once wrote in the Thirties that Leon Trotsky was superior to Winston Churchill in one sense, in the sense that the former had a philosophy of history which the latter had not—a profound judgment which was approvingly quoted in the Sixties by Professor Carr. It is interesting, this enduring opinion of historical savants, especially in view of the recently published diaries of the exiled Trotsky, which suggest that in judging the events of the Thirties their writer was a bigger ass than Harold Laski. And Churchill *did* have a lasting philosophy of personal convictions. Only it was not a Philosophy of History: it was something profounder and more modern: Churchill's philosophy was the reverse: it was an historical philosophy. I say "more modern" because, true, Churchill was a reactionary: but only in the sense in which his quick impatient mind and his convictions instinctively reacted against the prevalent stupidities of modern progressivism; because Churchill's view of history was ahead of Trotsky's in time, precisely because it was not a rigid philosophy, not a Germanic system. "A splendid anachronism," wrote a British intellectual in one of the Sunday papers, trying to reconstruct his attitude toward Churchill during the war. Who were—and who are—the peddlers of anachronisms, the real reactionaries? Were they not those who believed (and who still believe) that history is a process of vast economic developments, who predicted that Hitler could not wage war because, as statistics proved, he would run out of oil or tin or rubber in a few weeks, the same people who had thought beforehand that his government would not last in face of the Concerted Opposition of the German Working-Class? Wasn't it Churchill rather who immediately understood that Hitler was a very modern incarnation of a very old evil, Churchill who almost always knew instinctively what it was that was really new and what it was that was really old?

A man by the name of Henry Fairlie wrote in the *Sunday Telegraph:* "Mr A. J. P. Taylor said last week that historians of the future would ignore at their peril the spiritual contact which one man found in 1940 with the rest of his fellow-countrymen . . . If Mr Taylor is not afraid to talk of a 'spiritual contact', I see no reason why one should be afraid to talk of a vision . . ." "Afraid" is good. For God's sake, why should one be *afraid* to admit the existence of something that was a matter of spirit, something that was not a matter of "production" or, at that, of "opinion" statistics? This is no longer the outcome of racial shyness; it is a kind of perverted crampedness of mind. It is this belated triumph of Josiah Bounderby that had laid the spirit of England so low that Churchill had to come to lift it up at its greatest danger: this Bounderby philosophy which, bruited now in the name of Freud and of Marx (how curious it is that both of them are buried here in London) is again abroad in this land?

What remains then, for England, on this Sunday? The nervous tic on the face of the man when he ordered a Wimpy. The essential, the uneradicable reticence graven into the hearts of the girls and of the women of England even as they leaf through the latest sex book or magazine. This Sunday stillness.

At midday we went to Mass in a Roman Catholic church on High Street in Kensington. It was not a very attractive church, set back between the brown brick houses. It was full of people: a few Poles and in the pew ahead of us the earnest and solicitous heads of Central European converted Jews: but the majority of the congregation was English, infinitely serious English men and women with their children. Living through the last phase of the Protestant episode, of the long unhappy chapter of Roman Catholicism in England, with the old suspicions and the mistrust melting away, with reconciliation setting in, these English Catholics, perhaps better than any other Catholics in the Western world, know what it means to be Christians in a post-Christian land.

In a superficially post-Christian land, that is. In England, the existence of something like Christian morality may have survived the decay of religion. And yet is it "Christian morality," this thing which is dissolving and changing into the pale fluid of a vague universal humanitarianism? Yes: and no.

In this people who ushered in the modern age there is still a mystical, a near-medieval strain, a strain that has been part and parcel of their Protestantism, of their Puritanism, of their Industrial Revolution, of their English socialism. It is there in this living strain of English Catholicism which, in the twentieth century—curious paradox in the spiritual history of England—has become one of the strongest subterranean streams of a peculiar Englishness. To be hounded by heaven was one way to put it— but it was not only the Gerard Manley Hopkinses who sensed this. Even Aleister Crowley. Or Malcolm Muggeridge. Hounded by the sense of Satan or of God in a new-old, post-modern way, preoccupied, unlike many other people in the Western civilization, with the living reality of the question of whence we have come and where we are to go. Even now.

Then to midday dinner in an English home; we sat in friendliness for a little while; after that the cold wind whipping the torn papers in the doorways; through the brown Sunday afternoon and the wide streets to the steel tower of the airways terminal, with its inscriptions in many tongues. In a foreign airplane we rose into the winter evening sky.

In the hot droning airplane the Sunday papers again. *His name.* *Churchill.* How the very sound and the shape of his name fitted him. Pouting, aristocratic, flecked by sunlight. The round and juicy sound of the first syllable, formed by lips curling to speak just as his, the air filling up the cheeks of a seventeenth-century boy with a young and churchy sound. The pout makes it human and humorous rather than churched (but, then, the sound of the English *church* is so much more attractive, rounder, than the high guttural Gothic of *Kirche,* than the cold Roman-law *église,* than the hard angular Celtic *kell*). The pout merges, in a genial way, into the second syllable. There is nothing chilly about that final syllable, it is short, shiny, even brilliant, that springy sound of a rill. The sound of the full name is serious and humorous: it has a male charm about it: it is like the baroque fountains of Blenheim. (English rather than British; an English name whose bearer is now buried in English earth; English earth with its Roman and Saxon and Norman layers; an English man who had a romantic and exaggerated, an expansive notion of Britishness perhaps precisely because he was neither Scottish nor Welsh.) The shape of the name, too: like the shape of his body: compact, slightly corpulent, with the glimmer of a single jewel, jaunty. The fluted cylindrical second portion giving clear form to the roundness of the first. Wearing his black 1940 hat, he looked like that dome of St. Paul's on occasion. Churchill. Churchill.

Sans Caviare

(1976)

Someone comes up and whispers to me:

"The Russians have been looking for you."

Then and there, a Russian—squat, dark, gold-inlaid teeth—grabs my arm. I don't have a moment to reflect, which is good, because here is the materialization of a recurrent bad dream: they are about to get me. At one time I fled Hungary when I thought that the Communist secret police, and, behind them, the Russians, were about to get me. I dreamed this typical dream, lodged in the collective unconscious of millions of displaced persons, for many years thereafter: I am back, and they are about to get me. And now they've got me.

But it is 1976, not 1946, and we are in a high-ceilinged room in Norway. The sun is streaming in, and the Russian is smiling. Broadly, humanly, Muscovitically smiling. He hands me an invitation that is engraved and gilded. "The Ambassador of the Union of Soviet Socialist Republics and Fru T. A. Kirichenko" (it is in Norwegian) "have the honor of inviting Professor J. A. Lukacs to a Buffet-Dinner." *"Tirsdag den 17 August kl. 19.00,"* it says. I experience a moment of relief. *"Tirsdag"*: Thursday, on which day I leave here. "No, no!" he says: "Tomorrow!" and points a strong, stubby, determined finger on the cardboard. *Tirsdag* is Tuesday.

"I shall be pleased to come," I say, or words to that effect. "I shall call the Embassy," I add, more than half-seriously, "or should I drop a card?"

"No, *no!*" the Russian insists. "You tell *me.*"

During the next few hours I make inquiries. About two dozen scholars—half of a scholarly conference—have been invited. Among the few Americans I am the only one. I ask one of my American colleagues, a former State Department man: If I don't show up at the conference Wednesday morning he'll report this to the American Embassy promptly, won't he? One must have courage enough to be a coward.

Tuesday morning. Through the groups of milling scholars the Russian comes, grabbing my arm again: "You *come?*"

"Sure. I come, and thank you very much."

And now it is a pearly afternoon in Oslo, with the summery Scandinavian sense of an everlasting luminescent noon, and I return to my hotel to bathe and dress, after having had one of those awful Norwegian beers with a Canadian friend on the terrace of a crowded café, where I had a painful glimpse of the most beautiful girl in the world, a waitress, on the other side of that thronged terrace, at an irrecoverable distance in space and in time.

As I descend in the hotel elevator I meet a colleague who is a military historian and a Swedish general staff officer. We order a cab and I drive off to the Soviet embassy with this safest of companions.

Description of a reception at the Soviet Embassy in Oslo, 1976. A large villa on the Drammensveien, in the villa and embassy district of this bourgeois city. A garden tended with great care and propriety. The back of the garden slopes down to Oslo fjord. Plashing fountain there. Red carpet up front. Ceilings medium high. Dozens of glass chandeliers. Dozens of oil paintings, mostly snowy forest scenes: icy running brooks, impassive trees. Green plush furniture. An incredibly long table, bedecked with all the comestibles for the buffet dinner. At the end of the long room a small table draped with linen, with all the drinks and bottles set out in the American fashion. With the solitary exception of a medium-sized portrait of Lenin over a corner chimney this is how the embassy of a Czarist Russia would look in a provincial northern capital in, say, 1976?

Yes and no. There is a 1926 sense about this place, with all of these richly framed oil paintings and upholstered *Stilmöbel,* the glass chandeliers and the apple-green plush: it breathes a kind of stiff Central European opulence, rather than bourgeois comfort. There is something German about it—the house of a rich Berlin industrialist around 1926—as indeed there is that German interior influence in Russia, whether Czarist or Soviet. Had there been no revolution in Russia in 1917, Russia would probably be a constitutional monarchy now, with embassies like this: half-bourgeois, half-opulent. Like the buffet table: a very large display of splendid dishes, including the first first-class salmon I have seen in Norway in three weeks, for Norwegian cooking is not one of the best, to say the least, and this is the best there is, not to speak of the excellent Soviet vodka in small crystal glasses that I keep knocking back with an increasing sense of comfort.

One of my expectations is unfilled: there is not one grain of caviar to be had, or seen. It dawns upon me: this is a second-class diplomatic reception, one for scholars. Caviar must be reserved for higher occasions. There is a definable sense of protocol throughout the evening. Most of the scholars congregate in the smaller drawing-room, sitting around a large coffee-table, talking. A coffee hour at the embassy. The ambassadress is large and heavy, wearing, however, a beautiful print dress, and there is something that is very nice in her smile. Her face shines with the happy contentment and catholic goodwill of Russian grandmothers. I learn later that she is the daughter of a famous Russian Field-Marshal: the natural choice, I guess, for a Soviet ambassador. The Soviet aristocracy. I try to charm her. As we leave, I bow: *"Madame l'Ambassadrice,"* I say, *"je vous suis très reconnaissant pour cette charmante soirée."* Next to her stands the Russian general, military historian, veteran of one hundred scholarly conferences across the globe. "Hah!" he says, and pumps my hand. "American professor!"

"Charmante soirée" may be too much. At ten o'clock everyone leaves. One has the sense that everyone is *supposed* to leave. With a young Norwegian couple we repair to an *Ølgarden*—beer-garden—where, again, I espy, from a hopeless distance, the most beautiful girl in the world, another one.

Description of my thoughts after this diplomatic event. Life is funny. If I had been told in 1946, in Hungary, that thirty years later I should be a welcome guest at a Soviet embassy in a Western capital, with my only complaint being the absence of caviar . . . Suppose the Russians knew that I was a vocal anti-Communist, their strident opponent, their . . . They couldn't care less. An American citizen, member of the international bureaucracy of scholars, this is what counts. Forget the rest. Besides, they are rather nice people. The chunky ambassador, his large wife, their son who speaks perfect American English (as most Soviet linguists do, the only Europeans to whom American English comes easier than English English, and there is an unwritten essay latent in this topic), the affable general, the secret-police *rezident,* whoever he is . . . If one day the revolution comes in Russia (a future event the date and the circumstances of which I am ignorant but the eventuality of which I am certain), I think I could feel sympathetic for some of these people. Suppose one day I were to receive a letter, from somewhere in Europe or Asia . . . I would, I think, be inclined to proffer some help.

That, too, does not matter. Marx was wrong. Hitler was wrong. Even Tocqueville was wrong. The wave of the future was not Communism; it was not anti-Communism. The age of aristocracy was followed not by the age of democracy but by the age of bureaucracy—a novel phenomenon, utterly different from the old bureaucracies of Roman or Chinese empires. This is why people such as Brezhnev and Nixon got along spankingly well. They recognized the successful bureaucrat in each other. What did Haldeman or Ehrlichman know or care about capitalism or republicanism? They liked the overheated pomp of those Kremlin apartments; the stiff attention of the close-cropped Soviet captain, master of protocol; the fact that they were to be escorted to dine in state with the Numbers One and not with the numbers two, Kissinger or someone from his staff having told them that this was the caviar dinner.

The trappings of honor are one thing, the trappings of status quite another. There was a time, not so long ago, when diplomacy represented the last glimpses from an aristocratic world; its representatives were bedecked with the remnant pomp of a bygone age, since they represented the most important and solemn reality in the modern world: the state. Now there are no longer Ministers, everyone is an Ambassador; protocol still exists, but bureaucracy and international Americanism have triumphed: there are only Very Important Persons, Important Persons, Persons, and, somewhere in the Soviet lists perhaps, unpersons. Full Professors, Associate Professors, Assistant Professors, and untenured instructors. CEOs, Presidents, Vice Presidents, and non-executives.

Two years ago, in the hall of a hotel in an Eastern European capital, I was standing with a friend at the bottom of a wide staircase, waiting for our wives who were getting dressed. It was exactly six o'clock. Suddenly there was an explosion of motorcycle outriders outside. A mechanical procession ensued. Every twenty seconds a car drove up to the hotel entrance, ejecting an ambassador and his retinue. Each car had a national flag encased in plastic on the left fender. Each car was a Mercedes. Each car was black. We found that a reception was being tendered in this hotel by the Canadian Ambassador, in honor of his country's Independence Day. My friend has a genuine red beard, and when he wears his porcelain suit he looks rather like an Anglo-Irish municipal councilor at, say, Epsom, *circa* 1907. Now he wore a dark suit and could, at least from a distance, be mistaken for an English or Irish or Canadian dignitary of small proportions but of no mean importance. Which is exactly what happened. As the ambassadors and their wives trooped in, Western or Eastern, they hesitated for a moment: whether to turn to the right to greet us or whether to proceed ahead along the red carpet, straight to the back of the hotel hall where the Canadian flag was draped over the portière. We stared impassively over their heads. It was all rather funny.

By 1984 invitations to certain diplomatic receptions may or may not specify Decorations; they also may specify that Name-Tags, encased in plastic, be worn. Another American custom will have conquered the world, something that will make Social Intercourse as well as Security much easier for everyone concerned. Even RSVP may disappear, having followed abbreviations such as p.p.c. into obscurity. There may be "Regrets Only," and I can see an old *fonctionnaire* going through the stacks of incoming mail at the Quai d'Orsay. There are the American receptions, and there are the Soviet ones. The American invitations are sorted into two piles, and he lightly pencils VIP on the corner of one, IP on the other. He sorts the Soviet invitations, too. On the larger pile he marks, lightly: s.c. *Sans caviare.*

Slouching toward Byzantium

(1976)

"The people of Greece," said one of Saki's characters, *circa* 1912, "unfortunately make more history than they can consume locally." Save perhaps for the Cypriots this may no longer be true. All of its recent political vicissitudes notwithstanding, Greece is one of the more stable countries in Europe. The Greeks are intelligent, quick-witted, not given to despair; and, with a steady eye on tourist income, they make all the history—all kinds of history—that can be locally consumed. On the most barren and empty islands, one is aware of the presence of a hardy and intelligent people. But, then, in Greece the landscape and the people are inseparable. Without the people the landscape would be somehow meaningless. Unlike the United States, Greece is humanly old and geologically young. It is all very different from the Grand Canyon.

With this in mind, I find it fascinating how the relatively short-lived era of European bourgeois civilization affected the Greeks. During the twentieth century, Athens, like Madrid or Marseilles, has become a modern city, large portions of which are now comfortable, as well as hideous. Athens, which fifty years ago was a southern Balkan capital of 200,000 inhabitants, has grown together with neighboring Piraeus until, now, they form a swelling and smog-ridden conurbation of nearly five million people, choked with automobiles, of course.

Oddly enough, World War I—of which Greece remained on the fringes—seems to have affected her more enduringly than World War II, when the Greeks were in the middle of it: invaded, occupied, bombed, left vulnerable to the horrible civil war that followed. The street names of downtown Athens echo the Francophile alliances of World War I. The French-style boutiques; the Parisian bars of the great hotels; the beautifully dressed children of rich Greeks, with their English nannies or at least *au-pair* girls; the suits of the men of the upper classes, cut in London clubland fashion—it all breathes the surviving strength of the social and cultural aspirations of the European bourgeois era. (When a Greek took the Orient Express to Venice or Trieste fifty years ago, he would say that he was going to "Europe.")

On the small islands there are the older bourgeois survivals, the statues of civic leaders, men of the Trikoupis generation, with their tight-fitting morning-coats, their sideburns and enormous moustaches and large beady eyes carved into stone. They are more than the remnants of the past. They represent respectability, family, civic repute: matters that remain dear to the hearts of all Greeks, for they are a democratic people— their entire aristocracy consists of a few patrician clans—and they know that with luck, perseverance, and a few connections, anyone can strike it rich. American and English intellectuals, contemptuous of what they (often mistakenly) take for the bourgeois in their own countries, repair to Greece where they decide to be charmed by a laughing, virile, voluble olive-skinned Mediterranean people, a breed of colorful and artistic peasants and fishermen. What a pity that they are not artifacts, to be brought home for conversation pieces, to be displayed in New Hope or Cape Ann or Kensington, together with Mexican pottery and home-woven rugs. If they only knew how profound are the attractions of bourgeois standards of status and comfort for the Greeks, for all Greeks!

I see no danger of Communism in Greece. The Russians are another story. Communism had a certain appeal to many Greeks decades ago, when the Russians were a mysterious entity, far away. But now the Russian presence is palpable in Greece, a kind of monumental influence, for the first time in long centuries. Who ever heard of a Russian cruise-ship as recently as ten or fifteen years ago? Now they are here: large white ships, with their stubby and streamlined funnels, they disgorge their passengers (who come from all over Europe) in ports such as Mykonos, Piraeus, Patras, where American and British and French ships are no longer in sight. On the islands, most of the taxis are Russian-made Volgas. They look like 1956 Checker cabs. They ride like trucks on the graveled mountain roads: the Russians must have offered them cheap. We saw but one American warship, a slightly rusty old Navy tender, riding the swells in the Piraeus roads. Thirty years ago the American Government made the right decision in helping the Greeks and defeating the Communist guerrillas; but should Greece, and Turkey, have been made members of the *North Atlantic* (!) Treaty Organization thereafter? I think not. And now many things have shifted, and the Greeks have come to terms with the Russians. For they are realists: when they see the future, they work it.

I had a sense, in Greece, of a great lurch toward Byzantium, of a return to a Levantine civilization: a sense that the fortunes of the peoples who live in the Eastern Mediterranean were rising for the first time in more than one thousand years. Fifty years ago these countries seemed the fag-end of a decayed Levant, hopelessly corrupt, backward, out-at-elbow, unclean. Just think of the career of someone like Michael Arlen, a talented Armenian who desperately wanted to become an Englishman in every possible way, hoping that not only he but others would forget where he had come from and why. Now these people are rising, full of energy and hope beyond the tired-out dreams of the peoples of the West.

The Greeks themselves have been transformed. Fifty years ago one million Greeks were thrown out of Asia Minor by the Turkish troops of the nationalist Kemal. They camped in the dusty streets of Athens, for a while even in the gardens of the royal palace. Their richer, and selfish, compatriots were appalled by their presence, but they were quickly absorbed into the bloodstream of the modern Greek nation.

Among other things, these Greek refugees from Turkey brought with them the wailing, Oriental bouzouki music, entirely Anatolian in origin and sound, which has since become a Greek national trademark. I find it wholly repellent, especially since the Greeks are possessed by a national mania for noise, and thus bouzouki is blaring everywhere—but then, after all is said (or, rather, heard), bouzouki is hardly worse than rock. It is ubiquitous and democratic and it has become the truly popular and national expression of this dynamic people. It was not by accident that the most legendary millionaire of the last thirty years was Onassis, a Greek boy-refugee from Anatolia, and that Greek shipowners are among the richest people in the world today—along with the new millionaires from Jordan and Lebanon and Turkey and Arabia. A certain breed of men are on the rise now, because of their talents which are ancient and their aspirations which are modern. Their coruscating abilities are sufficient unto the day. Something is involved here that is far more deep-rooted and, quite possibly, far more enduring than oil money.

On some Greek islands with no more than three thousand inhabitants, there are over three hundred whitewashed churches and chapels. They were abandoned long ago; but some of them are newly refurbished, and most of them are opened at least once a year, when a great popular procession and festival marks the day of the saint after which they were named. One often sees the handsome, hirsute, sleek Orthodox priests going through the streets. There is something stylized in their walk—the way they all roll and bowl along in their cloaks—just as all cowboys in American Westerns ride alike, or all baseball players chew gum and lope to the plate alike. These priests are unsmiling—none of that grin of the curate in the parking lot. They may well know that they are indispensable. They are the representatives of an ancient civilization that seems to be getting closer to the surface now.

Greek seamen tell me that when their ships put in to the Soviet ports of the eastern Black Sea, they find a primitive Levantine capitalism flourishing there again. Their Georgian friends show them their villas, with their modern appliances smuggled in from abroad, and their marble floors chiseled (in both senses of the word) locally. They like to trade in old gold, they collect and sell ikons, and some of the harbormasters can be bribed with cartons of cigarettes. These port towns are full of cars. An amazing number of people there understand Greek. It is very much unlike the rest of the Soviet Union.

Toward the end of an age, as toward the end of a lifetime, certain very old things reappear again. A civilization in its last stages of decay shows symptoms of primitivism—of infantilism—that reappear from within. This seems to be happening in the Americas today, in places like Mexico as well as in parts of our own United States. And it may be what is happening in the Mediterranean—for the first time in centuries the southern shore has reverted to the peoples of Africa, and the Eastern Mediterranean is becoming a combination of West and East again. Athens grows and flourishes while London and New York decay. Eliot as well as Yeats may have mixed things up. The slouching is toward Byzantium.

Russia may be in the ascendant; but Brezhnev had better not take too much comfort from this. There is a sunbelt rising across the Eastern

Mediterranean, probably even more corrupt than our American sunbelt, but it may transform a goodly portion of the world beyond its immediate horizons. At a time when the ambitions and pride of the French or the Germans are unsure, the peoples of the eastern edge of the continent may become the best Europeans yet. The Levantine fermentation has already affected parts of the Soviet Union; I believe that my children, perhaps even I, will see the emergence of ancient states such as Georgia and Armenia independent in everything but name, and perhaps even in name.* Brezhnev may yet suffer the Bellman's fate:

> *But the principal failing occurred in the sailing,*
> *And the Bellman, perplexed and distressed,*
> *Said he* had *hoped, at least, when the wind blew due East,*
> *That the ship would* not *travel due West!*

There is hope for us! After everything is said, *The Hunting of the Snark* may prove truer than *Moby-Dick.*

---

*1994. So it happened.

Cook's Continental Timetable

(1978)

My library is spacious and well arranged, but I have the same problem that other owners of books have, which is that certain books are constantly on the move. It is not enough for them to stand on a convenient shelf, within easy sight or reach; they tend to preempt an otherwise useful corner of an already overburdened table, ready to be picked up at the most random of times.

Books that qualify for such a privileged, though precarious, existence are either those whose contents give one instant poetic pleasure or those that are repositories of practical information. There is only one book which, for me, combines these two attributes in a miraculous way. It is a book printed on cheap paper, orangey and paperbound, costing about five dollars in the U.S. and less than half of that in England; three-fourths of each of its pages is covered by broken columns of numbers consisting of three or four digits; and a variorum edition is published each month of the year. It is called *Cook's Continental Timetable,* and it is one of the greatest book bargains in the world.

I open it, and the *frisson* is instantaneous and deep, independent of atmosphere or mood, whether on flannel-dark December evenings or sun-shot mornings in June. I fling open a page filled with serried ranks of numbers separated by lines and vertical arrows. On the side panels going downward I read the most brilliant, the most evocative, the most inspirational sequences of place-names: Orange, Montélimar, Valence, St. Rambert, Vienne, Lyon; *or* Piacenza, Fidenza, Parma, Reggio Emilia, Modena; *or* Gloucester Eastgate, Bristol Temple Meads, Weston-super-Mare, Taunton, Exeter, St. Davids, Dawlish, Newton Abbot, Torquay, Paignton, Plymouth, Penzance.

The numbers clatter with the fast rhythm of a forest-green train, the arrows interrupting this rhythm for a trice as it shoots across a switch. The train flashes through the station, there is a rush of geraniums in the stationmaster's windows, and of the rusticated brick of the building as it disappears and the blue mountains come into view again; after the precise steel tinkle of the station bell one hears the toneless bell of a village church. The speed had blurred the sign over the platform, but we flash past a sun-baked signal post: *St-Jean-de-Maurienne.* Or it snows.

During the last twenty years European trains achieved something of an inspirational reputation for American tourists, like Parisian chapeaux two generations ago, something that no one would have believed as late as, say, 1950, when, except for the *Orient Express* and the *Train Bleu,* the magical names of trains were all American ones, *The Chief, El Capitan, The Twentieth Century Limited.* The tables have turned, but this is not the point.

The practical point is that if you want to go by rail—or if you want to sail—anywhere in Europe (or in Russia, the Near East, the Far East) *Cook's Continental Timetable* is a must. Most American travel agents do not have much European rail information. It is possible to obtain—not without difficulty—the timetables of certain European national railroads, in the front of which the principal international trains originating in their country are listed; but that's about all.

Cook's Continental Timetable lists *all* the principal, and most of the local, trains within every European country, plus those in the USSR, China, the Near East, Turkey, Egypt, Algeria, Tunisia, and Morocco (and it also gives a bland seven-page summary of what Amtrak offers). It contains a number of detailed tables that may be available elsewhere—currency tables, temperature and rainfall figures, passport and visa regulations for all countries. It also contains a vast amount of information *not* available elsewhere: a complete list of trains with sleeping-cars; maps of all principal cities with their railroad stations; and the timetables and compositions of all international expresses, and of all the ships plying the English Channel, the North Sea, the Baltic, the Norwegian coastal route, the Rhine, the Danube, the Göta Canal, the Swiss and the Italian lakes, and the Greek islands, and of the burgeoning network of shipping lines, including car ferries, across the Mediterranean, serving the Near East and North Africa as well.

For the sake of travel agents, *Cook's Continental Timetable* is issued every month, listing every variation in the timetables or regulations. For the common traveler a copy ought to be good for two or three years, since most European timetables change little, and the variations are minimal. However, my admiration for the editors is enhanced by reading the insert for variations. It contains such items as: "The new morning fast trains between Bergen and Oslo have been given names, as shown in Table 481. The eastbound train is named *Henrik,* the westbound train is named *Pernille.*" "On April 14 and 15, passengers wishing to join the 11.45 Newhaven-Dieppe ship at Newhaven will require an embarkation ticket—see Table 51. This will not apply to passengers arriving by boat-train from London." "The *Varna Express* (Warsaw & Cracow-Varna and v.v.), which has previously run through the USSR without advertised passenger stops, now includes a stop at Lvov and includes a through car—see Table 84. This car will run until September 1."

The common traveler should be able to master the use of *Cook's Continental Timetable* in about ten minutes. To read a continental timetable is twice as easy as to read an American one, and three times easier than to read a red *Guide Michelin.* Anyone who wishes to travel by rail within Europe and, say, buys a Eurailpass for this purpose without attempting to get hold of *Cook's Continental Timetable* knows not what he is missing.

The English, with their numerous private railways, produced a unified national rail timetable during the nineteenth century, the famous *Bradshaw's,* whose name is known to readers of Sherlock Holmes and of other examples of Victorian and Edwardian literature. Bradshaw published a guide to Continental railways as early as 1847; this eventually grew to encyclopedic proportions. In 1873 a Cook's employee, John Bredall, convinced the Cook family to issue a small, condensed continental timetable. It was printed by Cook's themselves on their premises in London at 107 Fleet Street, which they shared during that period with Professor and Mrs. Fowler's Phrenological Consulting Rooms.

The *Continental Timetable* grew rapidly, doubling its size every twenty years. The early editions have a charm of their own (they included the timetables of stagecoaches in Switzerland, before the latter became the electric-train country *par excellence*). Starting in 1883 *Cook's Continental Timetable* was published each month. Before the Second World War it adopted the sensible international timetable symbols (the little wineglass for buffet service, the crossed knife-and-fork indicating the dining car, the made-up bed for the sleeping-car, the flat couch for the couchette, the little house for the frontier station, etc.). After the Second World War *Cook's*, like the British and American Armies, adopted the system of the 24-hour clock (23.11 instead of 11.11 P.M.). Since 1976 it has given distances in kilometers instead of miles. In spite of the proliferation of air travel it is selling better than ever; it is reported to be doing very well in Japan.

Read the *Nord Express:* Paris to Copenhagen via Namur, Liège, Cologne, Münster, Osnabrück, Bremen, Hamburg, Lübeck, and the Rodby ferry: a route that cuts through the history of Europe, with rich nineteenth century, seventeenth century, Hanseatic associations. But it is the *when* that gives life to the *where;* these names of towns are but a list without the magical evocation of their hours. The click of recognition springs into the mind through the punctuation of the timetable. Paris Nord 18.09 (it is raining, the evening lights have come on, the cabs crowd and congregate under the tower of the Gare du Nord, across from which the awnings with their beer signs glisten and darken. The train glides out of the station, there is that unique sense of excitement and comfort as it gathers speed and screeches past the yellow-lit windows of the dark apartment houses). Namur 20.12 (the iron shapes, the slag-heaps of the Belgian night, the rain streaking at an angle against the windows of the dining car). Aachen 21.44, Köln 22.32 (the steel swords of the Rhine bridges slashing across the dark). Münster 0.22, Osnabrück 0.41 (the empty, echoing long platforms, the arclights in the cold German midnight hour; one pulls the shade down). Bremen 3.00, Hamburg 3.32, Lübeck 4.07 (the half-frozen shape of the great harbor factories, the broad-hipped towns breathing in the last hour of the night). Rodby 6.50 (the wisp of the grey dawn, the taciturn dunes of Denmark, the soughing of the sea. Two hours later the ferry clanks into the harbor, awash with the morning light. The red tiles on the houses, the ozone odor of the electric wires, the glass cupola of the main station. A beautiful Frenchwoman combs her blonde mane in the corridor). Copenhagen 9.19. The *Nord Express.*

And where else can one read about the *Pushkin/Athens Express,* departing from the Kiev Station in Moscow at 15.15 on a dark and snowy December afternoon, running past the stubbled fields of the Ukraine during the night and during the better part of the next day, pulling into Budapest that midnight, with the lights of her European-style boulevards scintillating behind the smoky glass dome of the East Station; and after a tiring sunny morning across Thessaly, arriving in Athens—warm and blue, smelling of olive oil, anise, and the near sea. (Accommodations include hard and soft coaches, and a first-class Russian *wagons-lits* sleeper.)

The *Blue Gentian* is an express from Hamburg to Carinthia; the *Edelweiss* a super-train from Brussels to Zurich, cutting across all of Alsace during the afternoon; the *Espresso del Levante* runs from Milan to Brindisi; *L'Arbalète* from Paris to Zurich. There are three expresses named *Aurora,* a Russian, an Italian, and a Yugoslavian one; one of the super-trains from Paris to Marseille is named *Le Phocéen,* the other is *Le Rhodanien.* The *Transmaghreb* clatters across the North African night from Algiers to Tunis (couchettes and an Algerian dining car). Oh, *Amtrak,* with your ugly Russian spelling; or *Conrail,* which sounds like a task force made up by the Nixon Administration!

The *Mirabell* runs through the Vienna Woods, on its way to Salzburg. Evening has come; the train speeds past the emptying platforms, a bright streak flashing by, until it is swallowed up by the darkness. The light of evening: *Mirabell.* I am standing in my library, great windows open to the south. Armchair traveler my foot.

The Light from the East
(1979)

The Pope arrived in the United States on the first day of October.

Forty years before that day, on the first day of October in 1939, in Poland the thud and the boom of guns stopped. That day the last Polish soldiers, begrimed and ragged, dropped their arms. The pall of death spread over that melancholy country. The Germans, a new, brutal breed of Germans, had conquered it. Their then allies, the Russians, a new, brutal breed of Russians, poured in from the east. Between them they divided Poland. In Cracow, the sacramental city, the German viceroy of Poland, Hans Frank, set up his retinue and palace. The Russians would deport thousands of Poles. The Germans would tell them that they were slaves, close their schools and most of their churches, for the purpose of starving their spirit, and not only their flesh, into submission. Karol Wojtyla, a plain Polish draftee from around Cracow, was among those millions of potential slaves.

Forty years later he is the Pope, the ruler of the Catholic Church, the Bishop of Rome, the only remaining true monarch in the world. The cardinal-bishops of Germany worked in the conclave for his election. The Germans are gone from his homeland but the armed might of Russia is still there, having forced a Communist government upon the country. That government was constrained to receive this Pope, the former Archbishop of Cracow, when he elected to visit his homeland. Millions rose across the country, gathering to greet him. A generation of Communist rule had passed. Hitler and Stalin are dead.

Now he arrives in the United States on a triumphal visit. He lands in Boston, the hub-city of the American intellectual tradition, seat of the richest and most famous university of the globe, repository and representative of the scientific view of the world, according to which the economy of man is determined, his biological evolution ineluctable, democracy means the progress of education, men and women are programmable and their history ultimately predictable. Oh you ghosts of President Conant, Justice Holmes, Professor Skinner, watch the Polish Pope flying in from the East.

I am a historian, not a theologian. "How many divisions has the Pope?" Stalin once asked that rhetorical question. He stole the phrase from Napoleon. *Qui mange du Pape en meurt.* This was often true, perhaps even of Napoleon. I cannot take much comfort from it. The Catholic Church is good at arranging spectacles. What their consequences will be I cannot tell.

I remember the Eucharistic Congress in Budapest in 1938. What a glorious May week that was—resplendent Masses, with masses of people under a brilliant blue sky, the gold of the sun pouring through marble columns, shining on Cardinal Pacelli, who would be Pope Pius XII within a year, on dignitaries in ancient Magyar dress, on the Regent, on girls in peasant costumes, Boy Scouts, choirs, an outpouring of pride, sentiment, hymns, faith. Still: 1938 was Hitler's year. The Congress came and went, two months after his conquest of Austria, four months before his resounding triumph at Munich. Among the delegations of the visiting faithful there were Germans, carrying their holy banners and an occasional swastika flag. "These German Catholics give me a pain," my mother said—or words to that effect.

But all of that was long ago; and I remember one other sentence from our family party. That day we had with us a relative, Anna néni, Aunt Anna, a nun.

"It is not given to us to know everything," she said.

Ruminating in St. Helena, Napoleon said that the future may belong to the United States and Russia. Tocqueville had developed that prediction at the end of the first volume of his immortal *Democracy in America.* Ninety-nine years after Napoleon died, Karol Wojtyla was born. The predictions seemed to have come true. The two great prophets, world leaders of the twentieth century, were Wilson and Lenin. Neither had much respect for Popes. When Wilson, triumphant, visited Rome in 1919 he made it clear that he did not wish to call on His Holiness. Forty years later a call on His Holiness had become the necessary routine for every American presidential candidate; and the son-in-law of the leader of the Soviet Union would visit the Pope. Sixty years after 1919, a giant figure of a Pope will enter the White House to meet a skittish and anxious American President, four years younger than the Pope but somehow looking preternaturally old.

The visit is a milestone. But is it a turning-point? We live in an age of visits at the summits, of the airplane, of public relations. Air Force One meet Shepherd One. Number one meet Number One. The King and the Queen of England visited the United States three times during the last forty years. What difference did their visits make? In October 1965 a Pope, Paul VI, visited New York for the first time. Certain people tell me that the event was unforgettable; that day New York ground to a standstill. Perhaps. Ask other people from New York: remember 1965? What happened in October 1965? "Of course I know," they say. "The great blackout." The first city-wide failure of electricity blots out many things, including the first visit of a Pope. For millions it was the first whiff of the end of the modern age, of the end of the secure certainties of the technological order of the world.

On September 25, 1979, seven days before the arrival of John Paul II in New York, the Associated Press carries a story, which I read in my local Pennsylvania newspaper, about a Polish-American parish in Staten Island. Before the weekly bingo game in the church hall, the pastor of the parish raffled off 75 tickets for the Pope's Mass in Yankee Stadium. Of the more than two thousand people in the parish there were 213 applicants for tickets. "You know," the pastor said, "many people would rather watch it on television." The pastor put 213 numbered balls in a wire cage, pulling out 75, calling out the winners. "Many players never even looked up. They were busy reading the boards for the Early Bird Special, the evening's first game, or stacking their chips. As the drawing continued, the players' chatter grew louder. Finally, Father H. stopped calling out the names." The headline runs: "Bingo Comes First, Pope's Raffle Second."

This is one level of reality, television evolution in the age of the masses. But while evolution may be predictable, history is not. Who would have foreseen—fifty years ago, one hundred years ago, two hun-

dred years ago—that the giant figure in this world in 1979 would be the
Pope, a Pope from Poland, having come to the center of events from the
benighted and Communized eastern marches of Europe, from a people
that Americans have made a butt of their jokes? Not Hitler, not Stalin; not
Lenin, not Wilson; not Napoleon; not Robespierre, not Jefferson, not John
Adams, not Louis XVI. Perhaps Poe foresaw, Edgar Allan Poe, our tragic,
American, unfinished Poe:

> But there arose in our pathway a shrouded human figure, very far larger in
> its proportions than any dweller among men. And the hue of the skin of the
> figure was of the perfect whiteness of the snow.

These are the last sentences of the *Narrative of A. Gordon Pym;* a
vision of a Christ-like figure standing at the end of the world. We are now
about to receive the Vicar of Christ at the end of the modern world.

It is, alas, not the Church which stands out from the modern world
and shines in contrast to it. It is the Pope. *Pontifex triumphans,* not
ecclesia triumphans.

John Paul II is the last monarch in the world. There are a few kings
and queens left, here and there, almost all of them in northwestern,
Protestant, bourgeois Europe: but, let us be honest, they are, all, fig-
ureheads now. Even the Queen of England. Respected, remnant figures,
largely powerless, no longer governant, rarely governing, heads of state
for ceremonial occasions, they are traditional celebrities, no longer the
fathers and mothers of the families of their peoples; ready to resign any
moment if their peoples would so demand; like that proverbial Saxon
king, unready to grasp the reins, to command their peoples in the event of
a great crisis, of a monstrous threat.

And yet this abdication of monarchy has taken place at a time when
the democratic masses are waiting for a leader, for a father-figure whom
they could admire and trust and follow. Two thousand four hundred years
ago Aristotle saw this, that monarchy has a natural attraction for democracy. It is true of the democracy of the United States, in spite of its
legendary republicanism. This country has often resembled an elective
monarchy, whose people are forever looking for a fatherly figure and for
his family, in order to celebrate them as few monarchs have been celebrated in the modern age. When Franklin Roosevelt died people fell on

their knees in the street; a priest was quoted who said that the late President ought to be beatified. When John Kennedy died many people said that he was a martyr, and some of them thought that his martyrdom was a sacramental one. A king is a sacramental figure, not merely a ceremonial one; and in an age of atomized individualism, of mass democracy, of dissolving families, of untrustworthy politicians people yearn for the presence of a father.

See the pictures from Ireland, infinitely moving even on television: a crowd of people spreading as far as the eye can see, a youthful crowd out of that ancient and gnarled race, youthful because they are filled with joy. It is the greatest event in the history of their generation, and something more than ceremonial. Their faraway king has come to see them, to touch them, to kiss their ground. The last time something like this happened was in 1851, when Queen Victoria, three years after the passing of that awful catastrophe, The Famine, came to see her Irish people. It is recorded that the people of that tortured and depressed land, even after centuries of English insensitivity and oppression, even then in the wake of the greatest catastrophe that the English, albeit unwittingly, had allowed to be visited upon them, welcomed the Queen with a kind of quiet warmth. She was, after all, a Mother; not their real mother, perhaps, but not someone entirely different, either, a kindly Stepmother who is preferable to no mother at all. And now, again, this occurs, but differently. The Irish people are surprised by joy, their distant Father has come, to visit them for a day or two, flown in in the belly of a big steel bird. I can well understand the chill and the gloom that must penetrate into the hearts of certain Ulster Protestants as they watch the spectacle. It is, I fear, no longer the Old Contempt, the proud dismissal, the No Popery as they contemplate the ceremonial vestments, the popish idolatry, that double-peaked cathedral of a tiara on the head of the man. They must know, because they can see, that this man is a monarch, more powerful even than their Queen; he is the Distant King of the people of Ireland, and perhaps of much else besides.

My American Protestant friends and relatives—how different is their sentiment from that of their grandfathers! Their respect for the Pope is so great, so sad. Unlike their ancestors, they no longer question his authority, his saintliness, his goodness. What saddens them is not that the

Catholic Church is too rigid or too authoritarian, but that its representatives so often seem unspiritual, that they are trying to be of this world, assiduously impressing their fellow-citizens that they, too, are regular fellows, television-watchers, diners-out, credit-card-holders, convention-goers, eager businessmen, basketball coaches, football fans—accepting the television-Englishing of the Mass, divesting themselves of their religious clothes and habits and traditional convictions. My American Protestant friends and relatives yearn for the presence of men and women whose convictions spring from a spirit that they believe to be eternal and true, who can infuse meaning into this world because they are not wholly of this world. This is what they see in the Pope.

How strange and miraculous this is! A century ago the Pope was the prisoner in the Vatican, suspected and shunned by the government of Italy, a man in a gilded cage in Rome. During the last world war no one dared to touch him, not even Hitler. In 1943 Hitler said to his confidants that there were three powers in Rome: Mussolini, the King, and the Pope, and that the Pope was the most powerful of them all. In the midst of the war Mussolini felt obliged to allow eminent citizens of the Allies, his enemies, American diplomats and the Archbishop-Cardinal of New York, to pass through Rome, to and from the Vatican. In the midst of Hitler's Europe the Vatican was a safe house and an island of flickering light. The German writer Hochhuth, who wrote a long critical historical drama about the role of Pius XII during the war, criticized him not because he was too powerful but because he had not exercised his power enough. Great Expectations!

There is something in the history of civilizations that resembles the life of a man. A civilization, too, has its youth and its old age. The end and the beginning of life are two extreme conditions; and at the end of an age some of its beginnings appear again. Fifteen hundred years ago the civilization of our ancient ancestors was on its last legs. The end of the Roman Empire was in the wings. The emperors had long ago lost their power, and the ruling caste its authority. The Roman monarchy and the Roman aristocracy were wan and weak. And when the thunder of death broke over the Alps, when the Hun Attila appeared with his hordes in the north of Italy, there was no one who could go to meet him with authority except the bishop of Rome, the Pope, that elective monarch who a few decades before had been but the head of a small sect.

Something like this may happen again. I don't know. What I think is that there exists an element of something like this, an element of trust and hope and expectation, in the hearts, even more than in the minds, of many people who see in the Pope the last real monarch in the world, the last King in the West.

And he comes to America from the East, a witness to certain truths, like Aleksandr Solzhenitsyn—the erstwhile Polish draftee and the erstwhile Soviet captain. *Ex oriente lux:* from a portion of the world where not so long ago many intellectuals had chosen to see the new light of egalitarian justice for the masses. Stalin, that Asiatic monarch who had little more than contempt for them, put up some of these intellectuals, self-chosen émigrés and exiles, in the fleabag Hotel Lux in Moscow. There was not much *lux* in the Soviet Union, in those dark semi-Oriental streets. The true light has begun to appear now, a wholly different kind of light, at a time when the begrimed electric bulbs and the shameless neons have begun to flicker in the West, when the West is bedeviled by what people call with the idiotic name of an energy shortage, whereas it is, in reality, a shortage of the spirit.

I went to the office building—a skyscraper—of the Archdiocese of Philadelphia to pick up my press card. The place was humming; secretaries were chattering, wearing fancy boots, tight sweaters, red rouge, blue mascara. At a stop the elevator doors opened; before they closed again I had a glimpse of that particular floor. The brass sign on the wall read "Institutional Procurement Service." I glimpsed all kinds of revolting artifacts on shelves, behind them a motorized exercycle, with price tags, a useful thing for the rectory, no doubt.

Downstairs I got a large packet of a folder, the press release, produced by the Communications Center of the Archdiocese. (In the Beginning Was the Word. In the end is the Communications Center.)

There are all kinds of depressing things in that packet. The first of the releases ends with these two sentences: "In October 1979, Cardinal Krol hosted a celebration in Philadelphia for Pope John Paul II's historic visit to the United States. Approximately a million people gathered in

Philadelphia's Benjamin Franklin Parkway to pay tribute to the first non-Italian Pope in 455 years." Suppose they gave a party and only fifty thousand came? No matter: if it is in the publicity release, it must have happened, it will happen. The Word Was Made Flesh; the publicity machine does one better, it releases the future.

Monsignor Jaworowski, pastor of St. "Addlebert" Church (consistently misspelled in the release) "spoke fondly of the Holy Father."

"He has the charisma of a leader that makes you feel like a million dollars." There follows the description of a Polish-American banquet that some of the priests and their friends gave Cardinal Wojtyla when he last visited the United States. "The parishioners feasted on stuffed shrimp, filet mignon, and dishes of polish [*sic*] delicacies including golabki, peerogi, and kielbasa. The dinner was held at a local restaurant, The Casbah."

In the release entitled "Papal Visit Will Strengthen Ecumenism," a Dr. Rufus Cornelson, Executive Director of the Metropolitan Christian Council of Philadelphia, says: "I think the trip will be extremely important ecumenically. We are living in a world of pluralistic cultures. . . . I think that he, and the office he holds, is able to relate the Church most effectively to a pluralistic world." By which, I assume, the author means that the Catholic Church, Holy Rollers, Buddhists, Bolsheviks, believers in Hare Krishna, Lesbianism, Billy Graham, the Guru, all amount to the same thing.

A Dr. John C. Stetler, Conference Minister and President of the Pennsylvania Southeast Conference of the United Church of Christ, says: "We look at the visit of the Holy Father as fathering the hungers of the human family." Whatever Dr. Stetler means (this is not easy to assess), at least he did not say "parenting."

In the entire release packet Article # 1 is the Biography of John Cardinal Krol, Article # 2 is "Pope John Paul II's relationship with Cardinal Krol." There is a release on Copernicus, another on Kosciuszko, and two sheets listing the Polish-American parishes in Philadelphia and its surroundings.

Mother Teresa, not an ecumenicist, once said: "All our words will be useless unless they come from within—words which do not give the light of Christ increase the darkness."

The age of aristocracy has not really been succeeded by the age of democracy. It has been succeeded by the age of bureaucracy. This bureaucracy has now infected, penetrated, enveloped the Church. It is now devouring its organs of substance, much as sugar decomposes the sinews of the diabetic. There may be more bureaucracy in an American archdiocese than in the entire Vatican. What goes on in this skyscraper of a building is what goes on in the skyscraper of a huge business corporation. The cult of bureaucracy in the democratic age—and this is different from the ancient Roman or the Chinese or the Czarist or the Prussian bureaucracies—is the cult of popularity; and the cult of popularity is the cult of cowardice. It reeks of the decay of the spirit.

It is this bureaucracy, not the laity, that has debased the language of the Mass. The Pope said in Dublin: "The most sacred principles, which were a sure guide for the behavior of individuals and society, are being hollowed out by false pretenses concerning freedom, the sacredness of life, the indissolubility of marriage, the true sense of human sexuality, the right attitude toward material goods that progress has to offer." "Everybody wants the full freedom in all the areas of human behavior and new models of morality are being proposed in the name of would-be freedom." Are the bureaucracies listening? "Marriage for priests," one of them told me some weeks ago, "is just around the corner." This skyscraper is filled with people at the very time when there is but one seminarian in this country for every three twenty years ago. Many Catholics abandoned their habit of church-going during the last ten or 15 years; many priests and nuns abandoned their religious habits. The people may yet reappear in the churches. Will these priests and nuns reappear in their religious habits? I doubt it.

How many divisions has the Pope?

This monarch has now little or no control over the real beliefs of his aristocracy. Like other monarchs in great and tragic times of history, he still inspires the people, though no longer his bureaucrats and barons. He knows the limits of his power over those who pretend to believe in him. Like a monarch. He remains true to those who believe in him. Like a father.

In the darkening evening, I listen to the radio station which is tidying up the news of the Pope's day in Philadelphia. The newscaster mentions the long duration of the Mass and the length of the Pope's homily. A priest at the microphone comments: "Yes, it was very long. He brought in everything, didn't he? It was a little heavy for people who were standing there for hours."

How about the Pope? Wasn't it heavy for him? I had been there, a bit bone-weary, straining to hear his sermon as it came cracking and fading through the megaphones. Indeed he spoke about many things: Philadelphia, the Declaration of Independence, the Liberty Bell. The people clapped at times—an odd custom during a sermon—as he spoke. I, too, thought that perhaps he should not have talked about all of those things; it had a touch of the expected routine of a foreign dignitary on his visit to Philadelphia; and he quoted the triad of Life and Liberty and The Pursuit Of Happiness, including that last phrase of the triad that I had, and have, and will always consider as a gust of Jeffersonian guff, the emptiest phrase ever written in a declaration of *independence,* and the source of many things that are wrong in this country. But then I changed my mind. That distant figure on the platform, white but far from being spectral, robust and fatherly, kept on speaking in his booming, slow, careful way. Now he was speaking to these thousands of people against the kind of freedom that is, in reality, a kind of slavery, the very opposite of personal integrity and of independence: against the pursuit of material happiness, against the pursuit of sexual license, against the pursuit of the self-degrading preoccupation with the self.

How tired he must have been, after these interminable long hours, traveling, preaching, praying, traveling, preaching, again! But he was compelled to go on, to speak about these things, to try to exhort people to lead a better and more honest life, returning to this theme again and again. He did not demand these things from his listeners; I felt, deeply, that he was demanding this effort from himself, sacrificing his remnant strength for us, this Father.

There were unbeautiful things this day: the marshals wearing ugly tangerine-colored baseball caps which most of them forgot to remove during the Mass; the young woman of the television crew, giggling as she sat on the shoulders of a man, with another holding her bottom, with her pretty, sharp face, her hair done to a tee, furiously chewing gum; the many young louts in their sleazy sneakers and sleazier shirts, opened down to their bellies, all of them chewing gum, and obviously bored—but I ought to strike out that "obviously" because of what my wife said when I recounted that, too, at home: "They did go there, after all," she said.

There were beautiful things this day: the sudden coming of a golden autumn afternoon after a morning of dark, miasmatic rain; the gentle billowing of the pure and radiant vestments on the podium in that blessed breeze; the silent southwest flight of thirteen wild geese suddenly crossing the canopy of the blue sky during the Mass, after the whirr of the police helicopters had died away; above all, the white figure with his eloquent hands, this personal presence of the Vicar of Christ.

The sound of his voice too: that strong, meditated European diction, his careful use of English whose sound was different from the talking sounds we are accustomed to hearing, but somehow it was not really foreign. It was the very opposite of those foreign accents, like Henry Kissinger's, for example, which suggest that their speaker is determinedly trying to get inside the language in order to use it for his own mental purposes, but no less foreign for that. This Pope's accent meant nothing. He was not speaking for himself. He was speaking to us.

To us . . . but who are we? His divisions, his *franc-tireurs,* his guerrillas? His subjects, his followers, his children? How many of us will hear, listen, remember? And is it a matter of numbers?

It is not given to us to know everything.

Easter in Warsaw

(1981)

Holy Thursday. The plane from Frankfurt to Warsaw is empty. When I present my ticket and my passport I detect a flicker of surprise on the face of the woman at the Lufthansa counter, of the porter, of the German customs official. A long wait. I read a German news-magazine, in which the longest article deals with sex research—five or six experts assuring German manhood that they need not worry about the length of their penises, anything more than 8.5 centimeters ought to do. In front of me two Germans in Bavarian hunting suits, with pinched, high-colored Holbein faces and blue eyes, carry shotguns in fine leather cases. To go shooting in Poland, in a poor country, is a bargain now. The plane flies over Czechoslovakia, avoiding East Germany. Over Prague it changes course to the northeast.

Even before our landing, the poverty of Poland is visible. As the plane descends and swoops low I see smoke-darkened farmhouses, with faded red, battered roofs; an old, broken-down truck in the yard here and there. And now we roll to a stop on the runway. The bus is an aged German airport bus, obviously bought second-hand. The airport is reminiscent of the 1950s: a crowded, soiled hangar. Before me a Polish woman, coming from the United States or Canada, opens up her suitcase: it contains oranges and grapefruit, nothing else. They let her through. It takes me, with a single, hand-carried bag, half an hour to go through the passport booth and the customs. Through the rickety steel doors I emerge into a hall packed with people waiting for relatives to pass through the official sieve.

Immediately two young men corral me. "Taxi?" I say yes. Where? I give the name of my hotel. "Ten dollars," they say. "We change money. In taxi. We give you plenty of zloty." I shake them off and find a taxi on my own.

This is a grey city, peopled with weary faces. We shoot along the broad Eastern European boulevards, sliding in and out of the trolley tracks. The buildings are soiled cinereous concrete. We drive past a skyscraper in the Stalinist style, the Palace of Culture, foisted by the Soviets on Warsaw thirty years ago. It is half Woolworth Building, half Moscow gingerbread, immensely ugly, pock-marked with dirt, as if the relentless artillery of time were transforming it into something prehistoric, a tower melting into stalactites: concrete bent and deformed by time, a living example much better than that silly watch by Dalí. We drive up to the hotel. The driver pulls out my bag, sees a book in its outside pocket, reads the title (it is Maisie Ward's biography of Chesterton). "Oh," he says. "Very fine." I give him two dollars, obviously more than enough.

The hotel is an American block in the middle of the city, all cement and glass. It looks like an enormous underwater vessel, beached. To get my visa I had to pay more than $100 a day for my room in advance. The halls and my room have all the accoutrements of an intercontinental hotel, from plastic shower-cap to minibar. It is convenient rather than comfortable, and ugly to boot. And now it is early afternoon, and I walk out of the hotel into this strange metropolis with its large empty wastelands.

I see . . . a ruined hotel from the Twenties . . . soldiers with impassive faces and Soviet-style trousers tucked into their boots . . . the ashen face of the city that has suffered more than any city in this century, and this includes Leningrad and Stalingrad, Hiroshima and Nagasaki.

In the siege of Warsaw in 1939, one out of every four buildings was destroyed. During the Rising in 1944, one out of the remaining three. Then the Germans destroyed most of the rest in a fury at the Poles: had the Poles not resisted, the Second World War would not have begun as it did, and the Germans and Hitler would have been the masters of Europe yet, instead of facing defeat. When the Soviet Army finally moved into Warsaw (four months after it had stopped to watch the destruction of the city and of its people) nine out of ten buildings had been burned or smashed by the Germans. I lived through the Second World War in another Central European capital; now, nearly forty years later, in the nostrils of my memory I can still smell remnant scents of that war.

The rebuilding of Warsaw is still incomplete. The churches and the Old Town have been rebuilt. The baroque church of S. S. Wizytek is full of people, the afternoon Mass is ending. It has nothing of the warm spicy darkness of the Italian or Spanish Baroque churches, with people milling around their vestibules; there is an air of infinite seriousness about it. It is like the treasured possession of an old and battered, impoverished family, a place of sad and profound pride.

I walk out and along the wide boulevards, so very Central-Eastern European, with their Empire façades and windows but not more than one or two stories high. I go into the university compound: without knowing Polish, I attempt to read the wall posters and papers, and I can glimpse the expressions of freedom and of solidarity in the literal sense of those words. Night has come. I return to the hotel and try to sleep.

Good Friday. I wake up early and stare out into the grey asphalt desert where every hour on the hour three Polish soldiers in greatcoats march across to change the guard at the monument to the Unknown Soldier. Fifty paces before it they break into a parade step, reminiscent of the German and Russian goose-step but perhaps a tad less brutal, their arms swinging.

I begin my telephoning. I have four, five addresses of people I want to see. I do not know Polish but somehow I get through, with the help of the operator. The people answer with all the hospitality of the old Eastern European tradition, in halting English or in broken German. (The old Francophone upper class of Poland is almost all gone.)

Around eight, snow begins to fall, driven by the wind diagonally past my enormous window. It is somehow fitting, in this scene of wintry desolation.

I have a free morning, I put on a sweater under my thin raincoat and walk out into the city. I walk the entire length of the Krakowski and the Nowy Swiat.

This is a city of all-encompassing poverty. But the poverty has a smell that is acrid, not sour, like the proud poverty of a woman erect in her old fur coat. Again, there is the sense of a time that is past: this is how Vienna must have been in the late 1940s, or Budapest in the 1950s, and yet it is different. These are not the faces of a defeated people.

There are long lines before the stores: meat stores, bakeries, pastry shops, fish markets, even at the newspaper kiosks. (I am told later that there is a reason for this last: people line up not merely for cigarettes but because the newspapers, now reasonably free, are worth reading.) The people in the lines do not push or swarm, as in Moscow or Belgrade; they remind me of the stoicism of the queues of English during the war.

Many shops sell souvenirs—mostly amber from the Baltic—but, really, there is almost nothing to buy. These are privately owned shops: free enterprise breaking through, as in many other places of Eastern Europe. Again, I notice the self-composure of the people: when I and the few other tourists (mostly Germans) reach the counters and ask a few questions, there is none of the anxious servility of shopkeepers in a poor country.

The snow has stopped, and the sky is slate-colored; a few fast-scudding clouds, and once in a while the sun shows its face; but it is a distant face, bright without much warmth. I walk north, toward the Old City.

Warsaw was never a particularly beautiful or even pretty town, for many reasons, one of them being that the Polish aristocracy, with few exceptions, did not choose to live there: their palatial houses were in the country. Yet the Old City has a character of its own, like Saxon Dresden. Canaletto and Bellotto painted its vistas. Warsaw sits deep within the Polish plain, but the architecture has no Russian or Eastern marks: it is Baltic, Hanseatic, northeastern European, the gabled façades like Lübeck or Danzig (Gdansk) or Tallinn. Before the war, people of the Old City lived in the discomfort, clutter, and dirt of the eighteenth century, without plumbing, often on beaten mud floors.

The Old City was the center of the heroic 1944 rising. The Germans destroyed it, but after the war the Communist regime chose to rebuild it, with infinite care (it is said that some of the façades were reconstructed after minute studies of the Canaletto paintings). Now, twenty-five years later, the buildings have aged, they have none of the marks of facile or artificial reconstruction. I am chilly but I wish that the snow had not stopped falling, in these silent streets with their buttressed walls and sudden turns and leaded windows, in this compound of civic fortress and merchant-houses, military and bourgeois at the same time.

I return to the hotel, one of whose dining rooms bears the name of Canaletto: it is indistinguishable from a restaurant in an American airport, put together in three days by an expensive designer from New York.

In the afternoon I talk with my Polish acquaintances. They tell me many interesting things. One is this: much of what happened in 1980 began in 1979, on this asphalt wasteland, on this dreariest of cement squares in front of my window; here John Paul II said his Mass that June. Five hundred thousand people came. The government did not interfere, the militia and the police stood back; that enormous crowd was channeled and directed and organized by its own volunteers; there was a sense of self-discipline which was not only surprising and impressive but which may have been the initial coagulation of that silent and tremendous force latent in the present unity of the nation.

It is now evening and I go to visit a Polish home, relatives of Polish friends in the United States. This is in Zoliborz, a kind of suburb, and another center of the 1944 rising. Zoliborz is an eighteenth-century Polish adaptation of a French phrase, *joli bourg*. Well, it is not much of a bourg, and pas très joli. But again, as in so many other things in Poland, it is the interior which is touching: a destroyed house rebuilt, brick by brick, by the family, and the cosseted familiarity of their lives, worn as they are with daily cares, together with their constant protective attention to their children. We talk (with difficulty) and drink (with ease). They offer me food but I fast on this day. When I leave, the concrete cubes of the villa-like houses are dark square Cézanne shapes, with pale lights shining from the windows here and there. It is melancholy without being depressing, with the sense of life—of a very difficult, bruised life—going on and on.

Holy Saturday. Again I cannot sleep, and I have read everything I could lay my hands on. The cement square is emptier than ever. At noon I breakfast with an American friend. He is a professor of international relations, and very knowledgeable about many details of politics; but somehow I know that what I see here is not on the plane of International Relations.

Again I walk through the city in the afternoon. Again long, very long lines of people. (Why, I ask myself at first: the shops are all closed down for Easter.) They are standing in line before the churches, before each of the churches: all kinds of people, bundled up, men and women, old and young. They move forward with great patience, in the churches, to kneel for a moment and kiss a crucifix, or before a sculptured piece or a painting of Christ in the tomb. I want to record this; I lift my camera; I am embarrassed in doing so. But the people do not mind. They seem to be steeped in thought, infinitely serious people, like the lines of people I saw in London sixteen years ago, when Winston Churchill was to be buried.

An old woman comes up to me. She says that she will give me zloty for marks or for dollars. She says that she is an ex-nun. In the afternoon the lines stretch even longer, in places for half a mile. A faint sense of the old Poland is still in the streets: a few beggars; in that modern cavern of the hotel, young prostitutes. They look harsh and ugly. I have dinner with a Polish friend; it is very expensive (in Polish money which has lost much of its exchange value), and very bad. Now there is a great silence over the city, even though it is early night and early spring.

Easter Sunday. I go to the Holy Cross Church for Easter Mass. This church of the Lazaristes, built in the late seventeenth century, was destroyed by the Germans in 1944, except for its outer walls, a statue of Christ carrying the cross, and its great Salzburg organ. The church has been rebuilt. The walls are covered with marble plaques, one of them in memory of General Sikorski, the head of the anti-Communist Polish government in London during the war, a national hero whose name was taboo in Poland until very recently.

It is difficult to write about a Mass without lapsing into sentimentalism. So here are some observations on it which will make old-fashioned Catholics nostalgic: The Mass is partly in Latin, partly in Polish. The organ music is ineffably moving and beautiful. The priests wear their old cassocks, the nuns their old habits. Not more than 10 per cent of a hundred take communion—it is reminiscent of the Old Dispensation, of what we were taught in our youth: you ought not to go to communion unless you know that you are in a state of grace.

It is a joyous feast, the Easter Resurrection, but the people are deeply serious; this Mass has none of the emotional, communal, orgiastic jubilation of the Orthodox churches, the exclamation of Christ Having Risen. So many crippled people, so many people with worn faces: they must have personal knowledge of much of Calvary, that Christ has fallen and risen, fallen and risen, again and again . . .

The communion hymn is exceptionally beautiful, it touches me deeply. I would write that its beauty is "unearthly," except that there is something worldly about it, in the deep and faithful sense of that adjective; I am reminded of Bonhoeffer's phrase (that, too, in 1944, in the shadow of his martyrdom): *"Nicht von der Welt zu Gott, sondern von Gott zur Welt geht der Weg Jesu Christi."* "The way of Christ is not from this world to God, it is from God to this world."

Every people has the liturgy it deserves.

I know that I am in the presence of something profoundly historical: the existence of this nation, here in the eastern marches of Europe, is inextricably bound together with a belief that is Western, Catholic, Roman . . . and, in an odd way, modern. Like their famous Our Lady of Czestochowa, at first glance very dark like a Byzantine icon, but her face is a sensitive, European face; it has none of the round, pasty face of the Byzantine and Orthodox saints—big-eyed, yet expressionless, deadened and deadening.

The crowds stream out into the pale sunlight. Priests lope across the boulevard in their long cassocks; they wear berets in the French manner.

I go to Zoliborz to visit my new-found friends. An entire family sits around a table, twelve of them, on this one of the two great feasts of the year. The table is laden with food. Every few minutes a new dish is brought in by the women, and we drink small tumblers of vodka. The talk, in broken German and English, goes on. In the back of the room the Mass is celebrated over color television. After that the Pope: a priest reads his Easter letter to the people of Poland.

I am ready to return to my empty hotel but they won't let me. We go to the Powazkowski cemetery. They buy rush-lights for their parents' graves. The cemetery has that crowded darkness of European cemeteries, as if the dead would, sooner or later, burst from their graves, as if the earth were composed of rich black rust; the marble tablets are often split and broken. It is a cemetery of families and of martyrs. Generals of the anti-Communist and of the Communist underground armies are buried side by side. Behind it is the wall of the Jewish cemetery where people were buried even during the awful months of the ghetto siege. The cemetery is a museum, a living museum of the dead.

Now it is dark and I think I must go to the hotel; but I am the prisoner of these hospitable people. We return to their house, more food. The color television flickers on: the evening news. Again the first item is the Pope, the second item is pictures from Rome. After the news we watch a sensitive Polish film which I can follow even though I do not know Polish, a film by Wajda: misty scenes of a country house and dreamy faces of gentle young men and women from before the War; it suggests their latent nostalgia for the Second Republic.

I emerge to the dark cubes and shapes of the houses in Zoliborz and an empty city with few people on the streets. I am back in my hotel, in the empty lobby with the shiny paneling and the fake brass.

Easter Monday. This is another holiday: everything is closed. Snow flurries again. I breakfast with foreign journalists. They, and the people at the next table, discuss the prospect of Russian invasion openly. Will they intervene or not? During the past four days my Polish acquaintances spoke less frequently about that. In spite of the many bits of political information and gossip, I find the conversation uninteresting. It is all about the relations of governments and states, not about nations and their peoples.

My last walk through Warsaw. I cross it for hours. I see the desolate wastes of the ghetto. How much more animated this city would be with the presence of Polish Jews. I think that the Poles sense this. Some of their atavistic anti-Semitism may lie buried under the rubble of that ghetto. Whether they are *relieved* by the absence of their Jewish minority—a sad and cruel possibility of a thought which must be entertained—I do not know. What I think is that they know how, in the midst of their own Golgotha, they were the witnesses of an even greater tragedy, the enormity of which surpassed their own.

The streets are empty; but around the churches are little swarms of people. I walk into the church of the Holy Cross. And what luck: the Mass is half over, and the organist plays that most beautiful of hymns again. I am transfixed. The Mass is ended. I try to find a priest, find the stairs to the loft, find the organist, to ask for the music of the hymn. I cannot find my way, but the music swims in my ear for a long time. I return to the hotel and write it down. Here it is:

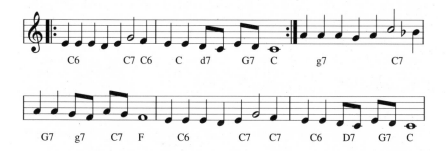

Later in the afternoon I drive to the airport. There, and perhaps there alone, I have the impression of being in a police state: the many soldiers, the grim and often senseless regulations. Sergeants in their uniforms, carrying briefcases in the Eastern European manner. On the terrace of the airport crowds of Poles are waving good-bye to their relatives and friends.

The Swissair plane begins to hum, and in a few moments we are over this desolate city and over the broken roofs of the barns and the dirt roads. Two hours to Zurich. I haven't seen a Western newspaper for nearly a week. The Swiss are wonderfully efficient; next to me on the rack are the latest American magazines. I pick the first one, the latest issue of *Esquire*. My eye is caught by an advertisement of the after-shave lotion I use. The text is unabashedly pornographic. The next article, by a noted literary critic, again dwells, among other things, on the size of penises. An article about what and who are in, even more vulgar than the pornography. The shiny pages of the magazine are tacky with mental filth. The Swiss airplane is clean, even the airplane food is excellent. But I am back in the West.

II

What happened in Poland, what is happening in Poland, is a slow earthquake, a development of tremendous dimensions. It involves, less than one hundred years after the death of Marx, the death of Communism, not only in Poland but in all of Europe, except that Poland, in this respect, is ahead of the rest of Europe: for in Poland not only has Communism died, it is there being buried.

The burial of an idea, of an ideology, of a governmental system does not happen overnight. The first shovelfuls of earth were turned long ago; but by September 1, 1980, the grave was open, and the ceremony could begin.

September 1, 1980, was a great event: the signing of the accord between the government and Solidarity in Gdansk, the minister of the Communist government shaking hands with Lech Walesa, their agreement meaning in practice that the monopoly of the party's power in the state was now finished, once and for all, because a new force had risen in Poland, representative of the nation. This happened on the first day of September, and in Gdansk: on the same day of the year and in the city, Danzig, where the terrible Second World War and the awful modern tragedy of Poland began—perhaps a sign of that "epic completeness which critics call the long arm of coincidence and prophets the hand of God."

What happened in Poland in 1980 was not what had happened there in 1956, what happened in Hungary in 1956 or in Czechoslovakia in 1968. This was not a revolution begun by intellectuals or by reformist Communists; it was the achievement of a conscious working class, standing Marx and Lenin on their heads. In 1956, in Poland and in Hungary, there was ample evidence that the workers had no stomach for Communism and that they would fight against the Sovietized state, if they must; but in 1980 in Poland the workers—of a younger generation, born and brought up under Communism—both led and represented the entire nation, including the Communists.

A few weeks later a monument was erected in Gdansk—with members of the government party at the ceremony, bowing their heads—to commemorate the workers who had died during the demonstrations in 1970 against the Communist government. It was as if, say, a few years after the Kronstadt uprising, the single rebellion against the Soviet government, Lenin or Stalin had been constrained to send representatives to celebrate the martyrdom of the Kronstadt workers who had been gunned down by Lenin's (and, for the sake of New York intellectuals, let me also add, by Trotsky's) orders in 1921.

The leader of the Polish workers, Lech Walesa, a simple electrician, said on one occasion: "We are not against socialism. . . . Where have the last 35 years led us? To a society of petty crooks, cheaters, tricksters, accommodationists. We must restore the morale of the nation. I have no power, I have only heart and faith. Every morning I go to Mass and receive communion. Why? Because that is the source of my strength." I have written it before, and I write it again: Walesa is the most impressive European personality since de Gaulle. He was born in 1944, in that most tragic year in the tragic history of Poland, a country which was the helpless victim of events then, and which may be the forerunner of great historical developments now.

Last September I quoted in *The New Republic* the sentence that the great French Catholic visionary and poet Charles Péguy wrote seventy or so years ago: "The true revolutionaries of the twentieth century will be the fathers of Christian families." He meant that the bourgeois state of France and the West was so rotten and corrupt that to be a Christian would take extraordinary courage, would require standing up against nearly everything in the modern world. And now, when the institutions of the West, including even some of the hierarchies and the bureaucracies of the Church, are infested with opportunists in whose minds the flame of conviction has flickered out, Walesa, with his six children, is the "true revolutionary"—as was de Gaulle, a student of Péguy, who, in 1940, rose in solitary revolt against the dreadful tide, against the corrupt surrender of France.

The present history of Poland is alone sufficient to refute Nietzsche.

Economics has nothing to do with it. "To be a person," the present Pope wrote many years ago, when he was a personalist theologian in Cracow, "means *to be* more rather than *to have* more."

To be more . . . This is the greatest aspiration of the Poles today. The great, the grave question is: can they do it alone? Three times in the eighteenth century Poland was invaded and cut up by her neighbor monarchs, because she stood alone. After Napoleon's defeat, the British and the French could not restore Polish independence against the resolution of the Czar; she was alone. Twice during the nineteenth century the Poles rose against the Russians; they were defeated, because they were alone. After the First World War Poland gained her independence, because Germany and Russia were defeated and convulsed, and because the victorious Western allies supported the Polish cause. Twenty years later the

Poles were crushed again, and twenty-five years later they were crushed yet again—because the Western democracies could not, or would not, help them. Now the Poles are more alone than ever. They know, and the Russians know, that if Russian tanks rumble into their cities the West Europeans and the British and the Americans will do little more than declare that they will—temporarily—halt their shipments of wheat and of chaff to Moscow.

They are alone in another sense, too. What has happened in Poland during the last ten months has not spread to other Eastern European countries, all the fears of the Russians—and especially of the East Germans and the Czechs—notwithstanding. As a matter of fact, until now the other Eastern European working classes have not been particularly sympathetic to the Poles. What we know of popular sentiment in the other Eastern European countries, including the traditionally sympathetic Hungarians, seems to be on the order of "The Poles are causing trouble again. They are rocking the boat. They won't get away with it."

Worse are the reactions of the Ukrainians and of the Russians. The Ukrainians hate and envy the Poles. So do the Russians. The Russian masses are not stirring. What they are saying, among themselves—and there is plenty of evidence for this, heard and overheard by Westerners in Moscow—is this: "The Poles are causing trouble again. Ungrateful wretches! We liberated them in the war, and we are giving them help. We have to stand in line, because all of our meat is going to Poland." That this is not true doesn't matter, at least in the short run: for this is how the masses of the Russian people think.

I have a very great and deep admiration for Aleksandr Solzhenitsyn, and I have written as much, but what is happening in Eastern Europe now is evidence that one of his fundamental beliefs is nonsense—somewhere between sentimental nonsense and absolute nonsense. For Solzhenitsyn has said, over and over again, that the tyranny of the Soviets is an alien imposition upon the Russian character; that the Russian people are enslaved against their will. How come, then, that not one Pole—and not one Russian dissident—expects any sympathy or help from the Russian people; that the reactions of the Russian populace to the events in Poland are, at worst, hostile and, at best, indifferent? (In accord with Solzhenitsyn's nineteenth-century forerunner, Dostoevsky, who hated the Poles to the end.)

So far as the Soviet leadership goes, it is divided. Their dilemma is truly difficult. During the "enlightened" eighteenth century, a neighboring state could be reduced by the cynical decisions of monarchs. But today's Soviet rulers face not a state apparatus, not even an army, but an entire people. To say that the Soviet solution will be an invasion by "osmosis," as Reagan's Defense Secretary, Caspar Weinberger, suggested repeatedly in April, is stupid.

The texture of history has changed; and all of this has little to do with that abstract study of states which is—inaccurately and wrongly—called "international" relations. After the First World War, the words of an American President assisted the creation of an independent Poland. During and after the Second World War, the United States could have assisted the restoration of an independent Poland—at the risk of war with the Soviet Union. By now, with space rockets and hydrogenated missiles at its disposal, the United States can, and will, do little or nothing. Rightly so: the Poles must do it themselves. Let us recall that few of the nations of Europe, surely very few of the Eastern European nations, won their independence without foreign help. Even such a large country as Italy, whose leaders more than a century ago said: *L'Italia farà di se*—Italy will do it herself—didn't. Italy needed French armies, and Bismarck's help, and the support of the Western allies during the First World War. But let me repeat: the texture of history is no longer the same.

The Poles may do it alone. They are not challenging the Soviets, certainly not for purposes of domestic posturing. Unlike Hungary in 1956, they do not proclaim their "neutrality" or their withdrawal from the Warsaw Pact, and not only because of political prudence. In 1956 the Soviets accepted the end of collective agriculture in Poland, allowing individual ownership of the land. They may have to acquiesce in the existence of independent trade unions. What worries them now is yet another step: the democratization of the Polish Communist—to be more exact, of the Polish governmental—Party. They may—I am not saying they will—accept that too.

The Poles are united and the Soviet leadership is divided. Is it not in our interests to pay more attention, and perhaps even some respect, to those among the leaders of the Soviet Union, probably including President Brezhnev, who are reluctant to plunge into Poland, who resist the proddings of their generals and of their police apparatus, aware as they may be of the incalculable and of the unpredictable element in the nature of history?

In any event, what happens in Poland was, is, and will be something quite different. The retreat of Communism will not mean an automatic triumph for capitalist democracy. Rightly so: why should the Soviets suffer a resounding defeat when the West doesn't deserve a victory?

And in one important sense—which is not measurable, either through popularity polls or through the number of divisions—the Poles are not alone.

"He who followeth me walketh not in darkness," saith our Lord. There are three important people in the world today: Reagan, Brezhnev, and the Pope; and it is at least possible that the strongest of them is the Pope.

Many in Poland say that it was the Pope's presence which crystallized this new kind of national resolution. All kinds of knowledgeable people agree—including the Russians, who have a great respect for the Pope and for the Cardinal-Primate of Poland, alas, very ill now. (When the shocking news of the attempt on the life of the Pope reached Warsaw, the churches were instantly filled with people and that evening all theaters, restaurants, places of public entertainment were shut down.) During the past eventful months there have been many instances when Catholic political personages and the Catholic party have been acknowledged as the moderates in Poland, trusted and listened to by the Party as well as by Solidarity, by many Poles, and even by certain Russians.

Two years ago, in 1979, and well over a year before the events in Gdansk, town planners and municipal authorities in the Polish town of Tychy decided to remove a crucifix from one of its squares. Instant resistance ensued; there were popular demonstrations and the authorities gave in. In early 1980—months before the Solidarity strike—people were invited to a retreat to fast for ten days in the church of Podkova Lesna outside Warsaw, in protest against some of the prevalent restrictions on civic and personal rights. A handful were expected: but hundreds came, including workers and intellectuals, young and old, a few from abroad. *They, including self-avowed atheists, fasted for ten days, and at-*

tended Mass every day. One lone Hungarian Catholic pilgrim wrote: "Those who partook in the Mass were completely united in spirit. One could sense the actual presence of the Holy Ghost. Of course the importance of this small temporary gathering of ours has been dwarfed by the tremendous movement of the united Polish workers a few months later. . . ."

What has been happening in Poland in 1980–81 is not a spring, not a thaw, but a kind of spiritual harvest. It is the rise of a people who have lived through Calvary, and who cannot be destroyed. It is not like that other Easter rising about which Yeats wrote that a terrible beauty was born. The terrible beauty of the Poles is within their past. The tree of their Golgotha is green with life, new life.

Postscript. 1 May. During the procession, for the first time, Party leaders walked with the people. A local newspaper wrote: "The crowds are reminded that it is the nation leading the Party, and not the other way around." *3 May.* The feast of national independence was celebrated for the first time since the war. The Constitution of 1791 was exhibited by Solidarity in the former royal palace of Warsaw, and the Church rededicated the day to the Holy Virgin, Regina Poloniae. *5 May.* I received a postcard from Owen Barfield, perhaps the greatest living English thinker of our times. I had sent him a postcard from Warsaw. Barfield now writes: ". . . I envied you your visit to Poland, which seems at the moment to be in something like the key position Britain occupied for a time in 1940."

So it is.

In Darkest Transylvania

(1982)

When I tell my American friends that I traveled in Transylvania, their response is predictable, automatic, universal: "Dracula!" with a grin. I am irritated by this example of the dismal influence of movies on entire categories of American knowledge—or, rather, anti-knowledge. "Dracula" was a Wallachian tribal chief who had little to do with Transylvania. His "castle" was outside Transylvania. For fourteen years he was imprisoned by King Mathias of Hungary, who was the real ruler of Transylvania then. In that gilded prison, "Dracula" (this means Little Devil in Rumanian; his real name was Vlad Tepes, the Impaler) allegedly gave up his Byzantine Orthodox religion to become a Roman Catholic in exchange for his freedom. This was the worst of the sins that the Russian historian Kuritsyn (one of the first chroniclers of Dracula's cruelties) held against him; but, then, Kuritsyn was the favorite chronicler of the immediate predecessors of Ivan the Terrible. Some humanists, these Muscovites! The Russians did not like the Rumanians then and do not like them now, and the mistrust is mutual.

The real trouble in Transylvania, however, is not between the Russians and Rumanians but between Rumanians and Hungarians, as we shall see.

Transylvania is a beautiful region, a beautiful part of Europe. I write "part of Europe," because this is essential, the key to its history, to the very configuration of its landscape and of its shapes, of its colors and scents, and of the taxonomy of its flora and fauna, including the human fauna. Transylvania had its high Middle Ages, cathedrals, Cistercians, a whiff of the Renaissance, its Reformation, its Counter-Reformation, its Baroque, its Enlightenment—the historical ages that made Europe, entire historical ages that did not exist in Russia or in Rumania, Moldavia,

Oltenia, Wallachia, Bessarabia, Bulgaria, Serbia, Macedonia, Albania, Thrace, Greece, the Ukraine.

Before Vienna the Alps peter out. But there are other mountains in the old Austro-Hungarian Empire, the largest among them the Carpathians. They form three-quarters of a ring around old Hungary, fir-laden dark mountains, not as young as the Alps but not very old either, black-green with sunlit clearings, mysterious rather than ominous, sparsely populated even now. On the map they resemble a tightly coiled wreath of the hair of an Eastern European peasant girl, girding the Danube basin as the girl's hair engirds her head. Eleven hundred years ago the Magyars (a name that I prefer to Hungarians) came into that basin. Its eastern portion was the land of the forests, Transylvania, Erdély, Ardeal.

To sum up the history of Transylvania in a page, or even a dozen pages, is nearly impossible: it is one long series of exceptions. The Magyars were, and are, exceptions, in a sense that they do not belong to any of the principal European ethnic families they have lived among—Germans and Slavs and Latins; and the Székely, the main Magyar tribal people in Transylvania, were exceptions among the exceptions. The Rumanians, too, are exceptional people: they claim to be descended from the near-mythical Dacians and from Trajan's Roman legions, which is near-nonsense. What is not nonsense is that their language is clearly neo-Latin, though for long centuries the Rumanian script was Old Slavonic, and until nearly 200 years ago the few Rumanian books were printed in Cyrillic. The Turks conquered almost all of the Balkans, including Wallachia and Moldavia (there was no "Rumania" then) during the fifteenth century. They conquered half of Hungary during the sixteenth. They did not penetrate into Transylvania; the Magyars fended them off. On two or three occasions the hot rake of war ran up several Transylvanian valleys, and Turks and Tatars ravaged scores of villages, but for nearly two centuries Transylvania was something of an independent state, governed for most of that time by Magyar princes. Transylvania existed between East and West. Its then status had remarkable similarities to that of Finland since World War II. The rest of Europe noticed this, exercised by a recurrent fear of the Turks. As in the case of modern Finland, the civilization of Transylvania was remarkable: there was religious toleration, decreed in 1560, and for most of the time Catholics and Protestants lived peaceably together. (William Penn knew this: impressed by the extant example of religious toleration, his original idea was to name his American Quaker colony "Transylvania.")

At the end of the seventeenth century the Turks left Hungary and the western fringe of Transylvania (though not Wallachia and Moldavia—that is, present Rumania). Transylvania reverted to a province of Hungary, which, in turn, was a semi-independent province of the Hapsburg Empire. The Rumanian population grew: Rumanians came through the mountain passes, getting away from the Turks, coming into that (often empty and open) land of the forests. In 1918, Transylvania, for the first time in its history, was given to Rumania—the gift of Wilson, Lloyd George, and Clemenceau, those pettiest and most hapless of middle-class statesmen in the twentieth century.

There are now about 2.1 million Magyars in Transylvania, amounting to perhaps one-third of the population. The Magyars have not been a very prolific people. They are badly suppressed by the Rumanians. Before 1918 the Magyar treatment of the Rumanians was hardly exemplary either, but the present kind of suppression is different. There are relatively few political prisoners in Rumania now, but the secret police is ubiquitous, more ubiquitous than in any Eastern European country excluding the Soviet Union—and, as Rumanians themselves will tell you, the Soviet Union is not really a European country. The number of Magyar schools is systematically diminished by the government. The largest university, until recently bilingual, is now entirely Rumanianized. The Magyar faculties are gone, though here and there Magyar professors linger on. This is in Cluj-Napoca, the largest city in Transylvania, which was originally Kolozsvár in Magyar (Klausenburg in German), then it became Cluj in Rumanian, and lately it has been renamed Cluj-Napoca, a resurrection of a Roman place-name from the time of the Emperor Trajan. Official Rumanian propaganda and official Rumanian historiography claim that the Rumanians are direct descendants of Trajan's legions, which is as if Ronald Reagan were to declare his descent from Pocahontas. Yet many Rumanians have something mock-Latin about them; they are curiously reminiscent of the mock-European quality of Argentinians (and there is something Indian in Ronald Reagan's face).

The broadcast and television slots allotted to the Magyar language on the Rumanian state network are distressingly brief, and hardly more than official Rumanian propaganda. The speakers and the interviewed and the musicians must identify themselves as "we Rumanians." In the predominantly, and sometimes purely, Magyar villages and towns, all of the inscriptions are in Rumanian—bilingual signs and directions are not allowed at all. Those Magyars who succeed in struggling up through the bureaucracy to acquire diplomas or qualifying degrees are given jobs in Wallachia, Moldavia, Oltenia, and Bucharest. There have been cases when patients in state hospitals in Magyar towns and with a Magyar staff were forbidden to talk to their doctors in Magyar.

On the Rumanian side of the frontier with Hungary, the wait is three hours. There are not more than seven or eight cars in line, but the hoods and the trunks have to be opened, the seats are pried apart, the luggage taken out and deposited on concrete slabs of benches. It is not my American passport that entitles me to a bit more courtesy from the Rumanian customs men, but the fact that I have only one piece of luggage; the other cars are crammed with people, children, and packages of food that they bring into Rumania. The Rumanian police are looking for foreign books, including books from Hungary, which are confiscated. I was warned about that in Budapest and left my books behind, but on top of my clothes there is an offprint of an article by a Magyar medievalist, printed in a German scholarly journal, about the commercial and diplomatic relations of the Caucasian principalities with the city-state of Genoa during the fifteenth century. The Rumanian customs people pore over this for twenty minutes, they take it into their booth, they study it. They return it to me, and one of them asks: "Where is this Georgia?" "A republic of the Soviet Union," I say. He is reluctant to believe me, but then he returns my passport and waves me on.

This is the frontier between two Communist states, two Eastern European states, two member states of the Warsaw Pact. The difference between them is enormous. Passing back into Hungary—and this is southeastern Hungary, a relatively poor portion of the country—I am instantly back in the West. The difference between Rumania and Hungary is much greater than that between "Communist" Hungary and "Western" Austria. This is not merely the difference between two states, but between two nations and two cultures—indeed, the deepest boundary is not on the map. It is unmarked and yet immediately palpable, there between peoples: the boundary between Roman Catholic Europe and Byzantine Europe, between Western Christianity and Eastern Orthodoxy. (The fact that many of the Magyars in Transylvania are Calvinist shows that in Transylvania the exception is the rule.)

I could regale my American friends and readers with stories about Rumanian corruption: the official who exchanges currency, but who wants a tip; the "luxury" hotel which has (finally) a bath, but which will not furnish a stopper for the tub except for extra consideration; the fundamental difference between the cleanliness of the places populated by Magyars and those populated by Rumanians. I won't continue, because my readers will already be saying that, of course, this writer is a Hungarian and that explains everything. I cannot help this. I am a Magyar but I am an American too, and I am writing for Americans. The most important thing in Transylvania, as perhaps everywhere else in the world, is this existence of deep national differences, something that is obscured not only by ideologues (including those of anti-Communism) and by their appalling ignorance of geography and of history, but by the dominant social-scientific pattern of academic and bureaucratic thinking that dismisses national character as a reactionary nineteenth-century myth.

What is happening in Transylvania (and what is happening to many other places in Eastern Europe) has little to do with Communism or anti-Communism. What is even more significant, it has almost nothing to do with the Russians. As a matter of fact, during the Russian occupation of Transylvania, the Magyar population was treated a little better; the Russian rulers wanted no trouble in that regard. As the Russian flood receded from Rumania the atavistic inclinations rose again, and the crude suppression of the Magyar population reappeared. The principal, and sometimes courageous, spokesmen for the Magyar people are members of the Rumanian Communist Party, who on occasion are persecuted and dismissed from their jobs. Whether or not you are a Communist makes little difference in Transylvania. What counts is whether you are Rumanian or Magyar; or, to be more precise, whether you are anti-Magyar or pro-Magyar, regardless of your party membership, regardless even of your native language.

In many of the Magyar apartments and houses the radio is tuned to

Budapest. The news from Radio Budapest does its little bit for pro-Soviet obeisances and propaganda, but for the Transylvania Magyars this hardly matters at all; it is so much more objective than the Rumanian radio. "Sometimes we listen to Budapest, sometimes to Radio Free Europe," they say. "It hardly makes any difference."

Rumania used to be the richest agricultural country in Europe. The American fliers who were shot down over Ploesti in 1943 and then parachuted in were amazed at how well they were fed. (They were the only prisoners in World War II who gained ten to twenty pounds in one year of captivity.) The Communist regime depleted the land. The oil wells, the largest deposits in Europe west of Russia, are running dry. The fields are speckled by children in blue smocks; classes in the fall are ordered out to gather potatoes. The state of the economy is as bad as Poland's. As in Poland, the shops are empty; unlike in Poland people often do not bother to stand in line. In most restaurants there are no menus. The waiter will tell you what there is to eat, and the food is foul.

The regime, however, is fairly solid and strong, and not only because of the secret police. In Rumania, not unlike the Soviet Union, the government is seen by the masses as a necessary evil, an unquestionable force of nature. The Rumanian government caters to mass sentiment by feeding it nationalism, suppressing the Magyars, and on occasion making sly references about the Russians. Thus the most rigid Communist regime in Eastern Europe is also the least pro-Russian one. The dictator of Rumania is Nicolae Ceauşescu, a former cobbler, whose wife and whose numerous relatives occupy dozens of the highest posts in the government. His private train has twelve cars. He had himself photographed with a jeweled scepter in hand, as well as standing over the carcasses of wild boars and bears which he shoots as they are driven before his august presence. He was also photographed dancing the Rumanian *hora* with Richard Nixon: the grinning, dark, and jowly faces of the Californian and Wallachian Presidents, both chief executives from the edges of civilization, oddly resembled each other.

The Eastern European landscape is now that of a valley where the flood and the fog are receding, and the ancient towers and turrets, broken and begrimed but nonetheless recognizable and standing, slowly emerge from under the fog. This devolution is promising and should not surprise anyone except for ideologues and theorists of international relations. Yet it is not as simple as that. In Russia, too, the towers and the turrets of Old Russia reappeared when much of the red chaotic fog of the Lenin-Trotsky years was wafting away. Yet in the streets of that Russian scene appeared not the New Soviet Man (that invention of intellectuals), but a people reminiscent of something old and dark, as was their leader, a new reincarnation of Ivan the Terrible. In Rumania, too, Ceauşescu is reminiscent of something old and rooted in the dark recesses of Balkan history, of those Wallachian and Moldavian *voivods* who knew the Byzantines and the Turks and how to get along with them or against them, depending on circumstances, people whose calculations of power are in their blood, and compared to whose life stories Machiavelli's *The Prince* was but an elegant theory spun out by a rationalist skeptic.

But Dracula was not a Transylvanian, and Transylvania is different. There is the Saxon minority, for example. As early as in the thirteenth century, the kings of Hungary invited Germans to settle in Transylvania. The latter called themselves the Saxons. They were an early variant of the bourgeoisie; they built admirable and industrious lives in their towns. They lived a tight little existence, disliking the Magyars and despising the Rumanians. With the Reformation they discovered their German nationalism in an instant and became the grimmest Lutherans in all Christendom. Four hundred years later they were proudest followers of the Führer. As I drive through a village, a young boy in lederhosen, seeing my Viennese license plate, gives the Hitler salute.

All over Eastern Europe after World War II, the Germans were deported to Germany. The Rumanians did not deport them (though many of the Saxons left for West Germany through the years). An intelligent Rumanian told me several years ago: "Who knows? The Germans may become a great power again." There is that Hollywoodian witticism about the Hungarian who enters behind you in a revolving door and comes out ahead. Nothing could be further from the truth. Hungarians, with all of their talents, are the least able politicians. The political history of Hungary is marked by a series of disasters. It is the Rumanians who are masters at politics.

Here are a few examples from our contemporary history. To a certain extent, the modern Rumanian state had been a creation of France, but when France fell in 1940 the Rumanians turned pro-German more quickly, and more shamelessly, than any other state and people in Europe. Well before the Third Reich demanded compliance with the "Final Solution," the Rumanian Iron Guard hanged elderly Jews on butcher-hooks in the side streets of Bucharest. They murdered, among others, Professor Iorga, the nationalist historian, whose only sin was his Francophilia. (Before killing him they tore out his beard, hair by hair.) Now, forty years later, Iorga is respected anew; and some of the former Iron Guardist historians occupy chairs in the Rumanian universities. Marshal Antonescu, a Rumanian patriot of considerable character and stature, succeeded in crushing the Iron Guard with Hitler's tacit approval; as a matter of fact, Hitler respected Antonescu even during their last interview in August 1944, when Antonescu suggested to Hitler that Rumania must now follow her own interests. As early as 1943 the Antonescu government made all kinds of secret arrangements with American Jewish organizations. The awful pogroms, perpetrated by Rumanians themselves in 1940 and 1941, were forgotten; the time had come to curry favor with the winning side. In August 1944 the Rumanians executed the most successful *coup d'état* during World War II. With an entire German army in their midst, they turned around within twenty-four hours and proclaimed their alliance with the Soviet Union, Britain, and the United States. (Again the comparison with Italy is instructive: compared to this acrobatic feat, the descendants of Machiavelli were mere bunglers.) A few months later the Rumanians installed a pro-Soviet government in full compliance with Stalin's wishes. Stalin gave them their reward: all of Transylvania was put back under Rumanian administration, the way it had been under the kings and the Francophile capitalists of Rumania. And just as two, three, or six centuries ago the behavior of certain Wallachian chieftains was the surest indication whether Ottoman power in the Balkans was waxing or waning, Ceaușescu's gestures of independence from Russia, the first of which were made seventeen years ago, indicated that the Russian influence in Eastern Europe was becoming less ubiquitous and fearsome.

It is because of this Rumanian political genius that the political future of my native people in Transylvania is largely hopeless. There may

be an occasional member of Congress with Hungarian-American constit-
uents who will insert an occasional item in the *Congressional Record;*
there may be an article or two in *Le Monde* (for the first time in more than
one hundred years, informed opinion in France is no longer one-sidedly
pro-Rumanian); but a change in the Rumanian sovereignty over Transylvania, or that noble dream, an independent and autonomous Transylvania, is so remote that it doesn't even qualify as a possibility. The
Magyar sovereignty is gone for good, and even some of its stones and
turrets are destroyed.

I drove off on a side road to look at Bonchida, the baroque country
house of the Bánffys, of the Transylvanian Magyar nobility (which was,
with few exceptions, the most liberal and cosmopolitan of perhaps all
Central and Eastern European aristocracies). They left in 1944. The Rumanians had gypsies settle in the house. I lived through the war in the
middle of Europe, but destruction such as this I had never seen. Untouched by artillery or by bombs, the interior of the house has been
scoured down to the bare brick, the very plaster scraped from the walls,
and the Italian putti from the parapets smashed to pieces, lying in the rank
grass. Unlike Dracula's "castle" (which the Rumanians have now built to
attract American tourists—there is a "Dracula Tour," a Rumanian variety
of Disneyland), places like Bonchida can never be restored.

Yet history is unpredictable, which means that the texture of history
changes. The obvious alternatives disappear, and new conditions arise, on
another level. Culture is no longer a luxury, the possession of a minority;
on certain levels of life it is replacing politics, and it becomes the precious
possession of many, not only of a few. Life goes on among the Magyars of
Transylvania, who are a bitterly serious people. They write their books
(published in Bucharest, but published nonetheless) and they teach and
they crowd their churches. Their presence, including their intellectual and
spiritual presence, has not been eradicated. In the midst of this wretched
Communist state the houses in the Magyar towns are restored and repainted; small municipal museums grow out of near-nothing, tended and
arranged with infinite care. When the long Transylvanian autumn and
winter set in, a kind of decent nineteenth-century existence is palpably at
hand, with stoves and larders, the Magyar teachers' houses with their

books overflowing from room to room, and two big healthy pigs scratching in the yard. It is a nineteenth-century existence because of the interior quality of this kind of life. Outside, Transylvania is dark. It is dangerous to drive after dusk, since the occasional ox carts and horse carts have no reflectors on their backboards; in the cities the streets are badly lit, because the electric current is poor and weak. The lights are pale, hardly flickering in the squares, reminiscent of a Central Europe sixty or more years ago. But in the sunny autumn mornings the plane trees are drenched with gold and the cities are real cities, with people milling in the old streets, visibly propelled by the difficulties and by the purposefulness of everyday life. And thus certain things in these cities still breathe the life of decades ago, when Magyar (and sometimes Magyar-Jewish) geniuses took wings to fly to the greater world of Budapest and Paris. It was then, in the coffeehouses of Kolozsvár and Nagyvárad that the Baudelaireans and the folklorists argued and drank into the night, a Transylvanian night in which the coffeehouse smoke instantly wafted away in the clean dark air in the narrow streets, between the uneven rows of the yellow-stuccoed, one-story provincial houses with their earthy odors and sometimes erotic promises and the lone swaying electric tram car lighting up the cobblestones at the far end.

The cityscapes have changed in many ways, yet the landscape remains almost untouched. By September the grass is down, the large, unpeopled, and untended hills resemble the nineteenth-century deer park of a great Anglophile lord. There are lakes in the mountains, agate-pure, secretive, and calm in bowls of pine forests, without a single inn or a house or even a tourist tent nearby. And beyond the mountain ridges lie Moldavia and the snow, a different world of bearded priests and gypsies and Levantine merchants in their cordovan boots. Ancient roads and mountain passes, which were used by Transylvanian craftsmen to haul their boots and finished goods and furs to the markets, are still traversed now and then by bullock-carts, a truck passing them every five minutes or so. On the other side of Moldavia, a mere one hundred miles further to the east, almost all of the roads peter out, disappearing before the Russian frontier where the few crossing-points are hundreds of miles apart. It is as if Russia were thousands of miles away; as if the Russians had never been there.

So this is the beautiful and the bitter end of Europe, poor beyond its deserts, rich with its past, and where the past is present not only in the remaining houses with their high-ceilinged rooms and tile stoves, but in the minds and the hearts of the people. In George Orwell's *Nineteen Eighty-Four,* Winston Smith, on one occasion, secretly and daringly offered a toast "to the past." In darkest Transylvania, as 1984 approaches, such a toast would be as out of place as a toast to Dracula. There the past is real; it illuminates the everyday necessities of life; it is the living hope not only of the oppressed Magyars but of those younger Rumanian writers and thinkers who, perhaps for the first time since the Turks, have something in common with the Magyars. They, too, despise the police state, the mechanical surveillance, and the senseless acres of chemical factories in the valleys of Transylvania, spewing sulphurous yellow and scarlet fumes into the air. The Russian flood is retreating, one day the Communist state will be gone, and when that miasmatic fog had lifted perhaps the multifarious people in the streets and squares of Transylvania will not be condemned to repeat the past, precisely because they, unlike the Russians, have learned to know it. There will be no place for petty Draculas in Transylvania. They will take their vampirish flight to Hollywood, to those Californian castles where they belong.

Gasteinertal

(1982)

The valley of Gastein—Gasteinertal—is a long crevasse between two stretches of high mountains in Austria, coming to an end at a still higher wall of mountains, snow-capped all year round, blocking it from the south. This is one of the two Austrian Alpine regions which are not yet crossed by stunning automobile highways poised on ferroconcrete gooselegs one thousand feet in the air; but an indeed spectacular rail line does bore through it, a triumph of engineering achieved during the last years of the Austrian Empire, the time which intellectual fashion demands that it be defined as "inevitable" dissolution and decay.

But then the history of the Gasteinertal has had its share of exceptions. Thousands of years after the Celtic peoples had settled in the far western islands and headlands of Europe some of them came to the Alpine valleys of the continent and left their marks of habitation during what is called the Austrian Late Bronze Age. As in other parts of Germany, the Christian missionaries came from the far west, not from the south: not from Italy and the Mediterranean but from the rainswept islands of Ireland and England. Eight centuries later Lutheranism took root among the gnarled, headstrong peasantry of the Gasteinertal, together with a tribal kind of prosperity: gold and silver were hacked out of the mountains through the enterprise of a few determined families. They had risen from the peasantry; in less than two centuries they would descend to the peasantry again.

At that time the Gastein valley was the southernmost portion of the Archepiscopal state of Salzburg. We are accustomed to regard the Germanies before Bismarck as divided, and the Habsburg monarchy of Austria as united; indeed, the Germanies consisted of as many as seventeen hundred states during the seventeenth and eighteenth centuries (of which even thirty-nine remained after the Congress of Vienna), while Austria was governed centrally from the grand capital of Vienna. Yet the Salzburg Archbishopric was a separate state until as late as 1816. Its destinies differed from those of the surrounding lands. During the Thirty Years' War a diplomatic Archbishop of Salzburg, Paris Lodron, a kind of Alpine Richelieu, succeeded in keeping the horrific armies of that war away from his domains. But one hundred years later, when the fires of religious wars had burned out elsewhere in Europe, another Archbishop, Firmian, chose to force the Protestants of the Archbishopric, including those of the Gasteinertal, to emigrate. By that time the gold and silver mines were closed down. A great silence fell upon the valley. The shadows of mountains made it remote again.

Another one hundred years later the name "Gastein" became familiar all over the Habsburg lands and the Germanies. The thermal waters of Gastein were known for a long time but few people availed themselves thereof. The waters were known for their healing properties to the extent that around 1800 there was a thermal pool for horses, not people. During the nineteenth century spas and watering-places became famous. A commonsense explanation of this is the swollen girth of the Bourgeois Age, including the swollen stomachs and livers of its beneficiaries. But there was more than that. The central belt of the European continent teems with thermal resources—potential spas—yet not all of them grew to fame during the nineteenth century. Gastein had an additional attraction: its mountains. This attraction was the result of Romanticism. As the great English thinker Owen Barfield once wrote in a memorable sentence: "A hundred and fifty years ago when mountains were still 'horrid,' the foundations of the present economic structure of Switzerland were being quietly laid by the dreams of a few lake poets and their brother romantics." Mountains had become beautiful. Consequently physicians discovered the healing essences of the mountain air, and of the mountain waters. The mountain spas came into existence. The Emperor Franz I visited Hofgastein. The water of Badgastein, four miles away and one thousand feet higher, was channeled down in wooden pipes. Except for the water, thereafter everything went uphill, from Hofgastein to Badgastein.

One generation after Kaiser Franz's visit, Gastein was in the league with the most famous European watering-places: Baden-Baden, Bad Ems,

Homburg, Vichy, Evian, Aix-les-Bains, far surpassing the reputation of the original Spa (in Belgium). General von Moltke visited Badgastein in 1859 and told his ruler about it. William I of Prussia (later the Emperor of Germany) came to Gastein twenty times during the next twenty-five years. In 1863 Franz Joseph and William met in Gastein for the first time. Its reputation now earned it a place in the diplomatic history of Europe. Bismarck (who suffered from gastric trouble throughout most of his life) maneuvered his Austrian counterpart in 1865 to the short war between Prussia and Austria. Thirteen years later it was in the Hotel Straubinger (it still exists) where Bismarck and the Austro-Hungarian Foreign Minister Andrássy signed the Dual Alliance between the two empires. The Kings of Greece, of Rumania, of Saxony were Gastein visitors; so was the Emperor of Brazil in 1876 (he must have been a forerunner of the jet-setters; he had visited the Philadelphia Centennial Exhibition in the same year). In July 1886 the last great meeting of the imperial families took place at Gastein, the *Kaiserbegegnung.* Franz Joseph, the Empress Elizabeth, the ninety-year-old William I and his grandson (soon to become William II) met there. During the next four years the melancholy Empress Elizabeth came to Badgastein every summer. She walked far into the mountains.

By the turn of the century Gastein had become more bourgeois than aristocratic. The Central European bourgeoisie, Lutheran, Catholic and Jewish, as well as occasional English visitors, were layered among the dozens of Kurhotels, cheaper hotels (especially for the frugal North German clientele), guest-houses and *pensions.* The North Germans particularly preferred Gastein with its mountain atmosphere, the pert waitresses with their easy manners, the green velvet aprons of the mountains and of the women, the Austrian *Gemütlichkeit* of domesticity, prettiness, and comfort. As the pretext of coming for the waters receded, the pace of the social life increased. Then, in 1909, the railway was completed and the Gastein boom went on.

There is a 1909 atmosphere in Gastein even now. The hotels of the turn of the century are still there, imbedded in the mountainside. The great Gastein waterfall thunders day and night; at night the hidden arc-lamps bathe its precipice at the bottom, and the spray of the crashing foam rises in a wondrous swirling cloud, as romantic and mysterious as anything in the paintings of Johann Caspar Friedrich. Principal walks still bear the names of the Kaiserin Elizabeth and of Kaiser Wilhelm. In the evening the promenades are deserted but the windows of the elegant shops with their expensive silks and scarves and the fine leathers glisten, a jeweled setting surrounded by the darker glassy shapes of more modern hotels, situated further down. If—all of the industrious nostalgia of the Austrians notwithstanding—the scene is reminiscent of Franz Joseph and of Elizabeth only on occasion, it is at least reminiscent of Stefan Zweig. (The bookstore carries all of his books in paperback.)

That was the first period of opulent prosperity in the Gasteinertal. Then came the catastrophe of 1914. In the vestibule of the parish church of Hofgastein there is a marble memorial tablet, and next to it, under glass the faded photographs of the men of that community who died in the First World War, faded grey and yellow photographs of sad, serious, wide-eyed peasant faces under their Austrian chakos. "Gefallen" or "Verschwunden": fallen or disappeared. But another decade later Gastein revived. It had survived the dissolution of the Habsburg Empire, as indeed had Austrian culture during its last high period. Tourism, that great industry of the twentieth century, reappeared again. Between 1926 and 1936 the prosperity of Gastein returned, together with many of the pre-war guests. There was a difference now. There were, for the first time, many Englishmen and Englishwomen, even Americans. At dinnertime the pianists and the trios played Lehár, Kálmán, Strauss, Millöcker, as of yore; but they also played the music of the Berlin jazzy operettas and tunes by Gershwin and Kern. The Austrian government allowed the opening of a casino.

There were now two seasons in Gastein, not only the summer one from May to September, but also a winter one. For every guest who came to take the waters there were now five or more skiers. Yet the scene and its comforts remained the main attraction: the hotels furnished with brown plush *Stilmöbel* as well as the handcrafted wrought iron gates and lamps and dirndl costumes, that discovery of the charms of Austrian peasant baroque which became fashionable in places as far east as the villas of Budapest and as far west as Curzon Street in London. It was a meeting place for two generations: that of my grandparents, both born in 1872 who came to Gastein several times with their serious bourgeois clothes and modest hats; that of my mother, born in 1902, hatless, with her shimmering short dresses and long pearl necklaces, who was in Gastein after and before her marriage, when she was still chaperoned by my grandmother, and who was asked to tea-dance several times by an English duke (or was he a viscount? or an earl?), a story which I heard more than once, which no doubt contributed to my beautiful mother's Anglomania, a consequence of which was her insistence that her son be taught English from the age of five and sent to English schools, one of the things for which he remains forever grateful.

But underneath this hotel civilization—and literally thus, for they lived in the basements of the great hotels—was the world of the waiters and waitresses and porters and mechanics, the sons and daughters of the Gastein valley peasantry riven by the national identity crisis of the Austrian people. Some of them were to be impressed with the fantastic success of their countryman Hitler across the Alps, whose fatherland was Austria but who identified himself with his great tragic mother Germania who took him for her husband. And on a cold March Saturday in 1938 Hitler made the union of Austria with Germany. Soon came the Second World War, in which another one hundred of Gasteiners lost their lives. There is no memorial commemorating them; and the histories of Gastein skim over those tragic years in a few sentences.

In the last week of the war, in the brilliant late spring of May 1945, the American Army arrived and occupied the hotels and the *pensions* of Badgastein and Hofgastein for a year or so. And thereby hangs the thread of this short essay, which is the Americanization—and the non-Americanization—of the Europe of Gastein, something that is intertwined with the existence and with the memories of this writer, whose mother is Europe and whose wife is America, whereto he came in the year when the Americans were in Gastein.

The Americanization of the world, of which the Americanization of Gastein is of course just a part, is probably the main story of the twentieth century but it is a story of such enormous proportions, so worldwide and so protean in its manifestations and evidence, that no historian will ever tackle it. It is a development which is cultural and social even more than political and military. Its main element is the emulation of the social order (and, at times, of disorder) that made the United States famous and rich.

Its economic and social substance may be summed up in a single phrase: giving credit to the masses. This, even more than the outpouring of American dollars, or the Marshall Plan, led to the democratic prosperity of Western Europe soon after the war. As in the United States, consumer credit became an everyday matter. *On ne prête qu'aux riches*—only the rich are able to borrow—was typical of European capitalism before the Second World War; this rings hollow now, a *bon mot* from a sunken time.

The third, and largest, wave of prosperity for places such as the Gastein Valley began around 1950 and has continued without abating until this day. (One example: the peak in the number of visitors occurred in 1974, the very year when the oil crisis hit Europe.) Every two or three years another soaring ski-lift is completed, wafting people to hitherto unreachable Alpine peaks. There are ever more hotels. The building regulations are very strict; there are but a few buildings, here and there (and usually down in the valleys), whose artless surrealist appearance disfigures the scene.

There are all kinds of results of this Americanization, good and bad, in Gastein. There is a Convention Center in Badgastein wedged in between the hotels, a great concrete turtle, as ugly as anything conceived by a graduate of the Yale School of Architecture; its bookstore contains the German editions of *Playboy* and *Penthouse* which are now, I think, the only American magazines published worldwide. Even in the Grand Hotel of Hofgastein, where the manager's beautiful wife appears at the weekly reception for the guests in a velvet-panelled long-skirted dirndl, the salad table features Thousand Island Dressing. The mimeographed program listing the daily events and the menus of the hotel ends with a Joke of The Day, as if the Grand Hotel were a Holiday Inn in California. But all of this does not matter against the long run: without the American contribution to the defeat of Hitler, without the American presence in Europe thereafter this kind of sunny, late-afternoon prosperity could not have happened. Material prosperity is often destructive as well as constructive: but here its destructiveness has not carried the day, the Americanization of the Gasteinertal left plenty of opportunity for restoration as well as for leveling, and this includes the Promenade Kaiserin Elisabeth and the continued presence of the human music of the past.

And now it seems, at least to this writer, that this Americanization is slowly, gradually, coming to its end. This change is beginning to appear on different levels of life.

There are two cultures in the life of the world now, not at all the Two Cultures about which the fatuous Lord Snow trumpeted forth his theory, which was the existence of two separate parallel cultures, the humanistic and the scientific-technological, whose representatives knew little or nothing about each other's "field." No: the two cultures are neither separate nor parallel. They overlap, and they exist on different levels. One is the international; the other is national. One is represented by the international language of the network of business, of technology, of conference centers, of sociological jargon, of computers, of telex, of airline and airport lingo; the other by the language of domestic life. The first language is Americanized and in many instances outright American: the phenomenon known as *franglais* in France has its equivalents everywhere in Europe, including Gastein. The second, in vocabulary as well as in tone, is as Austrian as ever; and there is no reason to believe that it will gradually disappear. Outward appearances, too, reflect this: blue jeans and fringed cowboy jackets come and go, while the local dress of women and men stays as prevalent as it was fifty years ago.

The American physical presence, too, is less than it was twenty or thirty years ago. For every American visitor or tourist in the Gastein valley there are one hundred, perhaps two hundred Germans. And when we drive on the Autobahn in Germany the occasional signs indicating an American military enclave or command post already give the faint impression of anachronism, a leftover impression from the era of the German-American symbiosis, when the principal political reality in West Germany was the American military presence stretching ahead to the Iron Curtain.

For nearly one hundred years, from the middle of the last century to the middle of this one, Austrians had an identity crisis: if they could not keep their position as the ruling nation of the Habsburg Empire they might as well join their German-speaking brethren across the Alps. It was because of this identity crisis that the inspiration of the Nazi movement was often South German and that the presence of the former Austrians in the SS was more than considerable. But now another identity, another role has come into being: Austria as another Switzerland, a neutral Alpine republic, a bridge connecting not Berlin and Rome but West and East, prosperous between the two power blocs, America and Russia.

Democratic and partially Americanized as she is, with a Communist party that is one of the least significant of Europe, Austria is moving slowly, imperceptibly toward the East. Vienna has already regained her former position as the great cosmopolitan Danubian central capital city, a meeting place of Western and Eastern Europe, in many ways and on many levels. To demonstrate this could be the subject of a long article, perhaps even a book: suffice it to say that the historical rhythm of Central Europe has begun to draw Austrians (and Germans) closer to the European East than to the American West; but Communism has nothing to do with this.

This is a relatively new development, the consequences of which are unpredictable, but I do not think that we ought to be unduly worried about it. The European East has been moving westward, too, for more than twenty years now. The Austrians know that the Soviet Empire (and the Russian danger) is not what it used to be; but, then *mutatis mutandis,* that is true of the American empire too.

The darkest writer and the darkest seer of this century, the Frenchman Louis-Ferdinand Céline, thought that the defeat of the German Army at Stalingrad meant the death-knell of European civilization; later, toward the end of his life, he thought that the Americanism and the democratization of Europe meant nothing; sooner or later the Chinese will be at the English Channel, *les Chinois à Brest.* Well, the Chinese now imitate America even more thoughtlessly than the Europeans ever had; they are not in Brest, and the Russians are not in Gastein. However, the latter may arrive one day: a new Russian tourist class, emerging from the transformations of Russian society. I cannot see the Chinese in Brittany, or even the green tunics of Russian soldiers in the Gastein valley; but I can imagine the Russian and Prussian tourists, in their heavy tweeds, eventually promenading on the Elisabeth and the Kaiser-Wilhelm alleys, sometime in the twenty-first century.

The fields are spangled with dandelions, the meadows with wildflowers, the Mercedes swish on the highways, the golden and wheat-colored baroque sconces and swirls are freshly painted around the window-frames, the bright red geraniums glow in the dark green windowboxes, the pastry-shops are chock-full with young people and choc-full tortes, the loden-coated visitors walk in the thin rain with their sensible shoes. In America the age of democracy is in its third century. Here the age of democracy has only recently begun. It was in the Gasteinertal, not in the United States, that one hundred years ago history began to accelerate. The imperial phase was followed by the bourgeois phase, after which came the short and painful Third Reich chapter, after which came the American phase, and that, too, will pass. In any event, the mountains, the skiing, and its Americanization notwithstanding, the Gastein valley is not at all like Colorado, and while Austrian-style chalets and German investors may crowd into Aspen and Vail, the lives of Hofgastein and Badgastein are less and less like those of Aspen and Vail every year.

All of this has something to do with the spiritualization of matter—a difficult phrase by which I mean simply that in the history of mankind the relationship of mind and matter is not constant, because the intrusion of mind into matter increases, something which, Darwin and Marx and even Freud notwithstanding, is the only meaningful evolution there is. For two thousand years the material existence of people in the Gastein valley depended on agriculture. They lived from the soil and the trees. Then came a century or so of hollow poverty. Then, five hundred years ago, they dug into the mountains for gold and silver. They could not eat silver: they lived from what they were paid for their industry. When the mines ceased to be worked there came another trough of poverty. Then came the prosperity due to the thermal water. That water was material; but what attracted the paying crowds was not altogether material. The people of the Gastein valley now lived off what they were paid for their services to visitors.

There are still the people who come to Gastein to soothe their bodies; but their numbers do not compare to the numbers of those who come for that kind of well-being which modern humanity wants, of which the beautiful landscape is as much an ingredient as is the comfort of hotels, and the peaceful rhythm of the day as is the mountain air: they seek the agreeable healing of their minds as much, if not more, than the agreeable pleasures of their bodies. Thus the people of the Gasteinertal now prosper from the very perception of the atmosphere of their valley. From agriculture through industry to service and maintenance—from the chancellors of the Archbishops through the Vienna financiers and the bourgeois and then to Americanization—and what is next to come? I do not know.

But I know one thing: mountains will never become "horrid" again. That is inconceivable: because it is unimaginable. Romanticism was not merely the reaction to rationalism, a swing of the pendulum. We are—for better or worse—all Romantics now.

The Gotthard Walk

(1985)

Goethe was twenty-six years old in 1775, when he first went to Switzerland. "Werther" had been published the year before. His fame had flared across Europe. Within a year, the Duke of Saxe-Weimar would invite him to take up residence in Weimar, the Athens of Germany; it would be Goethe's home and princely seat for the rest of his life. But before that Goethe had gone through months of storm and stress. The phrase, while not precise, is apposite. *Sturm und Drang* was the name given to that first, elemental German wave of sentimental expression and creation of which Goethe was the principal embodiment. Eventually— within him and because of him—it became transformed into a more mature, serene, discerning classicism. Evidence of this transformation was already there in the style of the great dramas that Goethe composed with furious speed in 1774 and 1775. It corresponded, too, with developments in his private life. He had fallen in love with Lili Schönemann, the daughter of a rich Frankfurt banker. She was his third great love within five years, and for the first time he became engaged. But he had also become more worldly-wise. He began to think that the Schönemann family, the stiff social circle of Frankfurt patricians, and perhaps marriage itself, would not suit him. He fled to Switzerland.

He had been, he wrote, suddenly and surprisingly attracted to the romantic image of the Swiss. He wanted to see this "land of free peasants," with their "old-fashioned habits and mores [*Sitten*]," and he wanted to see the mountains. All this was something new. "Old-fashioned" was a bad word in the eighteenth century. More important, in that century mountains were still objects of horror to most people. In 1741, Lady Mary Wortley Montagu—no mean traveler—wrote that she was "inclined" to return to Italy again and again, but the Alps were "very disagreeable." In

1765, the English radical John Wilkes—surely not a classicist—wrote, "The Apennines are not near so high or so horrible as the Alps. On the Alps you see very few tolerable spots; and only firs, but very majestic." In 1769, Casanova went to Lugano, for the sole purpose, as he said, of having something printed there. But there was a change in the air—including the very appreciation of the air itself. Lady Mary had written, "I think this air does not agree with my health." Less than a century later, people discovered that the mountain air, instead of being dangerous, was salubrious. A century after that, the English philosopher Owen Barfield wrote, "The economic and social structure of Switzerland is noticeably affected by its tourist industry, and that is due only in part to increased facilities of travel. It is due not less to the condition that . . . the *mountains* which twentieth-century man sees are not the mountains which eighteenth-century man saw." Thus the prosperity of Switzerland—until 1800 it had been one of the poorest countries of Western Europe—and the love of people for mountains began.

The Swiss Alps, Goethe wrote, "at first made so deep an impression on me that I was bewildered and restless. Only in later years . . . was I able to consider them with composure." In 1777, William Beckford, the English gothic novelist, wrote, "Were I not to go . . . to the [Swiss] mountains very often I should die." In 1789, the Swiss writer and painter Hans Heinrich Meyer crossed the St. Gotthard mountains: "For a traveller who does not fear fatigue, how much more agreeable are the narrow and tortuous paths of the Alps than the wide roads of the low country, drawn as straight as a die." In 1820, William Wordsworth took much the same route. He wrote that "the arbitrary, pitiless, godless wretches, who have removed Nature's landmarks by cutting roads through Alps and Apennines, until all things are reduced to the same dead level, they will be arraigned hereafter with the unjust." His sister, Dorothy, added that it was *"heavenly glory* that hung over those cold mountains," and that their companion, Henry Crabb Robinson, "was drunk with pleasure, and made us drunk too." No one had written—or, presumably, thought—that way a mere generation before. It was a revolution of sentiment and of perspective comparable to another great revolution: the rediscovery of perspective at the beginning of the Renaissance, in Italy, four centuries before.

On his first trip, Goethe walked and climbed as far as the summit of the St. Gotthard Pass, where he spent a night with the Capuchin monks at the hospice. He looked to the south longingly, toward Lugano and Milan, before he turned back; this was eleven years before his famous descent to "the land where the lemon trees bloom." The Gotthard Pass, about sixty-nine hundred feet high, was for centuries (and still is) the most direct route from northern Europe to the South. In 1356, Petrarch went through it from south to north, on his way from Milan to Basel; he did not waste a word on the mountains, spilling his prose on the beauties of Basel and the Rhine. In 1402, Adam of Usk, the English lawyer and chronicler, went through "Mount St. Gotthard and the hermitage on its summit, where I was drawn in an ox-waggon half dead with cold and with mine eyes blindfold lest I should see the dangers of the pass." In 1432, Enea Silvio Piccolomini, later the humanist Pope Pius II, went through the Gotthard, *aetatis* twenty-seven. He did not like it, but it was the shortest route. And when mountains were no longer horrible all kinds of people followed: Generals Suvorov and Desaix; Turner and Ruskin; Henry Adams and Horace Greeley; Renan and Rimbaud; conventicles of English travelers; groups of German tourists; and innumerable others in the nineteenth century—at least until 1882, when the great railway tunnel under the Gotthard mountains was completed. Even after that, this approach to Italy continued to inspire people. As late as 1905, E. M. Forster, in "Where Angels Fear to Tread," wrote of "the supreme moments of her coming journey—the Campanile of Airolo, which would burst on her when she emerged from the Gotthard tunnel, presaging the future." "Promising Italy" would have been a better phrase, I think—even though that campanile happens to be a small one.

Hilaire Belloc and D. H. Lawrence walked over the Gotthard Pass early in the present century. And now, in the century's twilight, it is still possible to walk the entire two-hundred-mile route from Basel to Lugano, in about fourteen days, thanks to the well-preserved and well-marked paths *(Wanderwege)* of the Swiss Arbeitsgemeinschaft für Wanderwege and to its recently reprinted booklet of the route, to the superb Swiss topographical maps, and to the presence, at the end of each day, of inns and sometimes hotels, even in the smallest of villages, with a hot bath in or adjoining one's room—a prime consideration for this aging scholar and traveler, in the sixty-second year of his life, and for his daughter Annemarie, *aetatis* sixteen.

So here we go, out of Philadelphia, boring our way through the dark May night above the Atlantic, changing planes in Heathrow, to rain-shrouded Basel. We need a good rest to defeat jet lag and to prepare for the long journey ahead, especially because the first walking day will be difficult—nearly twenty miles. So I have a room booked at the Drei Könige, one of the last great traditional hotels, established almost a thousand years ago (in 1026) as Zur Blume (At the Flower). At that confluence and crossing of early medieval Europe, three rulers met within a year, including the last king of Burgundy. Then and there the name changed to the Three Kings, and it has remained so ever since, except for a few years during the republican flood that followed the French Revolution, when its then owners thought it politic to rename it the Three Moors. Bonaparte, Metternich, Dickens; the kings of Italy, Spain, Norway, Rumania, and Bulgaria; and the young Princess Victoria of England stayed there in the nineteenth century. In our century, Field Marshals Montgomery, de Lattre, and Mannerheim were among its guests. It is a very good hotel, breathing great comfort rather than luxury. The concierge, a courtly young Oriental, smoothly arranges the sending of our luggage to Lugano, for our return journey. Now we are traveling with backpacks. We are in our walking clothes—boots, no jacket, no tie. We shall not avail ourselves of the elegant hotel dining room, with its crystal-decked tables. We walk across the street to a town restaurant that was recommended by a charming Swiss woman on the plane. The porter accompanies us with a protective umbrella.

And here in Basel, in the warm, beery fug of the restaurant of the locals, with the rain pouring outside, I think of the last great world war, from which the Swiss were exempt. There is a sense of continuity—continuity even more than tradition—in this wood-panelled, high-ceilinged middle-class restaurant. Oddly, or perhaps not so oddly, it has a nineteen-forties touch. The great divide of 1939–45, which parted the lives of almost all Europeans (victors as well as vanquished), did not divide the lives of the Swiss. The year 1945 was no Year Zero for them, as it was for their great, tragic, bedevilled neighbor to the north. They had their emergencies during the war years, but their lives went on, and they stuck—sometimes thoughtlessly—to their customs of the past. Years ago, I read an article about the Swiss published in November 1940 in Goebbels' literary magazine, *Das Reich*. "What time is it in Switzerland?" the article's Nazi author asked rhetorically, and continued:

> At times, it seems that it is 1840, not 1940. The past breathes from the old pieces of furniture, the ticking of an old clock—a dream of comfort and happiness in a close family circle, including the security of their possessions, of solid industriousness, of honorable family life. . . . If it were only possible to halt the march of history, the wheels that are rolling across the world. . . . It is difficult to make us understood here.

Even in that article one can detect the seeds of a kind of exasperated respect for the Swiss. And, as the war went on, the contempt that the champions of the heroic new Europe had been professing for the antiquated virtues embodied by the Swiss would change to a rueful admiration. Pierre Drieu La Rochelle was a brilliant French Fascist writer, who excoriated the bourgeois. Yet in 1943, in "Notes sur la Suisse," he wrote, "Switzerland is the plane of Europe, the plane where all the physical and metaphysical crossings meet, the crucial plane—it is not in vain that her emblem is a cross—it is a sacred place." In 1940, after the Germans had conquered all of Western Europe, some of the Swiss leaders said that Switzerland must accommodate itself somehow to the realities of a new Europe. No, said others: we did not accommodate ourselves before, and we shan't now. They prevailed. Their people prevailed. This place prevailed. It is strange and melancholy for someone born in Europe before the Second World War and raised there during it to find himself in a place whose spirit is the same as it must have been before and during the terrible storm, and among people in whose lives the war was not a monumental chasm.

And now the first day of our wandering begins. The rain has lifted, but the sky is still grey, and so, under our lace-curtained window, is the quick-flowing Rhine, which I watch as I finish what I think will be our last breakfast served in a hotel room for a while. According to the "Wanderbuch Gotthardroute," we must take the No. 14 trolley to St. Jakob, where the Swiss peasants and burghers fought a bloody battle in 1444 against a feudal army. At the bridge over the Birs River, our eyes meet the first of the small oblong yellow markers that indicate the route all the way to the Italian border. Even with our compass and maps, we will find these markers to be a great blessing. Not one of them has been defaced or bent or destroyed. When the path reaches more than four thousand feet above sea level, the markers include a red stripe. These colors are also painted on the trunks of trees and on boulders; they will enlighten our path till the end.

We begin to cross the northeastern Jura Mountains. For the first few hours, the ascent is not steep. Great beech trees stand over us as we trudge southward in the misty morning. We are alone; not until after the Gott-hard will we see others making the same journey. When we are fifteen minutes out of Basel, the last joggers disappear. We are not high up and not many miles away from a great city, but we see only a few houses in the distance now—an odd experience for wandering Americans. The Old World is densely inhabited, but there are these long valleys of fields and forests between the swelling towns—a consequence of an age-old need for economy of space. In the New World we are avaricious of time but spendthrifts of space.

Here and there we pass military signs on fences, and bunkers built during the Second, and perhaps even the First, World War to guard the northern approach to the central alpine redoubt. Most of them are still kept up. "Blessed are the people who have no history": a Chinese proverb, and, like some other proverbs, not true enough. The Swiss have their history, but it is different from that of their neighbors. Their national heroes during the last hundred years have been two military men, Generals Ulrich Wille and Henri Guisan, the commanders-in-chief in the world wars—military heroes because they kept their country out of war. A third hero is General Guillaume-Henri Dufour, who did fight a war—the minuscule war of the Sonderbund, in 1847, out of which the united Switzerland, with its national flag and national government, was born (more than five centuries after the first establishment of Swiss independence: something that enthusiastic advocates of a united Europe ought to keep in mind). But this is not why General Dufour, monuments to whom stand in many Swiss cities, is a national hero. He established the scientific mapping of Switzerland, and he was instrumental in the founding of the Red Cross, whose original purpose was to care for wounded foreign soldiers in foreign wars.

A soft patter of raindrops on the myriad leaves changes to a steady splashing. This is our longest day of hiking. We must reach Waldenburg, nineteen miles from Basel. But "hiking" is probably not a good word. It is inadequate to describe this kind of progress, a combination of walking, marching, and climbing. "Trekking" would be better, except for its unattractive Afrikaans shape and sound. At any rate, this is our first experience of the kind, and it is less difficult than I feared. But I have a few irreverent thoughts about my famous predecessors. "The road is better than the inn," Cervantes said. This is the kind of Spanish heroic figure of speech that sounds better than it is (the opposite of what the English wit said about Wagner's music). *We* keep thinking—and I challenge other wanderers not to do the same—of how the inn at Waldenburg will be. I also think about Belloc, who walked out of the smoke and steam of England in the great railroad age, tramping to Rome alone. "The Path to Rome" is a grand book. He was full of spunk, history, and *propaganda fides.* Yet there is no word about *how* he walked. Did he have a backpack? What did he do with his clothing? Did he carry more than one change of clothes for the months it took him to walk from France to Rome? He spends many pages describing the hearty food and the honest red wine of Catholic peasants, but what happened when his tramping clothes were soaked? A sensible thought, because we are getting quietly drenched. Since I, too, will write about this wandering, there is now, as far as I am concerned, a literal truth to what Sir Walter Scott said about his harried financial existence: "Literature is a good staff but a bad crutch."

At noon, we descend in a rocky riverbed, having crossed the first saddle of the Jura. My daughter is thirsty and hungry. We reach Büren, the first village. In Büren, all is closed. But one of the inns opens up, we have a bowl of soup and something to drink, and I have a small cup of black, heart-and-mind-quickening espresso. (I am too tough on Belloc. There was no espresso in Switzerland in his time.) We are triumphant. This is the longest day, and we are more than halfway to Waldenburg. We shall be there by six, having done the day's walk in eight hours, exactly as the experienced walkers of the "Wanderbuch" do it. But we are too sanguine. We have to cross two, three more mountain saddles. Twenty minutes of sun alternates with forty minutes of rain, and the climbing gets more wearisome as the day gets longer.

Ziefen and Titterten: two Alemannic Swiss villages, with their share of medieval houses, and with the pleasant smell of horse manure and hayricks in the stony yards. There is little of that in Germany now, except in the East. (It is curious that Germany is "l'Allemagne" in French: at least half the Alemanni of yore lived in what is Switzerland now.) Once more, we trudge up the shoulder of a mountain, opening and closing trestle gates on the path. At a high point, we stop and see the undulating green wall of the Jura in a semicircle, and the little town of Waldenburg ahead of and below us. We are not yet in the Alps, and there is nothing particularly dramatic about the view, but its very peacefulness exhilarates: as you lift your eyes, your spirits rise with them. How strange is the evolution of our consciousness. Two hundred years ago, this landscape meant nothing to people. They averted their eyes from the snowy Alps, and ignored mountains such as the Jura. For the great landscape painters of the seventeenth and eighteenth centuries, landscape had to be either classical or familiar. Their paintings are filled either with the magic of a mythic past or with the shining presentation of the everyday. Our lives are different, of course. But the way in which our lungs fill up with oxygen as we look at this kind of scene is not simply attributable to the smoke of cities in the nineteenth century or to the automobile pollution thereafter. It is the result of a mutation of our consciousness, beginning about two hundred years ago—part and parcel of the history of Western civilization. I respect the Japanese tourists who crowd into our museums and look at the Constables and the Poussins, but I don't think they see them—or the mountains—the way we do.

For my American daughter, too, things are different. She loves the tinkling of the cowbells, flat and toneless in the mountain air. They sound "like African tribes," she says. This is what her ear is used to, what she has heard on television or on records. To me they are the pastoral music of a sunken time: not of cathedrals but of parish churches *englouties.*

One must, as I said, *stop* to see the landscape. This is why traveling by foot is not ideal. For the purpose of seeing, hearing, smelling, contemplating things, it is, of course, preferable to whisking through large frames of time and space in an automobile. But walking is arduous, and one must keep one's eyes on the path rather than look at the surroundings. I suppose horseback or muleback was best. On foot, one does not get soaked with the day's images. Goethe traveled on horseback as far as Lucerne. But when he started south in Switzerland he was interested in people rather than in views. It was only after Lucerne that the Alps began to strike him as spectacular; he looked at them with a new eye, and began to stop and think how to paint them in words.

In Lucerne, we spend the night in a comfortable commercial hotel, where one can loll in the tub. Uneasy question: Why is it that European hotels are now more comfortable and better appointed than American ones? I am not thinking of Europe's great luxury hotels, or of what remains of Old World service. But thirty years ago everything in a good New York or Chicago hotel was big and solid. Now the bathrooms, the appointments, the closets, tubs, toilets, hangers, towels are less substantial than those of a two-star, or even a one-star, hotel in Central Europe. In any event, the Europeanization of America and the Americanization of Europe have become palpable phenomena during the last hundred years. Before that, such phenomena were intellectual. In 1853, Harriet Beecher Stowe passed through Lucerne. She recorded that her hostess, and "even the servant maids," expressed "tender interest for the slave," and she continued, "All had read Uncle Tom. And it had apparently been an era in their life's monotony, for they said, 'O, madam, do write another! Remember, our winter nights here are very long!'" Now, in the underpass of the Lucerne station, a long-haired Swiss boy sits on the spotless floor bawling "Mrs. Robinson" and plucking his guitar.

We march along the sunny littoral of the Lake of the Four Forest Cantons, the path running for a while beneath modern apartment houses; on their balconies, large, shiny-faced young women appear in morning wrappers to water their geraniums. The lake "sparkles" with coruscating sunlight. The alpine meadows are "spangled" with wildflowers. (Writing is difficult because certain clichés *are* true.) A roadside church in Meggen is a small version of the great baroque churches of Bavaria and the Tyrol—a kind of Swiss Family Baroque. (Here "the externals of religion do not rejoice the eye and heart of a Catholic as they do in the Tyrol," Herbert Cardinal Vaughan wrote in 1885. Perhaps he was wrong.) We round the lake at Küssnacht: this name—"kiss night"—sounds funny, but then I read that the Romans had been here and called it Villa Cossiniaca. Here, a generation after Goethe, the travelers gave up their horses and

coaches to cross the Rigi range on foot. On the suggestion of the "Wan-
derbuch," we shorten the ascent by taking the first portion of it—to the
Rigi-Seebodenalp—in a cable car, at the end of this relatively easy day.
The small hotel there is pleasant and cabin-cozy, with a faint, steamy
smell of pinewood. We arrive just after the last busload of ubiquitous
German tourists has left. (The paved road ends here.) The hotel is full.
There are many English people, their presence recalling the century pre-
ceding the Second World War, when they were the principal tourists in
Switzerland. They began coming here about the same time their aristocracy discovered the French Riviera. They had small colonies in Europe in
the oddest places: Pau, in the Pyrenees; Dresden, in Saxony. There are
Anglican churches and chapels here and there in Switzerland—mostly in
the Grisons and the Engadine—to which Church of England pastors and
their reverend wives translated themselves in order to accommodate the
spiritual needs of their traveling compatriots. They kept to themselves
and kept well. Trollope once wrote that everything suffers from translation except a bishop, to which add the pastors of Anglican churches
strewn across Europe in his time. Samuel Butler (who traveled our route
in 1869) disliked the tourists and their pastors: "I keep away from En-
glish-frequented hotels in Switzerland because I find that if I do not go to
service on Sunday I am made uncomfortable. It is this bullying that I want
to do away with." Even in the nineteen-twenties, when the Age of Respectability had vanished, there were particular Swiss places visited
predominantly by Englishmen and Englishwomen of the upper middle
class—Maloja, for example, where high tea was served every afternoon,
and where I remember their sun-reddened faces, their smart sweaters and
caps and knickerbockers, the yellow scarves of their handsome women
ruffled by the wind. A splendid train, the Berne-Oberland Express, met
them at the Calais boat three times a week, spiriting them from the smoke
of Victoria to the champagne air of Chur overnight.

The Rigi (the name has a Swiss-Alemannic sound and means "rock-
ribbed") is a chain of a pre-Alpine ridges, its modern history inseparable
from the evolution of Romanticism and tourism. Goethe was one of the
first writers to cross it; he was properly enchanted with the view of the
lake below, rather than with the prospect of the Alps. A few years after
Goethe, more and more travelers began to consider the Rigi as a point of

excursion from Lucerne; for the first time, people climbed a mountain not only to get across it but to see the view and to enjoy the air. The first inn on the Rigi-Kulm, the highest of the Rigi peaks, was built as early as 1816. (Fifty years later, one of its waiters was César Ritz, who proceeded from there to even loftier things.) In 1837, Prince Albert sent to the young Princess Victoria—they were not yet engaged—a pressed alpine rose from the Rigi. A little less than a century after Goethe's first journey, a Swiss inventor stretched a cogwheel railway up one of the Rigi slopes.

We have a difficult path from the Rigi-Seebodenalp up to the Rigi-Staffel, the first high saddle. But it is early in the morning, and the air is liquid and sweet in the shade of enormous firs. We must stop every ten minutes or so to rest and pant. Our lungs seem to prosper from the sight of the emerald meadows and the emerging prospect of the lake below; in the western distance the sun glitters on the creamy peaks of the Bernese Alps. After we have passed over the Rigi-Staffel and the Rigi-First, the path opens up, thanks to the efforts of the Arbeitsgemeinschaft für Wander-wege. This is the Felsenweg, or "rock road"—a beautiful and agreeable and quite dangerless path carved into the rocks five thousand feet above the lake. According to geologists, the entire Rigi is formed of giant boulders that slid down aeons ago from the glaciers of the Gotthard mountains, thirty miles to the south. However, my imagination (and there-fore my eye) is historical, not geological. We are so high above the lake that the few sailboats appear as tiny white flecks, and when my gaze wanders west, beyond the town of Vitznau, the landscape is arcadian rather than majestic. It cannot have looked very different a hundred and sixty years ago, in that Biedermeier age of Romanticism, during the last calm decades of Old Middle Europe, before the revolutions of 1848 and Wagner came, tearing Biedermeier to shreds. (In 1859, Wagner worked at "Tristan and Isolde" in a Lucerne hotel. "The last act promises famously," he wrote. "I drew profit for it even from my excursion up the Rigi. At four in the morning we were roused by the alphorn—I jumped up, saw it was raining, and returned to bed to try and sleep; but the droll call went droning through my head, and out of it has arisen a very lusty melody which the herdsman now blows to signal Isolde's ship, making a sur-prisingly merry and naïve effect." "Merry and naïve" does not sound quite right.)

This is our second-longest day; and, as on the first, our exhilaration is premature. When we begin our descent from the highest point of the Rigi-Scheidegg, we find that we still have a rounded hump ahead of us, through the Gätterli Pass to the Brunniberg. It is a rise of a mere three or four hundred feet, whereas we mounted nineteen hundred during the first hours of the day; but, compared with a morning ascent, an afternoon one sometimes seems interminable. We go past a very large radar station of the Swiss Army, probably in the proper place for scanning the approaches to the Gotthard. Then we glide down the last stretch on a cable car, to Brunnen. As we float through the air, we cross a botanical frontier, the firs succeeded abruptly by tall, feminine beech trees and lindens.

Brunnen is at a turn of the cloverlike Lake of the Four Forest Cantons—at the end of the Lake of Lucerne and the beginning of the Urnersee, the Lake of Uri. We are now in the very heart of Switzerland, geographically and historically, where the three ur-cantons—Schwyz, Uri, and Unterwalden—meet; where the legend of William Tell was born; where, in 1291, the Swiss peasantry first won its independence from the Hapsburgs. In 1797, after his fourth and final journey to Switzerland, Goethe wrote to Schiller, "I feel almost sure that the story of Tell could be treated epically." Yet it was not Goethe but Schiller (who had never been to Switzerland) who would write "Wilhelm Tell." These small cantons are still resolutely patriotic. The Uri flag, which depicts the head of a steer, flies from houses here and there. I understand that in Switzerland there is a cachet in driving a car whose license plate shows its provenance to be one of the old, small cantons—Uri or Nidwalden, say. (Elsewhere in Europe, some people would give an eyetooth to have their car registered in Liechtenstein, that "FL" plate being so much smarter than any other— even the Monaco "MC," whose days of chic are past.) More important, this is where Turner's country begins. The great English painter discovered the beauties of this region around the time that the non-Romantic Stendhal, who came through the Gotthard from the Italian side, wrote, perhaps dyspeptically, *"Occupé du moral, la description du physique m'ennuie."* Turner was deeply impressed by the Lake of Uri, with its mountains forming an immense and yet not quite overpowering overture to the scenery beyond Flüelen, at the lake's end, where the great V of the approach to the Gotthard begins, between higher and higher snow-laden peaks. ("A rough, clumsy man," Turner's Swiss innkeeper said of him. "You may know him by his always having a pencil in his hand.") He came back to the dark beauty of the Urnersee twice, and made many sketches of the Gotthard approach. These were the ones that the young Ruskin tried to buy with some of his father's money. Still, as Turner's first biographer wrote, "notwithstanding the magnificence of Swiss scenery, it is not generally popular amongst artists, and a very experienced London pic-ture-dealer told me that it is not popular amongst the purchasers of land-scapes." In 1845, two years after Turner's last visit, Dickens came down to the Urnersee from the Gotthard. The road through the pass was open for only eight days during that entire year. He had ascended from the Italian side, and he was lucky enough to travel by carriage, winding "along a narrow path between two massive snow walls, twenty feet high or more," as he noted in a letter to a friend. The letter continues:

> Vast plains of snow range up the mountain-sides above the road, itself seven thousand feet above the sea; and tremendous waterfalls, hewing out arches for themselves in the vast drifts, go thundering down from precipices into deep chasms, here and there and everywhere; the blue water tearing through the white snow with an awful beauty that is most sublime. . . . Oh God! what a beautiful country it is!

We are not there yet. We spend the night and a late morning in Brunnen after the rigors of the Rigi. We are lodged in a big pile of a hotel, which is set in a park where tables and loudspeakers are being put out in anticipation of the arrival of an American rock group. (In 1814, Shelley came to Brunnen with Mary Godwin, hiring "two unfurnished rooms in an ugly big house, called the château." Next day, they discovered that they had little money, and "decided to return by the cheapest possible route to England.") We find that the lakeshore is very pleasant. At the after-dinner hour, the air is still clear and light. The promenade is filled with tourists, most of them old people. "This is a country for old people," my daughter says. In a way, she is right. History consists of three strata in Brunnen. There is the still and awful beauty of the Urnersee, its shores largely unchanged, undefiled by housing: evening falls, the mountainsides darken, but the picture is relieved by the illuminating sun-glitter on the incredibly white peaks of the Gotthard mountains in the distance—a near-sacramental scene, the prospect of Light rising beyond Darkness descending. The second level is the buzzing bumble of the promenade, with its crowds of old visitors to this old country. The third level is the raucous din of the loudspeakers in the park as the rock group gears up for the night's *Konzert*. The mountains, the old people, and the young: the triad of the Romantic, the middle-class, and the postmodern Switzerland. (And why are the young—and so many of the old people, too—filing toward the park so serious? No one smiles.)

Next morning we are off to Flüelen, the last town on the lake and the beginning of the Gotthard valley, where Goethe wrote that he had to have more nails put on his shoes, and where Ruskin stayed with Mr. and Mrs. Burne-Jones in the best (or worst?) Pre-Raphaelite fashion—"sitting together . . . in a room with an exquisitely clean bare-boarded floor," Mrs. Burne-Jones wrote, "and Mr. Ruskin reading Keats to us." We pass the Rütli, which for Tell and his band was the Valley Forge of Switzerland. I am surprised to find that the famous plateau of the Rütli is not high up the mountain but only a few hundred feet above a small wood-carved dock. Here in July, 1940, six hundred and fifty years after Tell, General Guisan convoked the handful of regular officers of the Swiss Army. He instructed them to hold themselves in the utmost readiness to defend the independence and the liberties of their country. I once saw a photograph of the scene: this general of a democratic citizen army speaking without notes and without a microphone to the officers, who stand in a circle, leaning forward in their long greatcoats, listening earnestly, on a grassy cliff above the silent lake, on a cloudy day.

From Flüelen to Erstfeld the path is flat, winding slowly southward. Close by on our left is a four-lane autobahn, which was built a few years ago; on our right, the running mass of verdigris water of the Reuss River. For long stretches, this bucolic path is separated from the concrete autobahn by high sheets of metal and masonry—presumably in order to mask the roar of traffic, and perhaps the view. It is pleasant to record that we have walked from Flüelen to Erstfeld an hour faster than did Goethe, who used—as far as I can find—the same path. All day we have marched in the relentless light of the alpine sun, but now the mountains paint long shadows on the streets of Erstfeld, even in mid-afternoon, for here the great way from north to south narrows from a broad cleavage to a narrow crevasse. A hundred and thirteen years ago, construction of the Gotthard rail line began here. We sit on the sunlit southern terrace of the Erstfeld railroad station. On the other side of the tracks is a monument on a single pair of rails: a preserved example of the traditional Swiss mountain locomotives, the last of the famous Crocodiles, so called because of their long, snoutlike hoods both fore and aft, a 2-4-4-2 engine. For a long time, trains had to be coupled to a second engine at Erstfeld: it is here that the Gotthard gradient begins.

The Gotthard line was one of the great engineering achievements of the nineteenth century, like the American and Siberian transcontinental railroads or the Suez and Panama Canals. (With all the talk about the technological "revolution" of the twentieth century, with all our soaring bridges and highways and airports, there has been nothing comparable to those feats of the nineteenth century which changed the geography of entire continents.) A great achievement, but full of tragedy. In 1871, the Swiss invited investors and engineers from Italy and Germany to meet in Lucerne, to plan a nine-mile rail tunnel under the Gotthard mountains. The tunnel was built in eight years. Louis Favre, the engineer who designed and built it, died before the borings from the two ends met. Four thousand workers, almost all of them migrant laborers from Italy, dug the tunnel day and night. Nearly three hundred of them died on the job. In the small cemetery of Göschenen, at the northern portal of the tunnel, a stone stele has been erected as a monument to these nameless dead, with an inscription hardly legible now: "MARTIRES LABORI COMUNITAS CRISTIANA." For Airolo, at the southern end, the tunnel's completion was a disaster. For centuries, the citizens of Airolo had been innkeepers, cartmen, muleteers, coachbuilders, farriers, wheelwrights. They prided themselves on their industry and honesty. (Trollope's brother found that his portmanteau had been stolen from the stagecoach, but the people of Airolo caught the two thieves, "each of them clad in three or four of my shirts and as many coats and waistcoats.") The people of Airolo scorned the artless crowd of poor laborers from Italy. The first train chugging through the tunnel brought the tidings of an existential catastrophe for the town, whereafter entire families left in droves for California.

From Erstfeld almost to the end of our walk there are four, sometimes five, routes carved under and over the Gotthard. Down in the valley is the railroad, a pretty sight from above, with trains winding through every few minutes. Next to it is the autobahn, its white double ribbon disappearing and reappearing through innumerable tunnels and galleries. Above is the old motor road, narrower and darker. Higher, along the side of the mountains, is the still older mule and coach track. These last two are sometimes identical with the *Wanderweg,* falling away from it and rising up to it. From Erstfeld to Göschenen, twelve miles to the south, the ascent is beautiful but wearisome: a long day, always uphill. At Göschenen, we are at the foot of the Gotthard Pass itself, and are already at an altitude of more than thirty-five hundred feet, with sun and shadows alternating in sharp patterns. In Erstfeld, we were in the V of two great mountain chains; in Göschenen, we are in a narrow three-dimensional double U. Göschenen, unlike Airolo, was an unimportant place until the trains reached it, a century ago. The northern portal of the great tunnel is but a few hundred yards south of the Göschenen station. The trains go through the tunnel in fifteen minutes; the walk along the footpath to Airolo, over the pass, takes eight hours. In the past, it took as long as two days if a traveler elected to spend the night at the Gotthard hospice, as Goethe and Turner did.

Most of the path follows the old mule track. But "mule track" is misleading, and not only because some of it is paved with cobblestones. The term suggests something distant from history and from civilization. But the Gotthard mule track is marked by the history of Europe. Not from its beginnings: it was not used during the Roman centuries, and not even in the early Middle Ages, because a deep ravine athwart it horrified and turned away travelers. Sometime during the late twelfth century, the stone arch of the Teufelsbrücke was built, and the traffic over the Gotthard Pass began. In 1599, the Spanish Infanta Isabel crossed the Teufelsbrücke ("a bridge which is called after the Devil with much reason"). Two centuries later, during the years of the French Revolution, the traffic grew. The Duke of Chartres, later Louis-Philippe, walked across the pass in 1793, in search of a teaching job in Switzerland. (He found one in Reichenau, where he soon got into trouble for seducing the school cook.) In 1793, too, the Duchess of Devonshire composed a poem about her crossing of the Gotthard, the twenty-fourth stanza of which inspired Coleridge's "Ode to Georgiana Duchess of Devonshire." The next year, an Englishwoman named Helen Maria Williams reported in her travel diary that she had seen "a numerous retinue of horses, oxen, mules, and other cattle [which] had passed in the suite of a great man, whose carriage they had dragged, by his order, from the bottom of the mountain, that he might have the fame of crossing St. Gotthard in a vehicle with wheels." She continued, "As our countrymen are known to be the only travelling philosophers who make experiments of this kind, the Monks [of the hospice] had no difficulty in conjecturing on the approach of this long procession, that if it was not the Emperor, or the Burgo-master of Berne, the two greatest personages they had heard of, it must be an English Lord."

In 1799, General Aleksandr Vasilyevich Suvorov marched north through the Gotthard with his army—the only appearance of a Russian army in Western Europe in history, apart from a short-lived and ludicrous landing of some Russian troops from English ships along the Dutch coast the same year. The first American to traverse the pass was (perhaps) the artist Washington Allston, in 1804. In 1815, Sir Stratford Canning had a difficult trip: "One slides down the snow as the Gauls used to do; with this difference, that instead of a shield one has nothing better than what nature has given all of us, to slide on." The time had come to improve this business. The companies of mule drivers and their families got together to pave the track. By 1835, a stagecoach was going through three times a week in the summer. By 1842, the run was being made every day, weather permitting. (In the winter, small two-seater sleighs could be hired.) It was now possible to get from Flüelen to Milan in thirty hours. In 1864, a Cook's-tour party consisting of seventy people "employed nine diligences, 432 horses besides bullocks which assisted at some of the heavier stages, and 108 men" in order to cross the Gotthard in some comfort. Twenty years later, the cobblestoned path was deserted, because of the railroad. Thirty years after that, much of it was repaved to serve as part of the first motor route over the pass. The traffic began to disappear again forty years later, as the great autobahn opened up in the valley. But the old path is still there, for wanderers such as ourselves, and for an occasional automobile, taking its time, avoiding the autobahn.

"Scheidpunkt Europas" ("The Divide of Europe") says a tablet on the chapel in the village of Hospental. The chapel is a few yards from the old St. Gotthard Inn, Suvorov's headquarters in 1799. But the watershed—

the true divide—is a good three hours away, uphill, at the Gotthard hospice, which was commissioned by the convent of Disentis in 1230, and occupied by a Capuchin congregation in 1683. The fog rolls in. We cannot see far toward Italy. But we are in Italy of a kind—among the Italians of Switzerland. Within two hundred yards, the human scenery has changed. In five minutes, we have walked from the Germanic north to the Italianate south; Italy is here in the architecture, in the solid masonry of the houses, in the colors of the stones, and in the faces of the few people we see. Soon it will be evident in the vegetation, too, as the fir forests gradually fall away and the warm breezes move up the valleys. In 1902, Belloc wrote, "When I began to see somewhat farther and felt a vigour and fullness in the outline of the Trees, I said to myself suddenly—'I know what it is! It is the South, and a great part of my blood. They may call it Switzerland still, but I know now that I am in Italy, and this is the gate of Italy lying in groves.'"

Well, it is not yet the South, and no part of my blood, but I am glad to see Airolo at the end of the day, if not quite like Belloc. ("When I heard again at Airolo the speech of civilised men, and saw the strong Latin eyes and straight forms of the Race after all those days of fog and frost and German speech and the north, my eyes filled with tears and I was as glad as a man come home again, and I could have kissed the ground.") Still, I must hand it to Hilaire, who walked from Airolo to Faido in three hours. It will take us at least six, and we will do it in two mornings, spending the night in Deggio.

But Belloc took the old road. We follow the "Wanderbuch" and take a path called the Alta Strada, three thousand feet above the valley, snaking along the side of the alpine Ticino from village to isolated village. These villages are peopled by a hardy Italianate race, who chose four hundred and fifty years ago to break away from the Counts of Milan and enter into a confederacy with the dour Swiss peasant communes of the Uri, on the north side of the Gotthard Pass. (Intermarry with them they did not.) The old road is now a ribbon near the bottom of the valley, on a green stretch above the rail line and the autobahn. Contrary to my expectation, it is not the southward prospect that is exceptionally engaging but the ever-changing retrospect of the valley, as we stop and look back to the north. There is an ineffable harmony between the villages and the mountains, and even the roads, between the human habitation and the landscape, between what stands still and unchanged and what men and their machines have wrought. For us, it is not only that mountains long ago ceased being horrible. It is, too, that what people like Wordsworth feared did not come about. The greed and toil of "godless wretches" has, after all, not levelled the hills and made the paths straight. Here the human presence has not—or perhaps not yet—rendered the scene less calming to the senses, less beautiful.

Deggio, geographically the high point of our path on the Alta Strada, is something like a low point in our wandering. The innkeeper's wife (no "strong Latin eyes," no "straight form") is slatternly, and suspicious of someone who has an American passport with a non-Italian name and tries to speak Italian to her; the food is indifferent; and in the evening there is nothing to do but watch television. The Swiss-Italian network shows an endless motorcycle race and the great flower parade in Locarno—the *festa dei fiori,* with drum majorettes twirling batons and smiling relentlessly, as if in California. Next morning, on the Alta Strada, we come upon—sometimes passing them and sometimes falling behind—small groups of German tourists, to whom this walk is well known; according to the "Wanderbuch," the Alta Strada is "much frequented in July and August." It was also frequented by Samuel Butler, who wrote most of "Erewhon" in Switzerland: the path from the Gotthard to Bellinzona was the descent to Erewhon. Our walk is nearly over. It was not lonely; but it was a walk of aloneness. As we clamber down, following the yellow marks on the trees, through the forest of Osco (the only time I slip, grazing my knee), I recognize the odd and yet familiar combination of regret and relief.

The end of our Gotthard walk is Lugano, the traditional terminus of the route, though recently the Arbeitsgemeinschaft für Wanderwege added two more days, extending the route to Chiasso, the Italian frontier station, so that wanderers can claim they traversed Switzerland along the diagonal, from one of its corners to another—from the German border to the Italian one. Our end is Lugano for more than one reason: my daughter must return home to school, and we promised to stay a day or two with my father's cousin, an old gentleman, widowed and frail, who lives alone in a high, sunny apartment above the lake, in the Paradiso district. The name is fitting: this is a paradise for retired people, who have found safety, comfort, and sunshine in this sunniest place of all Switzerland, sunnier and warmer in the winter than the Lombardy plains to the south. Italy is very near, its curving frontier within sight a few miles away; it even has an enclave on the Swiss shore, Campione d'Italia, which is twenty minutes away by the white lake cruisers.

And yet Lugano, with all its Italian flora and fauna (including the human), belongs to Switzerland—and not only because of its clean alleys, the precise functioning of its various institutions, and the prodigious richness of its shops. A little more than a century ago, Switzerland (the only republic in Europe before 1870) was a haven for radical revolutionaries. There is a house here in which, in the eighteen-fifties, Mazzini, Kossuth, and Bakunin were lodged. In this century Lugano is a haven for the bourgeois. Lugano and Switzerland have become a living portion of bourgeois Europe, in the best sense of that much maligned word (whose stock, however, has begun to rise). What they represent within Europe now is what Europe one day may—I am not saying that it will—represent within the world.

Our luggage has arrived. We breakfast in our room again. We say goodbye to the old, bent uncle, with his silvery head, and wait on the station platform in the shining sun for the transeuropean express train, which slides in at the moment the sweep-second hand of the electric clock moves to twelve.

A Night at the Dresden Opera

(1986)

At the curve of the highway, there appears, some five miles below us in the valley, the famous city of Dresden. More thoroughly than any other city, Dresden was destroyed during the last world war. Now it glimmers and breathes in the sunlight. There is a whitish flatness about it: no architectural landmarks, and none of the giant smokestacks that herald the other cities of East Germany from afar. And from that distance we can see none of the famous ruins. As our car moves into the city, we begin to comprehend why this is so. Most of Dresden has been razed. We stop at a parking lot on one side of the Pragerstrasse, an enormous pedestrian mall. We cannot drive farther. Our hotel looms, fifteen stories high, on the other side of the mall, which is a half mile long—a flat, paved expanse between large concrete buildings of different heights: hotels, department stores, government offices. This mall has an Eastern, Soviet look rather than a Midwestern American one, but with an Aztec (or perhaps Mongol) element here and there: concrete piles of buildings without eyebrows but with outcropping cheekbones. The Russians have been here for forty years, of course. Our hotel is the Hotel Newa, and its address is the Leningraderstrasse.

So this is the new Dresden, a modern city got together on top of the rubble and situated within the imperial sphere of the Soviet Union—this once princely rococo Saxon city, which, with its music conservatories and cream cakes, was much favored by Americans before the First World War (and also by Russians of the czarist era). It is still very German. As so often happened during the Second World War, the bombers missed one essential target. The old railroad station is still there, beyond the mall. It was built in the eighteen-nineties, a massive, solid building with a roof of glass and steel; its profile suggests that of a First World War German battleship. Something of an older Germany is more visible and palpable here in East Germany than in the prosperous West. The government of the German Democratic Republic knows this. It has gone beyond earlier pathetic and servile efforts to establish its presence, and has reached a stage of self-consciousness wherein it proclaims the G.D.R. to be the legitimate successor of the old, the historic, Germany. Its banners, draped on the fronts of buildings, announce, "DIE D.D.R. IST UNSER VATERLAND!" In West Germany, the railroad and the postal service are identified as those of a federal republic: Deutsche Bundesbahn, Bundespost. Here the names are harsh and assertive: Deutsche Reichsbahn, Deutsche Post—the railroad, the post office of the German Reich. Meanwhile, some of the streets carry the names of international Communists of the nineteen-thirties; the hotel chain is Interhotel, and the airline is Interflug. This much remains of the erstwhile Communist International, nothing more.

This *Vaterland* is not prosperous. Along the mall, at two in the afternoon, we can buy lunch only in the bowels of an office building; beyond the plate-glass door, one finds oneself immediately in the midst of the sad grimness of a German communal restaurant during the war. We are in need of a road map of the G.D.R. There are none to be found, even in the large bookstores, which are crowded with people. The young women at the hotel desk allow us to borrow, for an hour or two, one that was printed in England many years ago.

They cannot procure tickets to the state opera for us. It is now five o'clock. We have come back to the hotel, tired after a long walk, having crossed the concrete desert of the mall twice. We went to look at the Altstadt—the old city—at the north end of the mall. It was not difficult to find. An hour later, we go back; there is nothing else to do. Beyond the Sovietish mall, beyond the new Dresden, the first ruins appear: a great semicircle of them, perhaps a square mile in extent, stretching from the mall to the flat banks of the Elbe. They are the largest reminder of the Second World War in Europe—perhaps in the world. In Hiroshima and in Berlin, a few buildings were left in ruins as a reminder; the rebuilt city flows around them. But this is different. In Dresden, the old city is a monument of ruins. In the West—in London or Nuremberg, say—the ruins were cleared away; ten years after the war little or nothing of them remained. In the East, in Budapest and Warsaw (the latter destroyed by the Germans in two installments), the old districts have been rebuilt almost completely—an outlet for patriotism and traditional pride, and an activity for which their unpopular governments got some credit. Here it almost seems as if the ruins were meant to be preserved, instead of cleared or reconstructed—as if the destroyed Altstadt were meant to be a piece of propaganda to show people what the war was like and what the Western enemies of Germany wrought. Restoration has been going on only desultorily, here and there.

For someone who lived through the war in Europe, these ruined acres are an instant reminder of forty years ago. Some things about the ruins, however, are different. Forty years have aged the walls. They are no longer stone-colored or burned black. Four decades of grime and smoke and rain have made them dark brown, so that they look even more startling than the ruins among which one trudged in 1945. They are sombre and macabre enough, but there is an element of beauty in their midst. Trees have grown up within these walls, among these toothless giant buildings. Trees, not weeds—we are in the northern half of Europe, where vegetation is not riotous. There is something melancholy and peaceful in these young and middle-aged trees filling with green light the courtyards of death. In the park of the palace of the Saxon kings, German and Russian soldiers amble about. One of the palace buildings is half restored. Band music is playing over loud-speakers. We walk down to the Elbe. Old-fashioned paddle steamers (bearing such names as Friedrich Engels and Karl Liebknecht) are tied up along the quay. With their paddle boxes, they are white and broad-hipped, like Saxon women of the past. Here, at least, Dresden looks as it must have looked in the past, the river surely reminiscent of the scene Bellotto painted two hundred years ago. (Warsaw, Dresden—the famous riverscapes. He must have appreciated that green-and-blue flatness, like the Venetian lagoons.) Yes, the afternoon sky over the Elbe at Dresden is pale-blue, fine, unbroken porcelain—a Bellotto sky.

In the Theaterplatz, the equestrian statue of Johann I, King of Saxony during the *Reichsgründung,* has been erected again, midway between the array of burned ruins and the opera house, which has been rebuilt. This is the Semper Opera, named after its architect, Gottfried Semper. It is an oval neo-Renaissance building, with a curious history. The first Semper Opera, built in 1841, burned down in 1869 and was rebuilt less than a decade

later; in 1945, the bombs all but destroyed it, and it has been completely
reconstructed—an achievement begun in 1977, finished in 1983, and com-
memorated by a tablet at the main entrance. *Fidelis Semper!* Around a side
entrance, its doors painted a shiny dark brown, men and women are gathering. It is half past six. The performance tonight is a "Klassischer Ballett-
Abend"—an evening of classical ballet—beginning at eight. People are
standing in line for the remaining tickets. I do not like standing in line for
anything—surely not at the end of the day. But I give in. There is nothing
else—absolutely, completely nothing else—to do in Dresden at night.

There are three public entrances to the Semper Opera. The main
entrance is for those who possess tickets or special passes. Another is for
those who have reserved tickets. The entrance in front of which we are
waiting is for people who hope for standing room, or for seats if any are
left. The gathering now becomes a small crowd. People come in groups,
and some congregate in front of the main door, too. Precisely at seven
o'clock—I look at my watch, because there is no sound of bells from the
dead, burned towers of the churches around us—something happens: the
Semper Opera bursts into light. Hundreds of electric candles glow and
glitter from their chandeliers through the great, palatial Renaissance windows. It is still light outside; all this grand illumination is interior. The
Semper Opera is a brilliant jewel box ablaze.

At once the main door is opened; men and women press in. More and
more people are coming out of the evening, across the broad, cobblestoned square surrounded by the silent, unmoving, darkening ruins.
The scene is semicircular, and probably unrecordable even by the widest-
lensed of cameras. It is unforgettable, a scene beyond the means of the
most imperious of theatre directors, a true piece of *Welttheater:* this
nineteenth-century jewel box drawing the stunned, the desperate, the
determined, the fortunate, the hopeful to its lights, and three hundred feet
away the gigantic backdrop of the ruins. They are black now, and the
green, living trees inside them have turned black, too—indistinguishable
from those ominous towers in the moonless falling night. A backdrop is
always a reminder of sorts. (For once, a German word is more telling than
the English one: "*Mahnung*" combines the meanings of reminder and
warning, its tone intensely sombre.)

Between the ruins and the theatre, the square is largely empty, except for the statue of Johann I and the groups of people arriving. Most of the people come on foot. On one side of the square is a paved roadway, where cars may pull up to drop off their passengers. Every few minutes, a Volvo or a black Russian-made limousine appears, carrying what are rather obviously members of the governing class of the German Democratic Republic—content, smiling men and women of the bureaucracy, who make their way with ease through the crowd and enter the golden light of the Semper's foyer to be led to their boxes and seats. From one of the limousines emerges a group of North Koreans in European clothes. They wear red badges bearing the enamelled portrait of their dictator, Kim Il Sung; they are smiling rigidly, their features, I am sorry to say, proletarian and cruel. Later, two or three tour buses pull up. One of them is from West Germany. Its license plate indicates that, but so do its passengers— middle-aged men and women who are much better dressed than their East German compatriots. But perhaps "compatriot" is not the right word; they inhabit a different world from the people of Dresden—different economically, politically, and ideologically, as well as in dress. They belong to another age of history, these prosperous envoys from the West, on a prepaid package visit to their impoverished relatives.

The opera-loving people of Dresden seem the older Germans, and not only because in the Eastern part of Europe life is harder and people age faster. The shapes, the clothes, the faces of so many of these men milling before the opera, waiting for their wives, are reminiscent of the Germans of Germany before the war, sometimes to the point of carica- ture. They are heavy, thick-necked, odd-lipped, with hard creases around their mouths, and heavy jowls. They have George Grosz countenances, though without the uniforms and high collars, and without the arrogance that that vengeful German artist attributed to them circa 1923. In the Weimar period, a German photographer, apparently full of hatred for his own people, brought out an album of monstrous portraits of the stiff and distorted faces and figures of ordinary German citizens; I saw it a few years ago, in an edition that was published in New York. Some of these men remind me suddenly of the faces in that album. But, I repeat, they are devoid of arrogance. Their wives have brought them along to the music and the splendor. I must bow my head before these wives of Dresden. Here they are, heavier than their coevals in the West, serious and patient.

It is they who have a sense of occasion. Many of them wear long skirts, which, for fashionable evenings, are going out of style in West Germany; but these women don't know that, and it's not important. They come to pay homage to a culture they hope is still theirs, to the high-bourgeois nineteenth-century virtues represented by an evening at the state opera. They come for the ballet and the music, but, beyond that, for the occasion: to spend three hours once more in their opera house, which—unlike the Zwinger, that eighteenth-century rococo palace, which lies a hundred yards away—has been redone with all the opulence of a century that for them is irrevocably past and yet not unfamiliar.

We are told that most people arrive at seven, an hour before the performance, because the buffets of the opera house open early, offering sandwiches and Russian champagne that is very cheap. It is now ten minutes before eight, and still not everyone is inside. The shiny brown doors are opened from time to time by an official, who admits eight or ten people at once. At one minute before eight, we are let in. We are among the last, and get tickets to the highest gallery, for a few cents—standing room only. So we enter the Semper Opera. It is the eighteen-seventies, to the last jot and tittle. Crimson carpets, crystal forests of chandeliers, monumental black marbleized columns with creamy capitals, enormous mirrors—all in the eclectic neo-Renaissance style of the nineteenth century but somehow all of a piece. Only the colors of the many frescoes on the ceiling are a bit too new, too sharp. (Gottfried Semper, that neoclassicist, was a great advocate of polychrome.) The opera house is stuffed to the gills, but there is little of the loud, titillating hum that reverberates in theatres before the curtain rises. The air is not still, however; it is full of the subdued sounds of a silent respect.

The performance is very good: excerpts from "Swan Lake," "Sleeping Beauty," "La Bayadère." In contrast to the florid richness of the interior, the spectacle is reduced to simplicity. The ballets are performed on an empty stage, on a black slate floor. The dancers of the Dresden State Opera Ballet are like white butterflies, flying and gliding above the dark slate. More surprising than the lack of stage décor is the fact that the orchestra is not visible; but perhaps an array of serious German musicians in frock coats and white ties—yet another image from the past—would have been too much.

The respectfulness carries over to the end, with no thunderous applause, no pompous bourgeois shouting of "Bravo!" There is something like a hushed thankfulness instead.

During the long wait outside I had seen an old, quiet German woman in the crowd at the door. Her grey hair was pulled back in a bun, and she wore a long grey evening dress. She waited patiently, holding her program and leaning with one elbow on a crutch. Sometimes she rested her thin frame against the rusticated stone wall. She must have had some difficulty hobbling up to the fourth tier of the opera house. There she stood, not far from us, wearing a little smile and leaning forward on her crutch. There was no need to speculate about her: this was clearly something very important in her life. After the intermission, fortunately, she found a seat. I had the urge to say something to her in my halting German. I did not do so; and perhaps she would have been embarrassed if I had. It was then that the meaning of the evening crystallized in my mind.

This must have been how the people of the Middle Ages entered the vast, magical spaces of their cathedrals for high Mass, the only splendor in their lives. There was, however, a difference. That experience in the Middle Ages came to people with no consciousness of history. For the people of Dresden today, the Semper Opera was the tangible presence of a better past—a past that some of them still remembered. They thought that they were being faithful to what was best in themselves. Did they shut out from their minds the dreariness of their present, of their everyday lives? Perhaps not. When the evening was over and they left that building burning with the fullness of beautiful things, these people, still stunned forty years after their defeat, found the black monumental ruins staring at them. Whether they stared back or not, I could not see.

Hitler's One-Hundredth Birthday

(1989)

In March 1989 I went to Hitler's birthplace.

The town of Braunau, where Adolf Hitler was born one hundred years ago, is off the tourist-beaten track—that is, distant from the Munich-Salzburg-Linz-Vienna superhighway. It is in the Innviertel, a region of the province of Upper Austria, which, even before the Autobahn, had few tourist attractions comparable to the pretty shining lakes farther to the south, on the shores of which innkeeping had become a source of income for Austrians during the nineteenth century. About forty miles north of Salzburg and seventy miles east of Munich, Braunau is a good two-hour drive from both, on two-lane roads. There are few local trains between Munich and Simbach, the German frontier town across the Inn River. The train no longer comes to Braunau.

Partly because of this relative remoteness Braunau has been undamaged by the tempestuous ravages of the Second World War and by the less tempestuous but more endemic ravages of modern architecture. In 1874, three years after Hitler's father had come to take up his post as a customs official there, many of the wooden buildings of Braunau were destroyed by fire. But most of the houses of Braunau, built of stone, still stand in tight rows along the main city square, which serves as an open-air market once a week. They jut out more irregularly in some of the side streets. Many of them are buildings of the seventeenth and eighteenth centuries, and some even older. There are two particularly handsome prospects in Braunau. One is the remnant of the city wall (Braunau was a fortified town for centuries), with a few ramshackle gardens and houses set atop the grey stone ramparts in the cracks of which clumps of greenery have pushed their way through. The other is the view east from the large market square whose eastern edge is unobstructed by buildings and slopes slightly downward. The prospect is of a range of green-brown mountains under an unusually wide expanse of sky. But that bright lightness opens up away from Braunau, many of whose narrow streets, including the small square around its high-spired church, are seldom washed by sunlight. What is perhaps unusual is this combination: Braunau is both handsome and somber.

The somber quality resides in the darkness of some of its old houses, with their heavy buttresses. Their appearance is but a representation of the history of this town and of the complicated story of the loyalties of its inhabitants. The Inn River is the boundary between Austria and Germany; but that was not always so. For centuries Braunau was a Bavarian frontier town facing Austria. In 1706 it was a center of a peasant rebellion against the Habsburgs. It passed back and forth from Bavarian Wittelsbach to Austrian Imperial Habsburg rule. It was in Braunau that in 1810 Napoleon's new bride, the Archduchess Marie Louise, was festively transferred from her Austrian to her French entourage. During his campaigns against Austria in 1805 and again in 1809 Napoleon spent the night in this frontier town—in the same House Schüdl (and presumably in the same second-story rooms) where seventy years later Hitler's father came to live. It is a well-proportioned building on the south side of the large market square.

The house where Adolf Hitler was born stands a hundred yards farther down on the main street. In 1889 it was the Gasthaus zum Pommer, one of the two main inns of Braunau, an old hostelry once owned by a brewery—that is, a "Brauhaus." Hitler's father moved often, at least until he could buy his own house during the last years of his life; before that he had often preferred to live in inns. The Gasthaus zum Pommer is partially occupied now; it houses a hostel for handicapped children. Earlier it was a kind of public library. After Hitler had annexed Austria, Martin Bormann bought it for the purpose of ceremonial preservation. At that time, and also during the war, it was a place of pilgrimage for many people, most of them coming from Germany to contemplate the Führer's birthplace in awe. The house has something of a dual aspect now, almost as if it were divided against itself. The ground-floor façade is heavy and Germanic; the top two stories have the pale wash of yellow Austrian stucco. The back of this L-shaped house, with its arched corridors of the upper stories, seems abandoned and in poor repair. During my visit to Braunau the building was closed. I could not ascertain the location of the room where Adolf Hitler was born.

People in Braunau do not seem to be divided against themselves. They are a fairly homogeneous people, which is somewhat unusual, since during the 1940s (near the end of the war and for several years afterward) millions of the German-speaking peoples of Central Europe had moved from north to south and from east to west, leaving their great bombed cities, fleeing before the avenging Russian armies, expelled from their once homelands among other Eastern European peoples, eventually establishing themselves in postwar West Germany and Austria. (By 1950, for example, most of the inhabitants of Munich were no longer its natives.) But this great inchoate migration of peoples touched the Innviertel only marginally. Its people are stubby, gnarled, muscular, with some of the marks of inbreeding. (Hitler's father and mother, too, were second cousins.)

I came to Braunau in early March. A friend had reserved a room for me in the main hostelry of the town, Hotel zur Post, an old inn with gloomy rooms and a good sturdy cuisine. I ate my dinner alone, behind a table occupied by locals, including the owner, a man of a long line of Braunau innkeepers. I knew that they knew why I had come to their town; I was obviously a forerunner of the many journalists who had booked the Post solid for the nineteenth and twentieth of April. Their conviviality eventually spilled over the low back of the bench separating my table from theirs. As the dining room of the inn was emptying, one of them, a wiry little man, a bit in his cups, stepped over to sit with me. I told him that I was not a professional journalist but a historian, something that impressed him not at all. What seemed to impress him—and, I fear, not altogether agreeably—was that I knew something about the history of his town. I asked him where the Gasthaus zum Pommer was. We went out in the pelting rain. We looked at it. Then he invited me to go on drinking in another tavern. "My father was a Nazi," he said. "I don't know about myself." Then he added: "I am an engineer." At breakfast next morning the owner came over to sit with me. He started the conversation by telling me that "der Hitler" had lived but the first three years of his life in

Braunau. (Actually he lived there even less than that.) Then he went on to say that, yes, there were people around here who had been Nazi sympathizers in the 1930s, but this had been a depressed region then, and people were influenced by the prosperity and the high level of employment of factories in German Simbach, a few hundred yards away across the Inn.

That was typical of the few conversations I had with people in Braunau—which is why I write that people in Braunau do not seem to be divided among themselves. There is, at the same time, a division, a kind of split-mindedness, within their minds. When it comes to memories of the Hitler years, they are defensive but not remorseful. When it comes to foreigners, the attitude reflects what, to them, is a commonsense skepticism: foreigners cannot, and will not, understand those things. But this is not an attitude of the people of the Innviertel in particular; it is an attitude still widespread among the people of Austria at large. What is particular about the people of Braunau and the Innviertel is their insistence that Adolf Hitler was not a typical son of their city and their land, that he was not really one of them. And in this they are, at least to some extent, correct.

There are three things in Hitler's early years about which he misled people: about Braunau, about his father and about his years in Vienna.

He dictated—dictated rather than wrote—*Mein Kampf* in the winter and spring of 1924–25. *Mein Kampf* consists of (and originally was to be printed in) two volumes, of which the first is autobiographical. Hitler declared this in his preface: from his own history "more can be learned than from any purely doctrinary treatise" about the development of himself and of the movement. Now he had "the opportunity to describe my own development, as far as this is necessary for the understanding of the first as well as the second volume, and which may serve to destroy the evil legends created about my person by the Jewish press."

Mein Kampf begins with a paean to Braunau. "Today I consider it my good fortune that fate designated Braunau on the Inn as the place of my birth." Again: "this little town on the border appears to me the symbol of a great task." And again: "this little town on the River Inn, gilded by the light of German martyrdom." Yet it is not only that the Hitler family moved away from Braunau in the third year of Adolf Hitler's life. All of his repeated emphasis on his native roots notwithstanding, he did not return to Braunau until his forty-ninth year.*

He came back to Braunau on the twelfth of March in 1938, on a Saturday, the day of the week when he was born. That Saturday in 1889 had been grey. Now Braunau was washed by the sun. The resistance of the Austrian government had collapsed the day before. That night people poured into the streets; there was a triumphant torchlight parade. A large swastika banner was draped over the stone carving of the Habsburg Imperial double-headed eagle at the top of the arch of the old city gate. From the early morning of the twelfth German army units were coming over the bridge, passing through Braunau, cheered on by the crowd. A little before four in the afternoon there was a hush. In a big open Mercedes touring car Hitler came slowly across the bridge. He received a large bouquet of flowers. His face was unsmiling. The automobile halted before the house where he was born. He did not descend; he did not wish to enter. Braunau did not mean much to him. He never saw it again. After March 1938 party officials and other enthusiasts designed embellishments and commemorative erections in Braunau. Hitler was not interested.

That afternoon he drove on, in the direction of Linz. His triumphant progress followed, by and large, the route of his family during his childhood and early youth. The year after his birth his father was posted from Braunau to three different places in Upper Austria, eventually settling in Leonding, a suburb of Linz. On the thirteenth of March in 1938, more than one hundred thousand people crowded into Linz to cheer Hitler. Their frenetic jubilation made him change his original plans; he proclaimed the union of Germany with Austria then and there. Till the end he had a soft place for Linz in his heart. A few days before killing himself in the Führerbunker in Berlin, he looked dreamily at a plan of a future Linz that he had wished to make into a great cultural center (and to which in his personal will he had donated most of his paintings). Leonding is on the way from Braunau to Linz; yet it was Linz first and Leonding second. From Linz Hitler drove to pay a short visit to his parents' grave, in the parish churchyard of Leonding. I saw that grey gravestone, with his father's

---

*His companion and wife, Eva Braun, was born in Simbach. She killed herself together with him, a few hours after they had been officially married in the bunker.

photograph set in it under glass. In May 1945, after American troops had set them free from the concentration camp in nearby Mauthausen, a schoolmate of mine and a friend had their memorable first picnic lunch sitting on the wall of that churchyard. They saw an enormous wreath left on the grave of Alois and Klara Hitler, with a wide ribbon: the homage of the party of the district. In March 1989 there were two small pots of flowers on the grave.

Across the street from the churchyard stands an ochre-stuccoed one-story house where the Hitler family lived for eight years. Not far from the other side of the church stands another ochre-colored building, the tavern where Hitler's father was sitting when he was struck dead by a stroke. Adolf Hitler was thirteen years old then.

Hitler wished to obscure certain things in his youth. Unquestionable is the evidence of his love for his mother, a sad-eyed, oval-faced woman, the third wife of his father. This was a filial love about which Dr. Bloch (Klara Hitler's Jewish physician in Linz) said that he had seen nothing like it in his career. What remains contradictory (and these contradictions exist within Hitler's own statements) is his relationship to his father. Alois Schicklgruber was the first of his line to rise in the world. He was better situated and better off than his son would later admit. Without anything more than a lower-school education he rose to be a customs official in Braunau. He was a sanguine, willful, respectable civil servant: his photographs exhale the picture of an official of the Habsburg Empire, self-confident almost to the point of caricature. He was an illegitimate son (something that was neither rare nor particularly demeaning among Austrian peasant families then) and changed his name from Schickl-gruber to Hitler thirteen years before his son Adolf was born. For this alone Adolf should have been grateful. (The reminiscences of his school-mate Kubizek sound convincing: Hitler said that "Schicklgruber impressed him as too rough, too peasantlike; besides, too long and impractical.") He inherited other things from his father, too: the latter's restlessness (Alois's frequent moves), perhaps also some of his attractiveness to women; his handwriting and his signature resembled his father's for a long time. Yet he was vexed, perhaps painfully, about his father throughout his life. In *Mein Kampf* he wrote about his father with glowing respect, in phrases of superficial sentimentality that are otherwise absent in that book. "I honored my father and loved my mother," he wrote. But during a long nocturnal conversation, replete with memories, with the Austrian general Edmund von Glaise-Horstenau (who was also born in Braunau) in April 1939 Hitler said something different: "I feared my father, but I loved him not at all."

He wished to distance himself from his family as soon as he could. As he told Glaise-Horstenau that night, he wanted to break away, "with the definite aim to become something really great." In this, as also in many other things, Hitler was very different from Napoleon, whose ties to his family had bound him (often burdensomely) throughout his life. Yes, Hitler was an Austrian who wished to be a great German, just as Napoleon the Corsican wanted to become a great Frenchman, or Stalin the Georgian a great Russian, or Alexander of Macedon the greatest Greek. Yet Hitler was perhaps less influenced by Austria than Napoleon had been influenced by Corsica, or Stalin by Caucasian Georgia.

He wrote at length in *Mein Kampf* about his progress from Braunau through Linz to Vienna, insisting that it was in Vienna that his entire ideology had crystallized. Most of his biographers and commentators have, by and large, accepted his explanation, emphasizing his Austrian background and his experiences in Vienna. There is some truth in these explanations, but not enough. Yes: his five years in Vienna influenced him in many ways. The life of a great city opened his eyes, in more ways than one. He read all kinds of political and ideological publications and he was, at least to some extent, impressed with their contents. But there is evidence that even before coming to Vienna he thought of the Austrian state as corrupt and ramshackle, while he admired the power of Germany. When he was twenty-three he left Vienna forever. The painstaking researches of certain German historians have since established that the picture he drew of himself of a poverty-stricken young man in Vienna was not correct. His small inheritance provided him with more money than he would assert later. It is questionable, too, whether his encounter with Jewish people in Vienna (where 90 percent of the Jews of Austria lived at that time—he had known no Jews in Braunau or Leonding and very few in Linz) was as decisive as he declared in *Mein Kampf,* since we have virtually no evidence of his essential anti-Semitism before 1919. It seems that the sudden crystallization of his world view came relatively late, in his thirtieth year, in early 1919 in Munich. It was then and there that the critical mass of Hitler's ideology congealed, out of his feelings about the defeat of his beloved Germany but even more out of what he saw as hateful and ugly in the few agitated months of the short-lived Munich "Soviet Republic." The other matter that this formerly shy and reticent young man had discovered within himself was this: he was a gifted public speaker, a *Redner.*

He was not a typical son of the land he had been born in; not in his elective affinities, not in his temperament or even in his appearance. In that part of Upper Austria there is a sun-bleached toughness in the faces of the people: a subalpine race, taciturn, suspicious of authority, conservative in their traditionalism, combative but not revolutionary. But Hitler was very far from being a traditionalist or a conservative. He was that frighteningly modern phenomenon, the revolutionary nationalist. "I was a nationalist; but I was not a patriot," he wrote. That distinction, that difference between nationalism and patriotism, is often obscured in our modern usage. The two terms are often used interchangeably. Yet "patriotism" is an old English word, while "nationalism" is a relatively new one, appearing first in the 1840s. The difference between patriots and nationalists has marked some of the deepest rifts in the history of the twentieth century. Patriotism is traditionalist, deeply rooted, introverted and defensive; nationalism is populist, extroverted, aggressive and ideological. Adolf Hitler chose to uproot himself from his family and his homeland. He wanted to identify himself with Germany, and he did.

Consequently Hitler did not have an identity problem. But an increasing number of Austrians did. The political manifestation of Austrian nationalism was born in the same decade in which he was born—among other things, in the form of Georg von Schönerer's Pan-German party, which strove for the union of Austria with Germany and, implicitly, for the dissolution of the traditional Habsburg monarchical state. Thereafter a paradoxical linguistic usage came into being. *Ein Nationaler,* a nationalist, in Austria was someone who wished to see the abrogation of an independent Austria and of a distinct Austrian nationality, in favor of their absorption into a German *Volk* and state. When in 1918 the Habsburg monarchy ceased to exist and Austria remained a truncated state, many Austrians thought that such a small country was not viable. Not every

Austrian who thought so was a Nazi; conversely there were Nazis who wanted to maintain some kind of separate Austrian identity. Especially after Hitler had risen to power in Germany, a difference emerged among the Austrian people, between patriots who struggled to maintain the independence of Austria, and nationalists who fought for its union with the Third Reich. Added to this division between themselves there was a split-mindedness within themselves. The last Austrian chancellor who tried to maintain the independence of Austria from the Third Reich felt compelled to say that he stood for a "German and Catholic" Austria. After Hitler had marched into Austria, he chose to sanctify the union of Germany and Austria with a plebiscite. On 10 April 1938 only 5 people out of nearly 3,600 voted against Hitler in Braunau.

That was the year of his greatest and most convincing political triumphs. He was the greatest revolutionary of the twentieth century, whose entire political career was a refutation of Marx. In that year Simone Weil wrote this refutation of Marx: "It is not religion, it is revolution that is the opium of the people"—words fitting Hitler all too well.

Twenty miles to the south, in the small village of St. Radegund, only one man voted against Hitler. This was Franz Jägerstätter, a Catholic peasant, the father of a young family. More than fifty years later few people in Braunau wish to remember Hitler. Few among them know anything about Jägerstätter. But the number of those who know about him seems to grow every year. Earlier I said that Hitler may have been the greatest revolutionary of the twentieth century. But Jägerstätter was a revolutionary too—in the prophetic sense in which the great French Catholic poet and visionary Charles Péguy wrote, even before the First World War: "The true revolutionaries of the twentieth century will be the fathers of Christian families." In this sense the true revolutionary was Jägerstätter, not Hitler.

The village of St. Radegund is on the ledge of a low hill, away from the road running from Braunau to Salzburg. I drove there on a cold spring day. When the clouds tore away from the sun, the fields glistened in the cool green colors of a northern spring. Except for a small tractor here and there and the distant shapes of modern factories toward the horizon, the scene was reminiscent of a Europe fifty or more years ago. I saw a few women working in the fields, some of them (this is very rare in Europe now) in their traditional peasant clothes. Because of an enforced detour at Oster-miething where a crew was laying pipes, St. Radegund was not easy to find. Half an hour later I felt the errant motorist's customary sensation of relief as I saw the road sign for St. Radegund, below which I was pleased to see another marker: GRAB JÄGERSTÄTTER—*Jägerstätter's grave.*

St. Radegund was empty. There was silence everywhere. From some-where I heard the lowing of an energetic cow. After a few hapless minutes, across the road I espied a man who showed me the way to the little church in a hollow, against the wall of which lies Jägerstätter's grave. He was guillotined in Brandenburg Prison on August 9, 1943.

He had refused to serve in the German army; not because he was a pacifist, not because he was an Austrian patriot, but because of his Catho-lic convictions. This war, Hitler and National Socialism were causes of evil; he said as much to the military court, and in what he wrote both before and during his imprisonment. That was the last station in the pilgrimage of his otherwise unremarkable life. Franz Jägerstätter was the son of a servant girl who could not marry his father. Both were too poor for that—the unwritten law among the Upper Austrian peasantry at that time. His grandmother cared for the boy. Two years later a better situated peasant married his mother. He adopted Franz, giving him his name, Jägerstätter. That was near the end of the First World War. Franz Jägerstät-ter's formative years followed in a poverty-stricken land. He was a hard worker, respected in the village where he was the first to acquire a motor-cycle, a handsome young peasant, rambunctious and tough, with a taste for merrymaking. At the age of twenty-six he sired an illegitimate daughter. Three years later he married another young woman. They had three daugh-ters. It was a happy marriage. But trouble came between them in the spring of 1938 when he said that he would not vote for the Anschluss. Afraid of the consequences, his wife turned against him. He was deeply hurt. In time she learned not to question his convictions again.

The faith and goodness of his grandmother had left an impression on him; but he had not been very religious in his early youth. Sometime between 1933 and 1936 his religion had deepened. After his twenty-sixth year the meaning of his faith became a growing concern in his mind. The evidence is in some of his letters to his godson and in some of his own notes from his reading of the Gospels, recently published by his biographer. They are extraordinary because of their simplicity, purity and insight. They are untouched by the neo-baroque language and the otherworldly spirituality of much of the Austrian religious literature of his time. They concern the responsibilities of a believing Catholic in this world. For Franz Jägerstätter these responsibilities included his recognition of the dangers of National Socialism, and the consequent duty to oppose it.

This was not easy for him. In an important sense he was alone among his people. In 1931 the Nazi votes in Braunau had doubled. In 1933 an entry in the parish chronicle of Ostermiething reads: "Our people are devoured [ganz durchfressen] *by their enthusiasm for National Socialism, their inspiration for Austria about zero." In 1935 Braunau declared Adolf Hitler its honorary citizen, which was then countermanded by the government of Austria. Political parties had been outlawed but there were many illegal Nazi party members (though not in St. Radegund, where Jägerstätter was offered the post of mayor in March 1938, which he refused).*

His loneliness weighed upon him in another important way. The guidance that he received from his Church was often neither clear nor strong. He could draw sustenance from certain allocutions: until 1938 the Austrian hierarchy supported the Catholic Dollfuss and Schuschnigg governments against the Nazis; there was Pope Pius XI's encyclical Mit brennender Sorge *in 1937 condemning Nazi racism, which Jägerstätter would often reread and cite; and the bishop of his diocese, Gföllner of Linz, was an old traditionalist who said that a Catholic cannot be a Nazi and that was that. But on March 27, 1938, a pastoral letter issued by the entire Austrian hierarchy and read at every Mass welcomed the union with Germany, praised National Socialism and told the Catholic people of Austria that it was their duty to vote for Hitler. There were Austrian bishops (not Gföllner) who had been sympathetic to the nationalist-folkish persuasion; many others were unwilling to stand in the way of enthusiastic popular sentiment; and perhaps especially significant, in retrospect, are those passages of that pastoral letter which declared the bishops' trust in the compatibility of Catholicism and National Socialism: "We joyfully recognize what the National Socialist movement has achieved . . . [and] that through the National Socialist movement the danger of destructive and godless Bolshevism is being defeated." Jägerstätter came back to this pastoral often. "The Church in Austria allowed itself to become a prisoner," he wrote. Nor could he have gained sustenance from the allocutions of the bishops of Germany. In 1939 Cardinal Bertram of Breslau said: "Heil Hitler: that is valid for this world. Praised be Jesus Christ: that is the tie between earth and heaven." No neater formula could be imagined. In April 1940 Hitler answered the congratulations tendered him by the German Bishops' Conference on his fifty-first birthday: "I am especially pleased by your expression of your conviction that the efforts of the Catholic Church to maintain the Christian character of the German people are not opposed to the program of the National Socialist party."*

Jägerstätter was not completely alone. In St. Radegund the priest, Father Karobath, was Jägerstätter's close friend. He was arrested briefly in 1940. Several of the priests of the Ostermiething parish were taken away by the Gestapo. In the Innviertel, indeed in Upper Austria, more priests were imprisoned or executed during the war than in any of the other provinces of Austria. In 1939 a Gestapo official told the pastor of the Braunau cathedral church: "In the Braunau district [to which St. Radegund belonged] we're getting nowhere." There was only one convinced Nazi sympathizer among the clergy, Father Weeser-Krell, a native of Germany, who tried everything to become the pastor of that church in Hitler's birthplace; but Bishop Gföllner refused to appoint him. In 1941 the resident pastor, Father Ludwig (in 1989 he was still alive, in his late eighties), was arrested by the police. When Germany invaded Russia, Hitler and his government expected Catholics to support his "crusade" against atheistic Bolshevism. No matter how wrong the ideas and practices of Communism, Jägerstätter said, this was but another invasion wrought upon innocent people. There was nothing in the practices and doctrines of National Socialism that was preferable to those of Communism.

He wrote down his thoughts in copybooks at home, and spoke about them when the occasion arose, among his family and friends. It is to the credit of the St. Radegunders that he was never denounced to the police. Yet many of his neighbors were of two minds about him. The village men were doing their duty to the fatherland, serving in the army; Jägerstätter was not and said that he would not do so. His wife no longer questioned his convictions and his choice. His mother did, and was bitter against her daughter-in-law for failing to support her. His parish priest told him that he was not wrong when following his convictions. The two of them asked for an audience with the new bishop of Linz, Fliesser (Gföllner had died in 1941). He tried to dissuade Jägerstätter: it would be better for everyone concerned if he obeyed the order to serve in the army, he said.

In March 1943 Jägerstätter was called up. He went to the provincial military center and stated his refusal to serve. He knew where this would lead in the end. But in the prison in Linz doubts beset him. There was his responsibility to his family, to his wife—even though she did not ask him not to follow his conscience. There was the temptation to convince himself that what he was doing amounted to a choice of suicide, a mortal sin for a Catholic. By the time he was moved to a military prison in Berlin these tormenting thoughts had left him. His faith, his serenity, his concern for those other prisoners with whom he had some contact, impressed them. He wrote many letters to his wife, who was allowed to visit him once. He kept writing notes to himself. Among other things he wrote: "It is not given to the powers of this world to suppress the conscience of a single human being." And: "Whoever is ashamed of his faith shows that he knows not Jesus Christ." Jägerstätter was far from being a religious fanatic. It is natural for a true believer, and especially for a man condemned to death, to direct his thoughts to the world to come. Jägerstätter believed, and hoped, in the world to come; but even more he believed in a Christian's duties in this world. Many of his statements remind me of another of Hitler's martyrs, the Protestant pastor Dietrich Bonhoeffer, who wrote, also in prison and before his execution: "The way of Christ goes not from this world to God but from God to this world." Or of Simone Weil: "The object of our concern should not be the supernatural but the world. The supernatural is light itself: if we make an object of it we lower it." (She died in the same month Jägerstätter died.) Jägerstätter was beheaded on the ninth of August. That night the prison chaplain told two Austrian nuns that they must be proud of their countryman. "For the only time in my life I had met a saint," he said.

One year after the war Franziska Jägerstätter brought her husband's ashes back to St. Radegund. Father Karobath had returned to his pastorate. Some of the villagers did not know what to make of Jägerstätter's story. Many of their husbands and sons had fallen in faraway Russia; many of *them returned wounded or maimed. Centuries of tradition and custom had made them obey the call of their country's rulers. Why was Jägerstätter a special case? For some time the Austrian government rejected Franziska Jägerstätter's application for the standard pension of war widows: some bureaucrat declared that her husband had not been a soldier. For many years the widow and the priest were criticized by veterans and their relatives for honoring a man who had "abandoned" his fellow Austrians. Some of them said that Jägerstätter had "betrayed" his people. Sometime in the 1960s there came a gradual change. It had much to do with the growing up of a younger generation of people to whom the memories of comradeship in the war meant nothing, but also with the respect of the St. Radegunders for the widow who brought up her three orphaned daughters and managed their family farm in an exemplary way.*

An important part in the recognition of Jägerstätter was taken upon himself by an American. I first read about Jägerstätter more than thirty years ago, in an article by Gordon Zahn, who was a conscientious objector during the Second World War, a committed pacifist and adherent of Dorothy Day's Catholic Worker movement. He had read something about Jägerstätter and chose to follow it up. The result was a fine book, In Solitary Witness, *published in 1966—for a long time the only book about Jägerstätter. Many more documents and details have come to light since then; yet Zahn's book has stood the test of time well—as Jägerstätter's biographer, Dr. Erna Putz, told me. I found her in Ostermiething, in the parish house (where she is the pastor's helper, busy with, among other things, bringing up two small Vietnamese children of the boat people), an hour or so after my solitary visit to St. Radegund.*

The little white church of St. Radegund is lovely, perhaps remarkably so even in this part of Austria where onion-domed parish churches abound. I walked down to it on an alley of cobblestones. The church (founded in 1422) was open but empty. As in many other places of the world, in Austria there are now not enough priests to go around; the Mass is said and the other sacraments administered by the pastor who comes over from Ostermiething. Against the white wall of the church lies Franz Jägerstätter's grave. It has no marker except for the crucifix above it. But there is a single bronze tablet set in the church wall to the left of it. I translate its words from the German:

†

THANKS BE TO GOD FOR JÄGERSTÄTTER!
HE KNEW THAT ALL OF US ARE BROTHERS
AND THAT CHRIST'S COMMAND IS MEANT
FOR ALL OF US. HE DID NOT DIE IN VAIN!
MAY THE GREAT LOVE OF GOD
AND THAT OF HIS SON JESUS CHRIST
FILL THE HEARTS OF ALL PEOPLE!
MAY THIS GREAT LOVE MOVE THROUGH
THE WORLD, SO THAT THE PEACE OF GOD
ENTER INTO THE HEARTS OF ALL MEN. AMEN.
A BROTHER IN CHRIST
Missoula, Montana, U.S.A.
9 August 1968

I felt a sense of pride being an American.

I went back into the church. There was a guestbook of sorts, open near the entrance. It was filled with the handwriting of people from far away: Irish, English, Poles, Hungarians, Rumanians and many, many Germans. I copied only one of the entries. "I was a German soldier. I know now that Franz Jägerstätter was the one who did his duty to our people." That afternoon in Ostermiething Erna Putz told me that all kinds of people came to St. Radegund every ninth of August, the anniversary of the martyrdom. On that day there is a pilgrimage walk from St. Radegund to the church in Ostermiething. This has become, she said, a local tradition now—one hundred years after Adolf Hitler was born. I thought of those few flowers on Hitler's parents' grave in Leonding and of the somber fact that, alone among the historical figures of this century, Hitler had no grave. On that cold March day in St. Radegund, Franz Jägerstätter's grave was covered with fresh flowers.

Budapest Resurrected

(1989)

One of the small pleasures of life is unpacking—I mean physical, not mental unpacking, the latter often being an undertaking of dubious merit. What I have in mind is the emptying of one's suitcase in a good hotel: in a cool room, spacious and light, with plenty of discoverable drawers and hangers, with a bathroom gleaming white and enough shelf space for the bottles, creams, lotions, and salves of a middle-aged movie actress. To such a place I repair to regain my physical balance after long hours of traveling. There, stretching out in the tub, I read some of the pamphlets extracted from the big leatherette folder of the hotel. This time, in Budapest, most of it is in perfect English, but some of the items are a little disconcerting. The viscous wash of global public relations now seeps in, as this page from one pamphlet illustrates:

FROM OUR GUEST'S BOOK. [Yes, the apostrophe is misplaced.]

"With many thanks for a most comfortable and pleasant stay in Duna Inter-Continental and for a wonderful first visit to Budapest."—DAVID ROCKEFELLER

"Had a beautiful stay. Everyone was beautiful."—ELLA FITZGERALD

"Thank you for your great hospitality. We are enjoying our stay here immensely. Thank you again."—RICHARD BURTON and ELIZABETH TAYLOR

"It has been an interesting stay."—SYLVESTER STALLONE

I'll say.

It is hot, on a Sunday afternoon, but within this very first hour of my return to Budapest I sense the vibration of change in the air. Budapest is at another turning point in its history: not only a milestone, a turning point.

My room has a picture window and a balcony. As is the custom of hotels everywhere, the curtains have been pulled closed. Impatiently, I yank them back, open the glass door, walk out on the balcony. And there is the incomparable sight of Budapest, the thing for which it is famous. The entrepreneurs and the planners of modern Budapest know this. It is why every window of the new grand hotels has a river view. I write "new" because none of these hotels is more than twenty years old. Every one of the former grand hotels of Budapest was burned out during the siege of the city in January 1945.

A white bridge arches over a great green river. (The Danube: It is not, and has never been, blue.) Immediately at the Buda bridgehead rises the rocky mount of Gellért Hill, with its flat pancake of a citadel on the top. That backdrop—and the curve of the river with a glimpse of the iron fretwork of the next bridge downstream—is almost too theatrical. Less theatrical but more meaningful, at least to this native, is the row of stately buildings on the Pest side, leading to the bridgehead, with an eighteenth-century church wedged in among them. I am gripped by the realization that these things still exist, that they have not changed, or at least not much, after a world war, after a revolution, after a siege in which every one of the bridges, like the hotels before them, was destroyed.

But the city has been rebuilt. And standing on my balcony, I am startled by the crowds of people in the Inner City: by their size and by their bustle. They are not elegant, but they seem astonishingly young and energetic; there is little of the Eastern European grimness about the scene. I saw this during other visits to Budapest over the last fifteen years. It is even more in evidence now, since Budapest is in the midst of a democratic revolution—in the proper and original sense of that word.

Unlike in Rumania, its neighbor to the east, there have been no barricades in the streets, no clashes of crowds and armed police, and few signs of political agitation on the surface. But a *revolution*—that is, a turning of a wheel—has occurred. After more than forty years, communism—not only its appeal (if that ever existed) but also its force and the prestige of its institutions—is largely gone.

Parliament, in October, abolished the People's Republic of Hungary and adopted a constitution of the new Republic of Hungary, which, in one stroke, ended Communist rule. "All power," states the preamble, "belongs to the people." Earlier in the same month, the Party itself renounced Marxism and renamed itself the Hungarian Socialist Party. Now the very word *communist* is not merely abhorred by the people, it is rejected by the Party itself, as if this had been nothing but an unfortunate episode in the history of this city and is now passing away fast.

The main reason for this is that communism did not come to Hungary through a domestic revolt or even a coup d'état; it was imposed by the Russian army. That made everything Russian unpopular. Decades of Russian rule has left the culture of my native country largely untouched. Russian fashions have been nonexistent, Russian customs ignored, Russian art and Russian writing, both new and old, unpopular and left unread. Of course, this was but one side of the coin. The other side was the sovereign reality: The Russians were still the masters of the Hungarian state. But this is no longer so. The cultural (and ideological) independence of Hungary is an accomplished fact, and the political independence of Hungary is developing fast.

"I'd like to take a picture of a Russian soldier," an American woman says in the hotel hall. Easier said than done. Russian soldiers appear on the streets of Budapest very seldom. Many of the units have already left Hungary. In a way, Hungary can be seen as a bridge between East and West—certainly the migration of East Germans to the West via Hungary suggested this. But Hungary does not merely connect the East to the West. Compared with its eastern neighbors (the Soviet Union, Rumania), Hungary belongs to the West.

This is true of Budapest itself. Somehow, in no matter what language, the very sound of that name evokes something of its slightly exotic, Central European character. *BU-da-pesht,* say Hungarians, in the forever dactylic mode of the Magyar language. *Bu-da-PEST*—say the anapestic Germans and the French. (There is even a difference between the English and the American pronunciations: *Byudapest,* the English are wont to say.) At any rate, Budapest is no longer an exotic place-name. In the imagination of all kinds of people, its image accords with its place within Europe and its recent history.

Within the city itself, the seven great bridges do more than connect. They embrace the river between Buda and Pest. The two did not become one city until 1872. For a long time their characters were different—even, at times, inimical. As late as eighty years ago, Buda was sparsely inhabited, partly agricultural, Catholic, with a considerable German-speaking population, conservative; Pest was becoming industrial, not only Catholic but also Protestant, partly Jewish, Magyar, and radical. In Pest, only one of the more radical Hungarian political figures (Táncsics) spoke up against the union of the two towns. But he was almost alone. People in Buda grumbled, but they went along. Most of these differences have now disappeared. For the first time the populations of Buda and Pest are nearly the same. But the physical differences remain. Pest is a vast flat sea of houses, with patches of greenery here and there, the largest of these being the City Park, handsome in spots but nothing like the Bois de Boulogne in Paris; rather, it is dusty and municipal, like El Retiro in Madrid. In Buda the hills march straight up from the Danube; there are villas on their slopes and behind them real mountains still within the city limits.

There is one more thing: The Danube divides Budapest in the middle. It flows through the city, unlike in Vienna (or Belgrade), where the majority of the buildings are on one side of the river. That contrast between Buda and Pest, together with the bridges, forms the incomparable cityscape of Budapest. The odd thing is that without the bridges, without their embracement, the scene would not be the same. The bridges not only provided the municipal unity of the city, but they have created the unity of its panorama—more so than the pretty bridges across the Seine, or the monumental bridges of New York.

I look at the white, modern Elizabeth Bridge, which is the second, not the first, of the finest bridges (the first being the neo-classical Chain Bridge, rebuilt in 1949 exactly as it was in 1849). I take a deep breath of satisfaction thinking that eighty years ago, when Budapest was at its zenith, someone standing on a balcony at the same place (where the Hotel Carlton had then stood) would have seen the very same scene, the very same backdrop, the very same buildings. What would have surprised him is the traffic. Thousands of automobiles scurry across the bridge, small metallic insects speeding in an endless stream, day and night. Budapest, in the throes of democratic transformation, is all too frequently in the throes of enormous traffic jams.

It was eighty-seven years ago, in 1902, that the original Elizabeth Bridge was opened, during the great Budapest building boom that included not only thousands of houses but also a score of grand public buildings, a rebuilt royal palace, and what was then the largest parliament building of the world. That was when Budapest first became chic. More than a hundred thousand foreign visitors came to Budapest in that year. In 1989 the number of visitors to Hungary was more than 11 million; that is, at least one tourist for every Hungarian. At the beginning of this century the reputation of Budapest sprang from the attraction of a hardly known city that was both beautiful and modern. Foreign visitors were astounded to find first-class hotels, electric streetcars, a modern subway, smart shops, well-dressed men and women, an elegant bustle: For that was the noon hour of Budapest, when summer galloped on its streets and in its people's hearts.

But then came the First World War, and by 1920 Budapest had become dusty, dirty, dark. The Treaty of Trianon mutilated Hungary: Two-thirds of the territories of the old Hungarian kingdom were lost, and millions of Hungarians were constrained to live within the boundaries of its successor states—Rumania, Czechoslovakia, Yugoslavia, and Austria. The political, social, and economic consequences of these upheavals were enormous, and some people thought that such a dwarfed Hungary would not be viable at all. But then the Hungarian willingness to live came back again; and, too, the Budapest chic. Now it was a mixture of the old and the new. Its people were charmed by the neo-Baroque atmosphere of the city; by the old aristocratic houses on Castle Hill (largely ignored by visitors thirty years before), as well as by the jewel-box interior of the small Budapest Ritz; by the feudal remnants of the masculine manners of the men and by the silver-lamé smartness of the beautiful women of Budapest; by the leafy open-air restaurants of Buda, as well as by the dazzling nightclubs of Pest.

Ten years later Budapest was destroyed. For two months the largest armies of the Second World War, the German and the Russian, fought it out in the city's streets, houses, cellars. Most of the historic buildings were gutted and burned out. Not more than twenty-six of every hundred buildings remained intact. Then came the night of a fully sovietized

Communist rule, and the Iron Curtain. In 1950, there were fewer visitors to Budapest than in 1900, and hardly any from Western Europe and the United States.

But after 1960 the rebuilding began, and Budapest has, for the third time, become chic. This chic—a product of mass tourism—is different. The tourists of 1990 are different. Many of them trudging through the halls of the expensive hotels wearing shorts and sandals would have been waved away by the hall porters of a different era. But that is, of course, a worldwide phenomenon. What remains particular are the attractions of Budapest now. And the main feature of the attractions consists of their old-fashionedness—the very reverse of what had brought people to "modern" Budapest eighty years ago.

One element of this is the architecture. Budapest, and certainly Pest, is not an old city. On the Pest side the only medieval remnants are the foundations of the Inner City Church (which was almost razed ninety years ago, when it seemed to block the roadway leading to the Elizabeth Bridge). Most of the houses were built during the eclectic period of architecture between 1870 and 1920. Beyond their occasional interest as Art Nouveau decoration, they are the massive presences of a bourgeois past for which so many people in Europe (and now also in the United States) have developed a kind of nostalgia. The German and Austrian visitors are particularly attuned to this, coming from their newly built cities; their favorite hotel is the Gellért, a huge monumental pile built just before the First World War. Its cavernous rooms and halls, its ceramic facades and secessionist decor remind them—sometimes wrongly—of the Austro-Hungarian epoch before 1914.

Another attraction is what are, nowadays, old-fashioned comforts. The best places—restaurants, hotels, cafés—have not much of the chic of bygone days. But they are not yet standardized. The service in them is reminiscent of decades past, for the simple reason that tourism is a source of profitable employment, so in the better hotels and restaurants visitors find more porters and waiters and busboys than in the West. This will not last long, but there it is.

For many people, the favorable exchange rate alone is sufficient to avail themselves of small luxuries in the best of the hotels and in the restaurants. This brings me to a perhaps idiosyncratic but, I believe, honest disquisition about Hungarian cooking. I am deeply, stomachically, devoted to it. But I also know that the cuisine of Hungary is not one of the prime cuisines of the world. It is, at its best, in the first rank of second-class national cuisines—that is, ranking below the French and the North Italian, though as good as the Viennese. That, too, is a relatively recent development. It was less than a hundred years ago that French and Viennese influences began to vary and enrich Budapest—Budapest, even more than provincial Hungarian—cooking. Then the reputation of the Budapest restaurants began to spread. A very considerable part of that development is attributable to a grand bourgeois Hungarian family of restaurateurs, the Gundels. Their celebrated restaurant still exists but, alas, bearing their name only.* That delicate harmony of Gallic refinement with Hungarian solidity of food is no longer extant. There are, instead, strenuous efforts to decorate the rich Hungarian dishes with all kinds of accoutrements. But the result is, at best, a culinary cohabitation instead of a good marriage. The best dishes in Budapest may still be found in small, stuffy restaurants, unabashedly Hungarian in their fare: paprika-spicy, strong, pleasantly coarse, and truly filling.

To find all this, however, travelers must leave their hotel enclaves, for the true Budapest is not easy to find. As an example, the newsstand of my hotel had every American and Western paper but no Hungarian one. To buy a paper I had to go out and find a news kiosk in a public square. I was irritated and asked the concierge why this was so. The answer was disconcerting: "If we stocked these papers we could not stop all kinds of people coming in here." This is but one illustration that there are two Budapests now—the Budapest of the tourists and the Budapest of its people. Nine out of ten of the latter will not enter those first-class hotels and restaurants, not because they are not allowed in but because they cannot afford them. The exceptions are those friends and relatives who come to visit a returning Hungarian, such as myself, in his air-conditioned room or in the wood-paneled public rooms of those hotels. They are entering something like a foreign enclave. The economic distress in

*1994. Great improvement! Gundel has been bought and beautifully refurbished and brought back to very high standards by the Hungarian-American restaurateur George Lang. It is now one of the cultural—and not merely culinary—monuments of Budapest, indeed, of Central Europe.

Hungary is not as bad as that in Poland, but it exists. On the other hand, the incomparable panache and verve of my native people are still in existence: so many of them will afford things that they logically, financially, arithmetically cannot afford. But life in Budapest has never been governed by logic.

So, to get the sense of Budapest, leave the main thoroughfares and amble through some of the streets immediately behind them. There, in the Inner City, and in the old Buda streets, you will feel and smell some things that are peculiar to it. There are those monumental circa-1900 apartment houses, protective of closely guarded lives. Behind their heavily curtained windows one may glimpse the presence of a bourgeois existence—no matter how cramped—with its covers and carpets and pictures and many, many bookcases, glimpse family lives that survived wars and tyrannies and communism. So much of the old Budapest life has gone, and so much has, strangely and surprisingly, remained. Even some of that Budapest chic: the chic that is a result not only of sophisticated taste but also of sophisticated judgment, of people as well as of things, the knowledge of the unavoidable connection of image with reality, including a bittersweet and self-deprecating sense of humor. While masculine elegance has become very rare, the feminine elegance that once marked the women of Budapest is still there. They know where they are going, they know how they ought to look, and they know what they are looking for.

I left Budapest forty-four years ago, and my tastes (including my use of my native language) are even older than that, anchored—as are my past, my youth, and my memories—in a Budapest and a Hungary that was still half feudal. And I am amazed how the eyes of my friends of a younger and very different generation, perhaps especially those of the women, light up when I, after a few drinks, allow myself to slip into a stream of consciousness of sometimes frivolous reminiscences, mentioning an ironic bon mot from the past, recalling a smart nightspot, the name or the place of *the* tailor or *the* dressmaker of this or that time, the eccentricities of a long-departed snob, or the customs of clubbable people, all gone forever.

Two days before my departure I am to meet a woman whom I had last seen forty-four years ago and whom I had first met fifty-one years ago in a dancing class. She was beautiful then, and I (like more than one of my classmates) was a little bit in love with her. Now she is sixty-six, widowed three times, having lived through the worst of times, and working in an office still. I get her telephone number from a friend in New York. She will pick me up with her car at the hotel entrance Sunday noon; we will drive out of the city, to lunch in a country tavern. How shall we recognize each other? I ask her on the phone. "I will wear a dark suit and a green tie," I say. "I haven't," she says, "yet made up my mind what I'm going to wear."

Back and Forth from Home

(1990)

Sometimes after dinner I walk out to the grassy slope beyond our terrace. At those moments the charm of the present is inseparable from a deeply satisfying sense of the past, because it is good to know that nearly everything I now see is still the same landscape that the American ancestors of my children saw 50, 100, 150, 200 years ago. The sense of the future: I am afraid of it.

Will my children inherit this landscape? One hundred or 150 years ago our ancestors hoped that the railroad or the telegraph or the new highway would come close to where they were living, the sooner the better. In our time the news that a new highway or a new pipeline or a new development or a new shopping mall is coming close puts fear and loathing in our hearts.

I am not alone in this. Most of my neighbors feel the same. That is why, for the past 20 years or more, I have served on the Schuylkill Township Planning Commission. Each month my colleagues and I spend a long evening poring over the plans of subdivisions and of developers that we may or may not recommend to the supervisors. All of our discussions are constrained by the technical and legal categories of definitions— matters, however, that ever so often are thick cloaks thrown over deeper, personal, political divisions, divisions of differing views of the world. Most of us know how often development amounts not to opening up but to closing in, how it means the eager spreading of cement and the indifferent razing of the land. We know how often construction means destruction— not only of trees and meadows but of certain ways of life. "Are you against progress?" people sometimes ask me. I tell them that the time has surely come to rethink the meaning of that word.

I have been living in this township and on this piece of land for 37 years. But I am not a native American. I came here from my native country, Hungary, 44 years ago, fleeing the imposition of a communist regime by the Russians. I thought then that this would last at least 50 years. But history is unpredictable. I did not know then how its dissolution would happen. That it would happen I began to see many years ago. Yet I have not been involved in emigré politics, or in Central European academics.

At the same time I have kept close to a few old, trusted friends. One of them is an old priest, Monsignor Béla Varga, a leader of the pre-war democratic Small Holders' Party (of which I was a youthful member 47 years ago). He was the last chairman of the freely elected Hungarian Parliament and he fled Hungary 43 years ago. He is now 87 years old and in frail health, the chaplain of a convent in New York, where I go to see him every time I am in that city.

And now came another, unpredictable coincidence. Elections were held in Hungary this spring. The largest party would form the new government; their candidate for prime minister is the son of Monsignor Varga's ally and friend during the war, when both of them did a heroic job saving and protecting Polish refugees, escaped French prisoners of war and many Jews from the Nazis; and the candidate for the new foreign minister is a historian friend of mine. The Monsignor and I followed developments in Hungary, though not very closely. From 4,000 miles away we wished them luck.

And then, one day in April, the routine of our lives changed. Things were speeding up. I was at the Planning Commission meeting when Béla called my wife. The new, freely elected Parliament would meet on the 2nd of May. Its leaders wanted him—and me—to be there. What follows is a necessarily breathless (though perhaps not superficial) account of those days and of my thoughts in diary form.

APRIL 18TH, WEDNESDAY. Fairly long Planning Commission meeting. This developer (to whom I spoke on the phone yesterday) is unusually eager to push his development through. Try to pin him down on how much of the woodland he will destroy. This is not easy. Details to be attended to: Trees with a diameter exceeding 6 inches must be shown on his plan. Two of the building setbacks on each plot missing. Ingress and egress of plotted driveways; PennDOT approval required. Behind these things looms the menacing shadow of Big Brother, i.e. the Valley Forge Sewer Authority, not to speak of the restive steamroller of the Fernley tract. The latter is gathering strength before the bulldozers are ready to roar.

APRIL 19TH, THURSDAY. Béla calls from New York. Antall (the coming prime minister), Géza (the coming foreign minister) call from Budapest. They implore Béla to come and speak. Béla still reluctant. Doctor says he can go, provided that fatigue is kept to a minimum and all medications properly taken. He asks me to help with his speech. He says that I must come with him. Am reluctant—have millions of things to do here—but Stephanie says, "If he says so, you must." Details to be attended to: must get airline seat next to him. Hungarian visa (not easy: cannot go up to consulate in New York). Write and xerox circular letter to a few friends in Budapest. Have no idea where I'm going to stay once I'm there.

APRIL 28TH, SATURDAY. Wake up with a hangover. Reason: drank a bottle of champagne last night, in order to celebrate first harvest and glorious consumption of white—yes, white—asparagus spears cut last afternoon, something that I tried to grow for 19 years in vain. (White asparagus *is* green asparagus, except that it must be planted much deeper. Asparagus expert told me it won't work, white asparagus is a different strain. Expert was wrong.) I talk to R. and T. about coming supervisors' meeting on Wednesday, May 2nd. I'll be in Budapest then, at the first meeting of the new Parliament of Hungary. Plenty of problems at both meetings. Here: Big Brother, i.e. the Sewer Authority, at it again, with its local allies who long to develop, i.e. sewer, the entire township, pouring concrete over what's left of open space. There: Big Brother, i.e. the Soviet Union, largely gone, but plenty of ambitious politicians wishing to pour rhetoric over what's left of open space in Hungarian minds.

First day of historic journey, I take the train to New York, to Béla's convent apartment. Nuns stand on the steps, with tears in their eyes, waving goodbye. Limousine to America's number one concentration camp, i.e. Kennedy Airport. Thought occurs to me that I was in a sort of concentration camp in Hungary 46 years ago. Fellow inmates preferable to mob at Kennedy.

APRIL 29TH, SUNDAY. Arrival very moving. Bright windy morning; Béla comes slowly down the steps, leaning heavily on his cane. Government delegation on tarmac, with flowers, also Béla's old sister. His return to his homeland after 43 years. I keep back, with tears in my eyes. Must say that this way of arriving is agreeable. No customs, no passport examination, limousines waiting for us at the plane. Antall arranged that Béla and I will stay in a government house. We drive into Budapest, the industrial suburbs giving way to streets lined with those old, sooty apartment buildings, with their smoky, vinegary smell. We cross the Danube. Government House is high up in the Buda hills (not far from where my grandparents' villa was, 47 years ago). Now my big job begins—fending off people from this old priest, after this wearisome journey. I wave a reporter away, unsuccessfully. Turns out to be editor of a newspaper, to whom an interview *was* promised. So Béla sits on an uncomfortable sofa, answering silly questions. ("What did you think when you first saw a Hungarian flag?" Plenty of Hungarian flags in the United States. The township reporter of *The Evening Phoenix* much more intelligent.)

Staff of Government House more than helpful. They are evidently personnel of previous communist government, probably including former secret policemen, all worried about their jobs now. After we settle Béla down, I ask them to call a taxi for me. "Sir," they say, "there is a car and a driver and a bodyguard at your disposal here." Car at my disposal is a Lada (Russian Fiat), bodyguard a policeman in civvies for whom proper adjective is "burly." (There are clichés that *are* true.) Not knowing where I'll stay, I had telephoned I. to get me a hotel room, also told her that I'll come straight to her apartment. The streets leading down to the city are green and gold with all the trees in leaf. I tip the driver and tell him not to bother to come back for me, I'll just take a cab. I.'s small apartment, in which she survived more than three decades of communism, is a perfect combination of elegance and coziness. (Not *House and Garden* stuff.) *That* kind of survival is what is best about Hungary and Hungarians. Later that day I meet an American diplomat. "Tell me one thing," he asks. "Why is it that every Hungarian I meet is deeply pessimistic? But at the same time they enjoy life so much." That is a very intelligent question. Finally I come up with an answer. "I can't tell you *why*. I can only tell you *how*."

Back to Government House again. Large, semi-palatial, furnishings rather unbeautiful. Béla rests through the long afternoon. Telephone keeps ringing without cease. Staff keeps telling me that they will serve food and drinks for us, whatever and whenever we like. After all, only a few guests in the building. When George Bush came to Budapest last July (for a single day), his staff consisted of at least 500 people. (Is this what the Republicans mean when they say they are against Big Government?)

At night descend to town again. Dinner with I. and L. We are told about great economic distress in Hungary, but the restaurants are crowded. I fought jet lag all day and now take a sleeping pill and collapse into bed. I address a request to the former secret policemen: breakfast in my room, at 8 o'clock, please.

APRIL 30TH, MONDAY. I am awakened as huge breakfast arrives on a huge tray at 7:59:60. I had thrown off all my sheets and find myself naked on top of bed. (It is *not* always wonderful to have obsequious servants.) I dress and walk out on terrace, heavy smell of lilacs in the air. Between the trees the roofs and towers of the city, four miles away, scintillating in the sun. Garden not too well kept. Thoughts of all of the mowing I'll have to do when I return home. Staff, who had no idea who I was when I arrived (perhaps American secret policeman, accompanying the main guest?), now have been told by someone to call me "Professor." (Well, I've known many an American professor working for the CIA.) Read Hungarian newspapers, find them quite good. One cartoon worthy of the—old— *New Yorker.* Farms in Hungary were collectivized by communists, but through the years peasants have done rather well, everyone doing his own thing in those collectives. Cartoon shows well-dressed couple, in well-furnished apartment, with large TV, VCR, lots of furniture. Man reading the paper, turning with a worried face to his wife: "They are returning our land to us. What are we going to do?"

At night dinner at apartment of my friend, the coming foreign minister. Could not send flowers to his wife, since all shops closed, this being a holiday, the eve of May First. (Will it remain a holiday?) Dinner party consists of many of his friends, some of them future ambassadors and ambassadresses. Am impressed with some of them. I drink less than usual, to E.'s considerable surprise. Am flattered to hear that almost all of them know me, having read my articles and books published in America and England. Does not happen in Philadelphia or Phoenixville, but perhaps no great loss. Cannot find a taxi, but walk through the warm liquid midnight air to the Intercontinental Hotel, its doorway still crowded with loud—very loud—Germans. I say something to the doorman in Hungarian and get a taxi ahead of the Germans. Great improvement, this: not so long ago it was better to speak English if you wanted to arrange something in Budapest. Suggests a rise of national self-confidence, without which most political changes turn out to be meaningless.

MAY 1ST, TUESDAY. Hurried call from superintendent of Parliament Building, to look over and arrange Béla's arrival, seating and speech tomorrow. This superintendent is an excellent man. The building is splendidly refurbished. I am touched by a sense of historical continuity: the intaglioed woodwork, the 1900 lettering, the frescoes, the heavy, gleaming brass ashtrays set into the windowsills of the corridors for the convenience of the honorable members. The Parliament Building has 24 gates. Béla will arrive at Gate Six, from where the walk is shortest and there is an elevator close to the entrance. Then we will rest in a chamber and have coffee and refreshments; and then through the high, Gothic-eaved corridors into the main chamber. Below the rostrum are the red velvet armchairs of the government ministers. Will Béla speak from there? For there *is* a microphone at that place. Or will he be able to mount the rostrum? Well, yes: It is only eight steps, and has a strong brass railing. But there is no place there for him to sit. And now the superintendent produces a standing desktop that will be perfect; Béla can lean on it as he holds his speech in his old, lovable, trembling hands. *That* is how it will be.

This was the largest parliament building in the world when it was finally completed in 1901. Now I am playing a part in it, as I am playing a small part in the government of Schuylkill Township, which has one of the smallest township buildings in Chester County, surely bereft of intaglio, scagliola, marble and red velvet. Now—without so wanting—I am involved in politics here, too. There are pressures on us to do this or that with the speech, to add this or that to it. The pressures involve the historical prospects of an entire nation, of my native country Hungary. It is surely different from my involvement in the Comprehensive Plan of Schuylkill Township, Chester County, Pennsylvania. Now I am involved in the phrasing of summary judgments on previous centuries, on an entire nation's relationship with Europe and with the Russian empire, with allusions to some of the deep differences and fissures within the democratic Hungary now emerging, with suggestions heavy with meaning—

not with tree calipers, roadside berms, ultimate right-of-ways, sideyard setbacks and lot averaging. Two kinds of politics. Two very different places. Two very different occasions.

And yet: Ultimately the essence of these matters is the same. Allow me to explain why.

First and foremost: The history and the essence of politics is a matter of words. This may sound strange in this age of pictorial presentations and numerical computerization, but so it is. In the beginning was the Word, as the Bible says, and so it is still. It is words that move us, hurt us, inspire us, depress us, because we think in words. In this speech a change of one word or two, the omission or the addition of a single phrase, could make all the difference. It could affect not only the tone but the entire meaning of the message that this old and honorable man addresses to an entire nation. His words most probably will not change the course of world history. But within my lifetime there were words that did change the course of world history: Hitler's words to which an entire nation rose to respond, ready to bear arms; and Churchill's words that made another nation ready to respond, to resist Hitler even when they were largely bereft of arms.

It strikes me that the future of Schuylkill Township also depends on words. Not on "facts," because there is no fact in this world that exists apart from the words with which it is expressed, or thought. It is words— about zoning, about wetlands, about lot lines, about soil configurations— that decide the fate of what may be built and where, and of what may be preserved or where; it is words that a judge will use when he makes a legal ruling, deciding a case for a developer or for a township. The law consists of words.

Right now I am making a great deal of fuss because a friend wants us to change one sentence to be heard tomorrow in the Parliament of Hungary. Last year I made a great deal of fuss because the consultants whom the township supervisors had employed to draft the new Comprehensive Plan had chosen to define unbuilt parcels of land in Schuylkill Township as "vacant lands." I rose up against that. "Vacant," I said, means "abandoned," "empty," "useless." Does this mean that every single plot of land of 10 acres or more in this township that is not yet covered with buildings is abandoned, empty, useless? Some people thought that I was making a mountain out of an empty lot; or that perhaps I was only speaking as a professor of English (which I am not; I am a professor of history). No, the matter was not that of the traditions of language. It was the preservation of honesty and decency—in the Schuylkill Township building as well as in the National Assembly of Hungary in Budapest.

Words are inseparable from ideas. Communism is gone in Hungary because for many years no one believed in it, including Party members, and now including the present leader of the Russian empire. That is why Hungary—thank God—has gone through a bloodless revolution; not because Reagan and Weinberger forced the Russians into an armament race that the latter could not financially afford. In Schuylkill Township the battle will be won once people's ideas—not merely their feelings, those are already changing—will change to the extent that they recognize the outdated vision of technological progress that would make the entire world into one gigantic suburb, resembling a shopping mall or an airport.

The second essential similarity between these two places is that of the human element in politics. The main political division in Hungary now exists between two large political parties, the Hungarian Democratic Forum and the Association of Free Democrats. The literal sense of these words means nothing, just as in the United States, where there are no monarchists or aristocrats, only Republicans and Democrats. The real divisions go deeper. They exist within the parties, not among them—in Hungary as well as in Schuylkill Township. There are good eggs and bad eggs in both parties. And who are the bad ones? Well, whether in the Danube Basin or in Chester County, Pennsylvania, they are the same kind of people: people who are moved mainly by envy and resentment—envy for other people who are (or who seem to be) more respectable or success-ful than they are, resentment of people who are (or who seem to be) better off because they seem to know more of the world. Such people exist within the majority party in Hungary, as they exist among the majority party in Chester County. They are a minority, but sometimes a *hard* minority. *That* is exactly what is missing in the numerical configurations of the pollsters. A hard minority may—I am not saying that it will—exert an influence beyond its numbers, let alone the quality of its component men and women, because when there is not much more than a soft majority in its way, a hard group of people or a well-organized lobby can give the public impression that it represents the popular and respectable majority. *That* is the danger of populist democracy in Hungary, between East and West, as well as in Schuylkill Township, between Phoenixville and Valley Forge.

In the history of Hungary, Dr. Samuel Johnson's famous phrase has been, alas, often applicable—patriotism having been the last refuge of scoundrels. In America, too, to which I must add that "free enterprise" patriotism is often the last resort of developers. The danger to democracy is not political extremism. It is the kind of ambition that is fueled by resentment and greed—and greed itself is a consequence rather than a cause, a consequence of a sense of fear. That fear is not really a fear of financial insecurity. It is a fear of personal inadequacy. The father of greed is vanity—in Budapest and Hungary as well as in any American small town or suburb.

MAY 2ND, WEDNESDAY. A brilliant May morning, full of promise. I am worried about the arrangement: Has my old friend taken his pills along? Will he bear the strain of standing up so long? But all goes well, including my secondary worry: Since I am not a former member of Parliament, but only his companion, will there be a seat for me in the gallery once he is escorted to the Parliament floor? But then I am led to one of the six ceremonial boxes on the floor itself, each with four red velvet chairs. I sit next to Princess Walburga von Habsburg, daughter of Otto von Habsburg, who is also here. The son of the last king of Hungary, he is a well-liked figure in Hungary now. The Princess is handsome and tells me that she has one of my books on her night table in their house in Bavaria. Before I have a chance to feel flattered, we all stand. There is the national anthem. It could not be more appropriate at this moment. (At some of the supervisors' meetings in Schuylkill Township we recite the Pledge of Allegiance—which, I must say, I do not find quite appropriate there; but then here, too, an actor goes to the platform and recites a poem written "To the National Assembly" 140 years ago, and I find his tone and his declamation not quite proper.) Finally my old friend Béla rises and slowly walks to the rostrum. His speech lasts not more than eight minutes. They fly by. It is a strange experience to hear some of the things that he desired to say as they are expressed in some of my phrases. At the end there is a passage that is as appropriate for Hungary as it is for the

United States—for my native country as well as for my adopted one. He says that the Nazis and the communists incarnated a pagan barbarism from which Hungary is now freed: "but ahead of us are perhaps the shadows of a new, technological paganism, threatening the nature of our homeland, our continent, our mother earth."

There is a standing ovation. Two other, much longer, speeches. Then an intermission. There is a champagne reception in the presidential chambers, above the Danube. The sunlight pours in. The Monsignor is tired. He will not stay for the rest of the long first session of the Parliament; he wishes to go back to the house and rest. I will go with him; I say goodbye to some of my friends and acquaintances and to Walburga: "*Je vous prie de bien vouloir soumettre mes hommages à Madame votre mère.*" I wish that my mother had lived to see this day and that my American wife were here, but that was not to be. Back in Pennsylvania dawn is now breaking. It is the 2nd of May, the monthly supervisors' meeting. What is happening in Budapest is the celebration of the end of a long painful chapter and the beginning of a new chapter in a nation's history. What will be discussed in Schuylkill Township is many petty matters but, after all is said, the preservation of something that means more than a few acres here and there: the preservation of a countryside, of a landscape, of a way of life, of a country.

All of the world's great newspapers are here. I give the correspondent of the *Frankfurter Allgemeine* my English translation of Monsignor Varga's speech. The next day they print a very precise account of it. This never happens in *The New York Times* or even in *The Philadelphia Inquirer,* though it does happen sometimes in *The Evening Phoenix,* not to speak of the Schuylkill Township Civic Association Newsletter, where all the details do count.

A Winter Feast in Hungary

(1991)

In the Hungary of my youth two family rituals within bourgeois or gentry families (neither of the two adjectives is accurate, but never mind) involved one's sixth and sixteenth birthdays. The occasion of the child's sixth birthday was his festive admission to the family dining table. Before that children had, more than often, their meals separately, with their governesses. Customarily on the Sunday after the child's sixth birthday he was given a place at the family table during the Sunday midday meal (usually with his grandparents present); for the first time he was allowed to swallow a small glass of wine. Thereafter the child sat and fidgeted at that table whenever the family ate together, subjected of course to the recurrent torture of admonitions for his eating habits, for not sitting up straight, for handling the fork or knife improperly, etc., etc.

The milestone of one's sixteenth birthday was less precise and less formal. It involved the occasional permission of the youth to be present when there was a company of certain guests. It even involved the, less frequent, occasion to accompany his or her parents to a luncheon or a dinner or a christening, social events at the house of distant relatives. Nowadays a youth—let alone a normal American teenager—would, most probably, resent being dragged along to a boring company of adults. Yet some such occasions then were more memorable than boring.

I have a very vivid memory, both of the family midday meal at my sixth birthday, and of what was, perhaps, the first occasion of my accompanying my parents to the Budapest town apartment of distant relatives of ours, on a winter evening, for a big feast. That feast was the *disznótor,* translatable as the *Schweinsfest* or *La Fête du Porc,* or The Pig Feast. This requires explanation.

In Hungary (and in Transylvania; also in some other neighboring countries) pigs are slaughtered in November. Out of the butchering comes the rendering of lard, the instant stuffing and cooking of different sausages *(kolbászok)*, of meat puddings *(hurkák)*, the smoking of sides of bacon *(szalonnák)* and of the ribs *(oldalasok)*, chops and roasts, many of these immediately hung in cool, spicy larders, others salted away for the long cold winters. (Winters in Hungary have become less cold during this century.) This is performed during a single day in the country, dependent on a master butcher (not a professional: usually a man within the family or a relative or a friend); a slew of helpers, including the women working in clouds of steam rising from all kinds of tubs, busy with the making of the sausages and with the many side dishes. At times—depending on the weather—the feast begins around noon; the viands put on rough trestle tables on the porches or in the back yards of the peasants' houses. It is then that the scene may remind one of a Breughel painting. However, more than often the company gathers indoors, in small, hot rooms, with the windows steamed up, with a constant scurrying back and forth from the kitchen and from the vats and tubs set outside. It is the occasion for much drinking. From the list of those present quarrelsome family members may be excluded because of the obvious presence of sharp knives in many hands.

In the Hungarian country, among well-to-do peasants this annual gourmandizing still exists. But at least before the Second World War the Pig Feast (literally *disznótor* means The Pig's Burial Feast) was a late November or early December event in the city, too, for urbane people. Of course the serving, the form and the style of the meal were different, but the food was, by and large, the same. This was part and parcel of a peculiar condition. In many non-democratic and even partly feudal societies, such as pre-war Hungary, there was (and there is) not much difference in the diet of the otherwise so different classes. Many of the same national dishes were (and are) preferred, and beloved, by peasants, bourgeois, and nobles alike. We may see this phenomenon also in Spain, Italy, Austria—whereas in democratic nations such as England or the United States the cuisine of the upper and lower classes was, and often still is, different.

In December 1939, we were invited to the Budapest apartment of our distant relatives, the D.'s. They had a fairly large estate near Orosháza, in southeastern Hungary. (I had been there, with my mother, at the age of five or six. I remember one oddity: on the brilliantly waxed, but pine-rough, floors of their country house their maids were running around bare-footed; at dinnertime they appeared in their starched-white and shiny-black uniforms but barefooted still.) The D.'s were well-off, though not rich. Their tenants and their estate-keeper had sent the viands for the winter feast up to Budapest. They invited my mother and stepfather and myself; I recall two or perhaps three other couples being present.

The D.'s lived in an upper-middle-class neighborhood in Budapest, where most of the houses had been built between 1890 and 1910, semi-palatial villas having one or two apartments on each floor, with large, high-ceilinged rooms, stuccoed ceilings, French windows, parquet floors: an atmosphere containing soupçons of pretentious elegance and a solid essence of bourgeois comfort. With my innards awash with the hungry humors of a sixteen-year-old I was looking forward to this feast, unknow-ing of its eventual sequence. Obviously this was to be a dinner-party, beginning about seven (the Hungarian custom at the time was to arrive not less than a half hour later), and not an all-day, rollicking and bloody country roustabout. As we entered the apartment, the smiling maid whom we knew (in her starched uniform, now, unlike in the country, well-shod and with a white cap) took our coats, wraps and hats. There were (to be honest, let me write that there *must* have been) some very fine odors wafting out from the kitchen. What I remember precisely was that most comfortable, very slightly smoky warmth radiating silently from the porcelain tile-stoves in the corners, as cozy as any fireplace can be.

Let me now recall the sequence of the culinary and oenologic events of that Pig Feast. At the beginning there was much animated talk among the men and women, and the hosts telling us when and how the large packages (or sacks?) arrived from Orosháza; and some merriment about the odd sayings of this or that peasant retainer in charge of the meatpack-ing or the transportation. Then everyone sat down in a kind of faded biedermeyer drawing room, with a lot of Magyar peasant designs embroi-dered on the pillows and even on some of the wall-hangings. The maid and the chauffeur (a kind of factotum, serving also as a temporary but-ler) handed around plates of hot biscuits, freshly baked of flour mixed with pork cracklings *(tepertos pogácsa)*. These were smaller than customary, in view of what was coming. What were served for drinks were both Hungarian apricot brandy (*barackpálinka,* much favored by the then Prince of Wales on his visit to Budapest in the 1930s) and a Tokaj wine (*szamorodni,* a dry but rich wine, not really golden but yellow with a brown tinge). The men drank the former and the ladies the latter.

That was a light overture. Perhaps one might call it a Salon Appetizer, since it was not served at the dining-room table. What followed was the First Act of a Two-Act Drama, whereof the most unusual thing was the Intermission, to which I shall come in a moment. The First Act was The Act of The Groaning Table, with a fantastic array of dishes. Soon others were carried around by the maid, as if the feast on the table had not been enough. There were minimal spaces for the bottles of wine, wrapped in white napkins. Everything was gleaming white, the napery, the reflections of the small Bohemian-glass chandelier, except of course for the colors of the wine and the dishes, the latter ranging from smoky beiges through rich reds to glistening browns, the palest among them the champagne-colored (and white wine-steeped) homemade sauerkraut, dotted here and there with the black *pointillisme* of caraway seed. Thus stood before us an embarras de richesse that I cannot remember having experienced before or since in sixty-seven years of a long and arduous, though culinarily not unsatisfactory, life. There were the cold, dark-red, paprika-flavored hard Hungarian sausages, with their purplish mosaic slices. There were the warm ones, of different kinds, some strongly spiced with sage and thyme and with no more than a fine touch of garlic, the soft ones within a thick skin-casing, much like *boudins blancs* and *boudins noirs.* There were—to Americans perhaps somewhat barbarous—rectangular slabs of fresh bacon, one kind strongly smoked and ochre-colored, the other covered with a layer of brilliant, crimson paprika, its lardy essence snow-white, though of course streaked with meat. These Hungarians eat thin-sliced and cold, placing them on pieces of crusty white bread, and washed down with spirits, or in this case with plenty of white wine. One more thing: a plate of hot, freshly rendered cracklings, crisp and salted, requiring the instant ingestion of a piece of bread too.

This, I thought, was our splendid Pig Feast dinner tonight. But I was wrong. There followed the ceremony of what the French—in this case literally—would call the *relève.*

It did not consist of a citrus sherbet or a salad. The men emptied their wineglasses and rose. It was they, not the ladies, who now retired from the table. They were invited to step, through tall white winged doors, into the two large bedrooms of the apartment. The curtains were drawn, the rooms were dark. The beds had been stripped, except for their cool white sheets and white pillows. The men took their jackets off, they loosened their collars. We were supposed to lie on the beds and rest after the arduous gastric labors of the First Act. Oddly (or, from what follows, perhaps not so oddly) no one lit a cigarette or a cigar. The sheets and the pillows were wonderfully cool and smooth. On each night-table there stood a cut-glass decanter and small shot-glasses, containing apricot brandy; and bottles of *Unicum,* the celebrated (though only in Hungary) dark-colored Hungarian stomachic, or *digestif.* Some partook of either of those, others did not. There was some talk, and then the heavier hum of breathing; in one case, a soft and peaceful snoring. The gentlemen were resting.

Thus half an hour passed. Then a muffled stirring began. Some of the gentlemen stood up, and threw back a shot-glass of the *digestif;* some of them disappeared in the adjoining bathroom; there was the sound of running water, splashing on reddened faces. Then we returned to join the ladies, who were talking and gossiping in the dining room. Then I saw that on the table Act Two was already served. All the crumbs had been swept away, a new white tablecloth had been put on. In the middle of the great table now stood a golden-brown roast suckling pig, with a small garland of bay leaves around his thick little neck, and a lemon (not an apple) in his mouth. It was surrounded by aromatic, home-made red cabbage. Around the platter were two beautiful china dishes piled high with preserved plums and apricots. There was another large bowl of potato purée. On two other, not inconsiderable, platters rested a roast loin of pork and a side of smoked ribs.

Do I remember how much we partook of the Second Act? I do not, except that, stuffed as I already was, I remember having at least consumed some of it. More wine was drunk. Dessert was light: a choice of three kinds of paper-thin strudels (apple-, nut-, and poppy-seed-filled) and a fruit compôte. Then everyone left the table and took to the drawing-room, where strong coffee and petit-fours (then called *mignons,* from the famous Budapest confiserie, Gerbeaud's) were served. We—myself, my stepfather, and my fashionably thin mother—were full, but perhaps not uncomfortably so. In my case that was not the result of prudent partaking. It was the testimony, most probably, of my youth.

I am certain that *this* kind of an urban and urbane Pig Feast, as distinct from the still customary country one, no longer took place after the war; and that even now, with the Communist regime gone, and at a time of considerable economic recovery (almost every kind of food is now available in Hungary), *fêtes du porc* such as the one I have described, belong to a vanished world. A few times this past winter I walked through the very neighborhood where that memorable winter feast had occurred fifty-two years ago. It was a much same grey winter evening, with the street lights spraying a thin misty halo through the pearly fog. But there was little of the interior reassurance that these villas used to (or ought to) breathe. There were not many lights casting a pleasant glow into the street from the small bourgeois chandeliers of those second-floor drawing-rooms or family rooms. So many of the windows were dark.

Perhaps ten years hence much of this will change. A new bourgeoisie will rise on the ruins of Communism in Hungary, the latter having been a foreign-imposed episode that was unbearably long for those who had to live through it but, really, not so long in the history of a nation. I do not know. What I know is that *that* Winter Feast, in 1939, belongs to an irrecoverable—and unrepeatable—past.

Cold Comfort
Finland and Scandinavia
(1992)

Ambling through the Museum of the History of the City of Helsinki
I find myself in a small projection room where a film is shown about the
history of Helsinki during the last seventy years. It is poignant and
telling. There are shots from the late 1930s, young, smiling, large-boned
Finnish women in their long white skirts, chatting at the trolley-stops or
pushing their babies in prams, during a relentless pale Nordic summer of
1939. Then the Russian bombs start falling: the Winter War. The sound of
the air raid sirens; the fires crackling through the dark walls and windows
on December nights, their blaze more sinister in these black-and-white
pictures than on a color film. Then the stream of refugees from the lands
the Russians had taken. Then the Second War. More bombs. Hospital
scenes. Then the slow rebuilding. All through this not one critical word
about the Russians, which is remarkable as well as rare, since the history
of small nations is ever so often suffused with the history of their (often
deserved) complaints.

The Finns are an admirable people (except when they are drunk, but
that is a different story). They are stolid, courageous, civic-minded, patriotic rather than nationalist. They have many reasons to hate Russians and
to dwell on their injustices; they are not inclined to do anything of the
sort. The Russians, including Stalin, knew that. In turn, what the Finns do
not know about the Russians may not be worth knowing. That is why
Finland, alone among the western neighbors of the Soviet Union, could
remain independent even during the worst years of the cold war. John
Kennedy, who ought to have known better, asked a Finnish diplomat in
1961: "What puzzles us Americans, is why the Soviet Union has allowed

Finland to retain her independence." What is puzzling is Kennedy's ignorance. Later in the 1960s and 1970s came the American propaganda and fear about "Finlandization"—that is, the potential temptation of Western Europeans to secure their security and well-being by restricting some of their independence vis-à-vis Russia, *à la* Finland. "Finlandization," of course, was an idiotic term from the beginning. The Finns knew that independence, whether in the life of a state or of an individual, is inseparable from self-discipline, from a knowledge of one's own limits of behavior. I often said to myself then: if only American democracy itself were "Finlandized"—that is: clean, reliable, homogeneous, modest, honest, well-educated, knowing its own limits of national well-being and security, uninterested in and disinclined to rhetorical, let alone political or military, ventures beyond those.

Some of the Soviet archives are now open. I talk with a Finnish scholar who shows me photostats of secret conferences with Stalin, with Stalin's handwriting on the margin. Here is one of them. It is 1945; Stalin won the war; potentially Finland is under his thumb. He receives a pro-Soviet delegation in the Kremlin: Finnish Communists, fellow-traveling intellectuals, etc. Hertha Kuusinen, a leading Finnish Communist: "You won the war. We admire Russians."

Stalin: "We did not do it alone. We have our faults. But, yes, Russians are stubborn and tough. So are you. Finland is a poor country, full of swamps and forests. But you built a state for yourselves, you fought for it. Finnish people: village people, not like Belgians. Belgians: cultured people. They gave up. Had Belgium consisted of Finns they would have fought." Later, to a Finnish general in civvies: "Why don't you wear your uniform? You have a great little army."

(This is the Stalin whom the most respected American scholars of the Soviet Union still describe as a "revolutionary fanatic." Even Robert Tucker, Robert Conquest, who are not phonies. Conquest in his latest, *Stalin—Breaker of Nations:* Stalin was an extreme dogmatist, Marxism "was obviously well-tailored to Stalin's own personality." Marxism was obviously well-tailored not to the personality of Stalin but to the personalities of the late Sidney Hook *et al.*)

Marshal Mannerheim knew better. He was perhaps one of the two or three most admirable leaders of imperiled nations in the twentieth century (the other two were Churchill and de Gaulle). He was a Swedish baron, born in Finland, served in the Czar's army, fought in the Russo-Japanese war in 1904–5, sent after that to survey the still largely unmapped borders of the Russian Empire, a 5,000-mile journey, mostly on horseback, that took two years. In 1917 his allegiance to the Czar ceased to exist. He led the Finns in defeating their own Communists and then the Red Soviet army. In 1918 a German prince was about to become the King of an independent Finland. Mannerheim said no. The British will win the war, not the Germans, he said. Besides, we don't need a monarch who, in the twentieth century, is often not much more than a figurehead. We, in Finland, need a strong president. He did not become president. But he became the constable of the nation, the Marshal of Finland. In 1939 he was seventy-two years old. He told the Finnish government to negotiate seriously with Stalin about Finland's frontiers; he knew that Stalin wanted to regain the old frontier of Peter the Great. He was overruled, but then led the Finnish Army during the Winter War and what was later the Continuation War. When the crunch came in 1944 the Finns asked him to become their President. The Fenno-Swedish aristocrat made peace with the Georgian bandit Stalin. Throughout the seventy years of Finnish history it was not the Socialists but men of the Finnish Conservatives—Mannerheim, Paasikivi, Kekkonen—whom Stalin and the Russians trusted. True Conservatives, not neo-conservatives, light-years away in character and intelligence from the latter bunch, in charge of much of our intellectual commerce now.

Mannerheim never owned a house. He rented one on a flat hilltop in Helsinki, which is the Mannerheim museum now. It has all the marks of the life of an old nobleman-soldier, plenty of superb antlers, the skin of the tiger he shot in Nepal, the two tall silver-chased horns from Tibet, his medals and guns (well, two of them are Purdeys), etc. They are not dominant or obtrusive. Impressive is his bedroom where he slept on a narrow army cot, requesting that the heat be not kept higher than 60°. In 1918 he divorced his difficult Russian wife and lived alone. Most of the house is comfortably furnished, with a North European upper-middle-class feel to it. The two Italian chandeliers he bought are not very good. The main boulevard of Helsinki is named after him, his statue is at the end of it, overlooking a soulless modern glass box of a building, not a very good place. The long living room has a view of the harbor. That view is my only luxury, Mannerheim said. That kind of restraint and modesty bonded this aristocrat to the democrats of Finland, both defenders of Western civilization, the civilization that for the last four hundred years was a mix of aristocracy and democracy, not yet levelled down entirely to the lowest common denominators of popularity, publicity, and populism.

The statues of Russian Czars stand in the squares of Helsinki. There is a St. Petersburg look to the harbor quays, broad with cobblestones, well-proportioned, lined with low-lying neo-classical buildings of the Eastern European empire style. It is a provincial capital, under gloomy grey skies in the winter, with bourgeois touches. I walk into a confiserie with stout Finnish ladies wearing large fur hats; then I sit in a brasserie where the food is not particularly good but through the windows I see the street full of people walking around after eight on a weekday night, with the streetcar gliding outside. I have the feeling that this will remain so ten, twenty, thirty years from now. There is a tremendous bookshop, the Finns are great readers. "The Month in Helsinki" lists the various operas and concerts. In 1917 Finland achieved her independence. In the same year started the Philadelphia Orchestra. I fear that in 2017 the Philadelphia Orchestra will exist in name only: it will perform perhaps once a month at Wanamakers in a suburban mall, while in Helsinki the bookshop, the home-baked creamy cakes, the grandmotherly Saturday afternoons and the Helsinki Philharmonic will still exist twenty-five years from now.

I fly to Tallinn, capital city of the reconstituted Republic of Estonia. At the airport the first signs of the new, uneasy, as yet thin authority of a new sovereign state: the hastily assembled uniforms of the border guards, the girl at the visa checkpoint who cannot find the official stamp, the remaining prevalence of signs in Cyrillic Russian script, etc. Tallinn still has a Russian touch: one-story wooden houses, slightly askew, with their large double windows. In the lee of Soviet-style ugly concrete apartment houses a yellow-painted Russian Orthodox church, with its big bulbous pea-green onion dome, closed, suspicious, inscrutable. Men and women hurrying in the streets in their padded coats, Russian fur caps and hats. Inside the buildings Tallinn has a Russian smell, with its ingredients of damp greatcoats, boiled cabbage and cold grease.

I am lodged in Hotel Olümpia, the newest and biggest hotel in

Tallinn. It was built for the Olympics in 1980, twenty-six stories high, all modern Sovietish architecture. The usual Eastern European oddities: for some unknown reason there is an enormous empty refrigerator in my room, clanking periodically through the night. One must hunt for the stopper in the bathroom. As one travels east, toilet paper gets coarser and coarser. The elevators are gigantic but they do not always work. Each may accommodate as many as thirty people but once in a while the Russian-speaking help orders the crowded passengers aside to make way for steel carts filled with hundreds of dirty plates, exuding ever stronger smells of lukewarm leftover grease. A hive of people at the bar; one will not get the bartender's attention except when reaching out to grab a glass, while others are pounding and shouting. I stand in my American overcoat, my fur-lined gloves in my right pocket. A middle-aged Russian woman stalks up to me, with a crumpled face, exclaiming in English: "Come! Sit with us!" Across that dim amphitheater her group, moustachioed Caucasians, grin and wave, beckoning to me to join them. Pointing at my watch, I excuse myself. Later, out in the street, I find that she had stolen my gloves out of my pocket. The hotel is full of Georgians and Armenians, the young Estonian woman at the desk tells me many of them are criminals, the hotel detectives cannot dislodge them; they make passkeys, empty their belongings and move into other rooms that they have cased beforehand.

Are these the remnants of the Soviet era, of the past? Yes: and no. All around me are the awful premonitions of a global future. There is one kind of sound and one frenzied gunfire of pictures that throbs, rules, pervades, dominates all the public places on every floor, screaming and yelling throughout this monstrous prison-box of the Olümpia Hotel, at the bar, coffee-shop, in the corridors, elevators, halls, spilling out even from the small hanging telescreens over the receptionists' desk: the black and white niggers of MTV. That deadening diabolical beat, their endless writhings and screamings are not the results of pain but the creations of a new kind of barbaric self-assertion. The Anglo-Saxon age is going, the prestige and the power of the British is largely gone, the United States retreats across the globe, but English—well, a kind of English—is still and will remain for some time the lingua franca of the world (well, not much of a *lingua* and not very *franca* but let that pass); anyhow, MTV and

CNN are thin plastic cords, unceasing and repetitious, wound around and around the crania of newer and newer populations throughout the world. I have often found Nietzsche unreadable but sometimes he reminds us of the obvious: "Men believe in the truth of all that is seen to be strongly believed in." One hundred years later: that is seen to be seen everywhere. Or Goebbels in 1939: "We live in an age that is both romantic and steely. The bourgeois were alien and hostile to technology, skeptics believed that the roots of the collapse of European culture lay in it. National Socialism has understood how to take the soulless framework of technology and fill it with the rhythm and hot impulses of our time." Not National Socialism: the New Barbarians (of whom the former were but one variant of fore-runners).

Darkness arrives in Tallinn in the early afternoon. Then the huge doors of the Hotel Olümpia are closed; the only entrance is watched by a young staff of hotel detectives, allowing some people to enter, pushing others away. Here, too, is the contrast, the new world of two kinds of people, those within and those without. Groups of young men and women, the girls with greatcoats over their incredible clothes, endeavor to penetrate the Olümpia. This is their instant future, the central emanations of steam heat and loud sound and company and sex, the world of MTV. Outside the chilly cold, the dark city under a black starless sky, the sullen shut Orthodox church, the broken sidewalks, the older people huddled at the bus stops, going back to their hot pots in their broken, creaky rooms. Inside the Olümpia the instant future, heat, neon-glitter, rock, the promise not of bourgeois comforts but of the world of a proletarian Dionysia. Very far from New York and yet not so different from much of it. Eighty years ago John Butler Yeats (the poet's father) wrote that "the fiddles are tuning up all over America." It was not ragtime that he meant; but, in any event, the run from ragtime to metal-rock was shorter than he, or anyone else, could have imagined. It is near-global now. New classes, New Barbarians, and the future may be theirs. It is from their ranks that one day the new Alexanders and Caesars and the new feudal lords will rise, with beautiful young women around them, longing for their chains.

Next morning, snowstorm. Seagulls and seahawks fly across Tallinn, inland. The Estonian historians, the Estonian Academy of Sciences, all very nice people, as we talk about all kinds of historic details, including the smallest episodes, ransacking the dramatic story of the extinction of their independence by the Russians in 1940. Some of them are troubled by their present politics. It is not easier to be free than not to be free. A new form of government and state may be congealing everywhere in Eastern Europe, perhaps almost everywhere in the world: the one-party state of a new kind. Not the party-state of the Nazi or Fascist or Communist type: those were party-states as well as police-states. Now the tyranny of the state police will be limited (though far from disappearing). Here, as elsewhere in Eastern Europe, the pushy squeegee tyranny of the majority will prevail, as it indeed already prevails: a nationalist government party that will extend its rule over the entire state apparatus, including the television news (very important now). The minority will be allowed to grumble (within bounds), it will keep a newspaper or a magazine of its own, but its chances of becoming a majority will fade month by month, year by year; it will be about as effective as the American or the British or the French or the German liberal intelligentsia, a class gradually absorbed by the soft soapy sponges of the universities, irrelevant, on its way to extinction.

I spend most of the day walking in the old baronial, Hanseatic city of which Estonians are justly proud. Only: it was all built by Germans. It is appealing and beautiful as the old city melts gradually into the wider streets. Above and between the towers the stony passages, the strong and solid Germanic houses, still showing a sharp hierarchical sense: for the German guildmasters, burgesses, etc., here in the east of Europe were something different from *bürgerlich,* bourgeois. Many Lutheran churches, in some of them the impressive lodges—more than boxes—of the German or Swedish noble families, hanging above the church floor, across the pulpit, crystal-paned. I can imagine their women in their tremendous dark skirts and white ruffs, sitting there bored, stiff and haughty. There was a small and constricted and humorless but strong civilization here in the Middle Ages and later, even at a time when the words "civilization" and "civilized" did not exist. Please keep in mind that these very words and their meaning arose only three or four hundred years ago. "Civilized," in English, appears in 1601: "To make civil; to bring out of a state of barbarism; to instruct in the arts of life; to enlighten and refine." A century later (*OED:* 1704) appears the very word "civilization." How long will it retain its meaning? There are already hordes of young people—here and in Detroit and in New York—to whom not only the meaning but the word has become incomprehensible.

At night I take the secretary of the Academy to dinner. There is hope yet: a private restaurant, with the waiters well-dressed, etc. Only: it is in a cellar, and I fear that by the twenty-first century all good private restaurants may be in cellars. Three courses, for both of us, payable in rubels: the total bill comes to something like one dollar and twenty cents. They pronounce *rubel* in English as *rubble*. So it is. The wine I must pay in Finnmarks: that costs about twenty dollars, red rotgut served in brandy glasses.

Back in the West: Helsinki on an empty, chilly Sunday. I find the Catholic church beyond a frozen city park, a brownstone building, with a Northern touch (the very large Orthodox Russian church, on another, large hill, retains something of a brownstone-Nordic touch too). The church is cold, we sit and kneel in our overcoats, not too many of us, about half of the people serious Vietnamese women and their children. The Mass is in Latin, which is more than cold comfort.

In the afternoon the boat to Stockholm. I was looking forward to the ship, to the pleasure of a seaborne departure which is the very best (alas, now so rare) of departures. (After which comes, on a lower scale, the petty pleasure of finding one's single compartment in a sleeping-car and then leaning out the window in an old railway station of a European city. Being tied down to one's cramped seat in an airplane is no departure at all.) The rising throb of the boat is fine, and so is the haunting, beautiful whirl of the dark icy water. Then comes the departure ritual: going for the first drink at the first bar. The pleasance is, however, compromised by the pounding of the ubiquitous rock and by the cardboard signs proliferating on the counter: Tonight Our Special Is an Elvis Cocktail; every Thursday in January Is New Orleans Night; this month the program of the ship is pronounced to be a HULABALLOO (thus). This in the middle of the Baltic winter, on a ship where there are few Americans.

The ship is enormous, laden with all kinds of technological conveniences, including television with CNN in the cabins (the global equivalent of *USA Today*, the ceaseless pictorial bilge paraded as information for semiliterate people). Large coarse Scandinavian men and boys in the sauna, drinking beer. Four different restaurants in this ship, all of them acceptable, though quite expensive. Along one entire deck the inside of this tremendous ship has been gouged out for a shopping mall. The discos beat. I go to bed early and wake up early. The ship moves fast through low waves on an inky dark morning. Breakfast available only in the Scandinavian buffet manner, as almost everywhere now in the world. Droves of shuffling people, sleepy women, unshaven men, sidling uneasily with their plates, standing in line for the juice pitchers, speechless with a queasy mix of appetites and embarrassments. The waitresses come and go, whipping away the plates as soon as they can. The democratic feeding of travelers. It is all very middle-class. But that word has already lost its meaning: here, back in the West, there are virtually no proletarians and no upper classes left. Should one therefore distinguish the upper-middle from the lower-middle classes? None of that is important, or significant any longer, which means not only that the Ralph Lauren ads are ludicrous but also that fine writers such as Evelyn Waugh will soon be read only as period pieces. Cold comfort again.

The old town of Stockholm is very beautiful, and inviting, too, because it is still lived in. There is a Stockholm of broad avenues, giant department stores, electronic shops blaring, office skyscrapers, glass-and-steel buildings of the 1960s and 1970s, endless traffic; but there is a sense of carefully protected interior lives, too, an instinctive rediscovery of older virtues which is more than an interior decorators' fad or nostalgia.

Such impressions are reinforced when I talk with Swedish friends in their apartment after dinner. How different is this fin-de-siècle from the one 100 years ago! We talk about Knut Hamsun, whose fame burst upon the world exactly 100 years ago. He, even more than Ibsen and Strindberg, opened the windows of the world in the Scandinavian direction, bringing in a fresh strong wind, about the same time when the fame of the great Russian writers arrived in the West. But Hamsun had more to say to the West than had the Russians, to all kinds of people in the West. Even second-raters such as Hemingway were ruffled by the Hamsunian wind. Well, Hamsun hated everything about the bourgeois world, its cramped-ness, its stuffiness, its coziness, the interiority of those lives, their intellectual philistinism, their convenient liberal categories of thinking—all of these then stiflingly prevalent in the Norwegian townlets in Hamsun's time. His heroes were loners, virile individualists, men with minds of their own, with a heroic rather than tragic (Hamsun was not a Catholic) sense of life, admired and loved by young women (while elsewhere in Europe the cult of womanhood had entered the last phase of the Romantic Agony). He also hated England and the English, which is less well-known, though it is there in many of his writings: his contempt for the hypocrisy of the English, their puritanism, their cult of moderation and of fairness. Hamsun was a Nietzschean of sorts, though his talent was great enough so that he need not have read Nietzsche. So it is not surprising that he admired Hitler till the very end, sticking to his guns, embarrassing and upsetting his own countrymen. At the very end of the war, when Hitler had killed himself, Hamsun still wrote about him: "He was a warrior, a warrior for mankind and a prophet of the gospel of justice for all nations. He was a reformer of the highest rank, and his historical fate was that he flourished in a time of unexampled coarseness, which felled him at last." Justice for all nations? There is something very wrong with this. But it is not because of this that my Swedish friends and I, too, see Hamsun as not more than a period piece, as a rebel voice that sounded strong and clear at a certain time but that has little to say to some of us now. To those of us who know that we live in a world at the edge of the sinking Modern Age, now when all the real bourgeois virtues, their interiority and probity, have remained enduring, real, loveable and admirable, like a piece of family furniture that is both finer and more solid than we once thought, a more and more precious heritage as we are carried farther and farther away from its time. As a matter of fact, our only *tangible* heritage.

Next night, as I sail out of Stockholm, as the large ship wends its way among the outer islands, I see the serried lights of the social democratic apartment houses on the low hills, here where the nightfall in winter means the slow brightening of lights in people's windows. It is unlike the sharp exterior glitter of New York, of that "numb brilliant jittery city" (as Malcolm Lowry wrote nearly fifty years ago, and so did Julian Green: they must have meant the traffic and the hustle but now that jitteriness is all inside). Here the sense of a somewhat chilly coziness but still with a measure of interior tradition. Cold comfort.

Six years ago I met a Swedish girl in my ski group. She was a plain young woman with plenty of integrity. I was alone; we talked a lot. She told me how she resented the bondage of sexual "freedom," ruining the lives of many of her friends, and how she disdained hypocrisy but intellectual—and spiritual—dishonesty was even more ruinous than that, much more. The last night in Zermatt I walked her back to her simple hotel. Before saying good-bye I tried to put my arms around her. She said: no, better no. That was all right: I am a closet monogamist, after all. She sent me Christmas cards for a few years. She lived three hundred or more miles from Stockholm but I wrote her a note before coming to Sweden. I found this letter from her in my hotel:

> Dear John
> Thank you for your letter. It was nice to hear from you. But as you wrote, from where I live it's far from Stockholm, so I don't have the possibility to see you there.
> For the moment i work nightshift in the hospital in Simvighamn. I am pregnant and in the end of february I'm going to have a baby. Also I moved to the countryside outside Ystad, in a small village called Hedvigsdal. I met the great love from my teenageperiod and we found eachother again.
> I hope you will enjoy your stay in Stockholm and much good luck with the business whatever they are.
> All the best to you.
> My new address, etc.

I wrote her a few lines. I knew that I was in the presence of a child of light. More than cold comfort.

Up the Mountain

Zermatt

(1993)

One comes to Zermatt by train. There is no other way. Decades ago the community of Zermatt decided—wisely—to keep automobiles out of this town, at the end of a narrow valley. Those who make for Zermatt in their cars (and most people now do) must leave them on an immense concrete apron of a parking lot at Täsch, the next-to-last station on the mountain rail line going from Brig to Zermatt, and transfer themselves with their baggage and skis to the shuttle train that glides through the valley under many galleries, reaching the Zermatt railhead in about fifteen minutes. As they clamber out of the coaches at the Zermatt station they find themselves among a milling crowd, electric carts and a few horsedrawn carriages. On that sunny plaza they encounter the duality of Zermatt: old and new.

Old: because the Matterhorn dominates the scene still. It rises above Zermatt in an extraordinary way. It is visible from every angle, everywhere: stark, threatening, majestic. "The Matterhorn," wrote Gerard Manley Hopkins 125 years ago, "looks like a sea-lion couchant or a sphinx; and again like the hooded-snake frontal worn by the Egyptian King." Gerard Manley Hopkins was one of the most imaginative poets of the English language; but somehow this will not do. An anonymous Frenchman put it better, about two hundred years ago: "Le Cervin n'est pas quelque chose, c'est quelqu'un." The Matterhorn is not a Thing; it is a Personage. That presence has not changed, and will not change. (One reason: Old Matterhorn is more climbable than one hundred years ago; yet skiable it is not.) But Zermatt, unlike one hundred years ago, is now predominantly a winter resort. As late as sixty-six years ago—well after

209

skiing had become widespread—the hotels and inns of Zermatt were closed in the winter. Now the great majority of people come for the snow in the sun, for the Alpine glitter.

It is the glitter of the mountains, rather than that of the town. The latter is not determinedly glamorous—wherein resides the remnant of its old-fashioned quality. The main street of Zermatt is the same street that has met its visitors in the past, running up from the station to the foothills of the Big Mountain, the entrance to the Matterhorn. Along it are the main hotels, the three most famous (and most comfortable) ones the same as one hundred years ago: Monte Rosa, Mont-Cervin, Zermatterhof. Comfortable, rather than luxurious: because Zermatt is a bourgeois place, in the best sense of that once maligning adjective. I stay in the Parnass, a three-star hotel. It has its shortcomings: there is no elegant bar, no piano player, only a small lounge for chatting and drinking before and after dinner, no indoor swimming-pool, no sauna. But the food is invariably excellent, the staff is amiable and respectful, there is familiarity and camaraderie among some of the guests, returning year after year.

Zermatt is not Gstaad or St.-Moritz, coruscating with the glamour of the most expensive chalets, hotels, boutiques and fashions of the world. There *are* beautiful young women, trailing their fantastic fur coats and jackets as they traipse up and down the pre-dinner promenade on the main street; but there are not many of those tigresses. Outside the hotels there are no remarkable restaurants in Zermatt, and no excessive après-ski hullabaloo, except for the young, of course. To me, the most glamorous place in Zermatt (for which I have sometimes a nostalgia at home, in Pennsylvania) is the Pharmacie Internationale on the main street, for which "pharmacy" or "apothecary" or, God forbid, "drugstore" are wholly inadequate translations. It is packed with people, and with emphatically lovely specimens of Swiss womanhood behind the counters: on the left a long brilliant array of the perfumes of the world; on the right a no less inspiring array of cosmetics, vitamins, and esthetic medicines; at the main counter the solicitous ministrations of apothecaries advising you of the virtues of every possible Swiss medicament, from inhalers to salves and pills, preventives or instant cures for an ominous sniffle or for a sore knee or thigh. There is an atmosphere of haut-bourgeois elegance, with a pervasive aroma of velvety and lemony scents.

No building in Zermatt is allowed to rise above four stories. But the perils of property are there. No gas-powered automobiles are permitted (except for the town doctors); but the electric buses are packed. The cement roofs and the platforms of the railroad station are extended every year. Each year there is another large condominium or a new hotel, some of them, alas, in a style of Heidi-baroque. 110 hotels and pensions; 36 trains and ski-lifts. Some time, some day, this expansion will have to stop; but God only knows when and how. A few steps from the Pharmacie Internationale is the first McDonald's on the main street, inaugurated last year. Discos abound, and they are *very* loud, though their ear-splitting noise seldom wafts out into the streets. There are masses of people pressing ahead for a seat on the cable cars or the cogwheel railway going up the Gornergrat; there is an Alpine subway (yes, subway), shooting up through the bowels of a small mountain to the plateau of the Sunnegga. But the slopes are not crowded and there are 65 ski runs, *pistes* groomed and marked, of every possible kind, which is why Zermatt is a skier's paradise, snow-packed and sun-baked, with the Matterhorn always above.

Often I shoulder my way out of the train at the Rotenboden stop, and not only because the two variant runs down from the Rotenboden to the Riffelberg are easy (I am, after all, sixty-nine now). There is the temptation to pause at the small Rotenboden plateau, but not for the sake of resting. There is a sudden stillness after the electric whine of the train dies away, and the voices of the few skiers starting downhill fade. I, too, will fasten my skis and start downhill, relishing the cold rush of the air in my face and in my lungs and the developing prospect of the red dots of the 200 chairs on the Riffelberg terrace two miles below. But sometimes before that I sit on a solitary bench, in the hot pour of the sun, entranced with the view of a gigantic Alpine amphitheater formed by the amazing crescent of one beautiful mountain peak next to another, with their whiteness unscarred by any path or any trace of skis.

Mountains! Two hundred years ago people hated mountains. Mountains (like winter, like ruins, like the Middle Ages) were *horrible.* Consequently most of Switzerland was poor, and this narrow tongue of a valley one of the poorest, a forlorn German-speaking recess of the French-speaking canton of the Valais. But 150 years ago this began to change. The English Lake Poets had discovered the romantic beauty of mountains; Englishmen and women discovered the beauty of the Alps. That English affection for Switzerland is a long story, and perhaps particularly in Zermatt. The first Alpine climbers were English. The Alpine Club in the Hotel Monte Rosa was English. Soon Zermatt had an English church. (One historian of Zermatt was Cicely Williams, wife of the later Bishop of Leicester.) The Matterhorn was first climbed by an Englishman, Edward Whymper, a difficult and morose man, especially since the descent from that first climb, in 1865, was marked by tragedy: a rope broke, and three of Whymper's party died. In the town cemetery are the graves of many climbers who died as they fell; there is at least one American among them. But then Ruskin and Mark Twain came to Zermatt in the 1870s (Twain did not attempt anything near the Matterhorn), and the young Winston Churchill in the 1890s, and a Mrs. Aubrey Le Blond, the founder of the Ladies' Alpine Club, truly a Victorian woman of both spunk and discretion who ascended the Matterhorn in long and abundant skirts— that is, until she ascertained that she and her party had passed the last cow on the high pastures, whereafter she would take off her crinoline, under which she wore her woolen mountaineer trousers. Leslie Stephen met his first wife (Thackeray's daughter) on the road from Täsch to Zermatt. (His daughter Virginia Woolf was no climber at all.)

Around the turn of the century the first skiers appeared. Many of them were Englishmen still. But the English predominance came to an end with the Second World War.

Now the majority of foreign visitors are German: ambitious, often superb young skiers as well as middle-aged couples in the dining-rooms and bars of the richer hotels, the women perfectly dressed, the men in their dark suits, wearing silver-colored ties, with champagne cocktails in hand before dinner, sometimes a little loud. There is a smaller but noticeable number of Italian families from Milan, with their smartly parkaed and sweatered women gossiping merrily on the sunny terraces, chic to the hilt.

But there has been a long continuity in the history of Zermatt. "Prato Borni" was a late-Roman and medieval name for the valley, where not so long ago Roman coins were still found under the snow and the rocks of the Theodulpass leading from and to Italy. There were cowherds and goatherds, many of them living in sheds and stalls on the high pastures, congregating eventually in a few more durable cottages and houses on the east bank of the brawling river Visp. They would become a village under the Matterhorn: "Zer-Matt." It was a cramped wintry existence for a few families who formed the core of an Alpine democracy, a "Burgerschaft," a community of burghers—which, to this day, is distinct from the "Gemeinde," the municipal council of the village. So many of the present hotels and shops bear the names of their owners, Julens and Perrens and Biners—well, they were the founding families of Zermatt two, three, four centuries ago. About 150 years ago hardy young members of these families found another vocation, a new source of income: they became "Bergführer," mountain guides, for the eccentric English. Two generations later their descendants tied on their first skis. Now, another two generations later, their descendants are the prosperous owners of hotels and shops and boutiques and confiseries; some of them are doctors and poets; but there are still champion skiers and mountain-climbers and ski instructors among them. Alexander Seiler came to Zermatt from another part of Switzerland 150 years ago. His career resembles that of the famous César Ritz who started out as a busboy in an inn on the top of another Swiss mountain, the Rigi. Seiler built the Monte Rosa, the headquarters of the English Alpinists. Then he built the Mont-Cervin. He enriched Zermatt. The Burgerschaft disliked him. They would not admit him to their ranks. To compete with Seiler (and to spite him) the burghers built another splendid establishment, the Zermatterhof, straight across from the Monte Rosa. It is still one of the three top hotels in Zermatt; and it still belongs to the Burgerschaft that leases it out.

The Swiss are not a romantic people. It is their land that is romantic. So here is a suggestion. You need not climb the Matterhorn to find high romance above Zermatt. Climb into the cogwheel railway up the Gornergrat on one of its last ascents in the evening, when the lights of Zermatt have begun to gleam below in a cobalt blue twilight; step out of the train at the end of the line into the sharp cold of the high mountain night, walk up (a few steps but quite steep) to the old hotel on the top of the Gornergrat to spend one night there and be sure to wake or to be wakened early, to see the incomparable rise of the sun. Dawn over the oceans of the world, sung by poets, is a tepid spectacle compared to this. What a pity that Shakespeare did not see it! In *Romeo and Juliet* he wrote: "Night's candles are burnt out and jocund day / Stands tiptoe on the misty mountain top." *These* mountains are not misty. They are aflame with the sun—rising behind, then pouring red and gold over the eternally white crests of the Monte Rosa, of the Castor and Pollux, of the Breithorn; and, finally, on the rock of the Matterhorn.

Index of Names

Credits